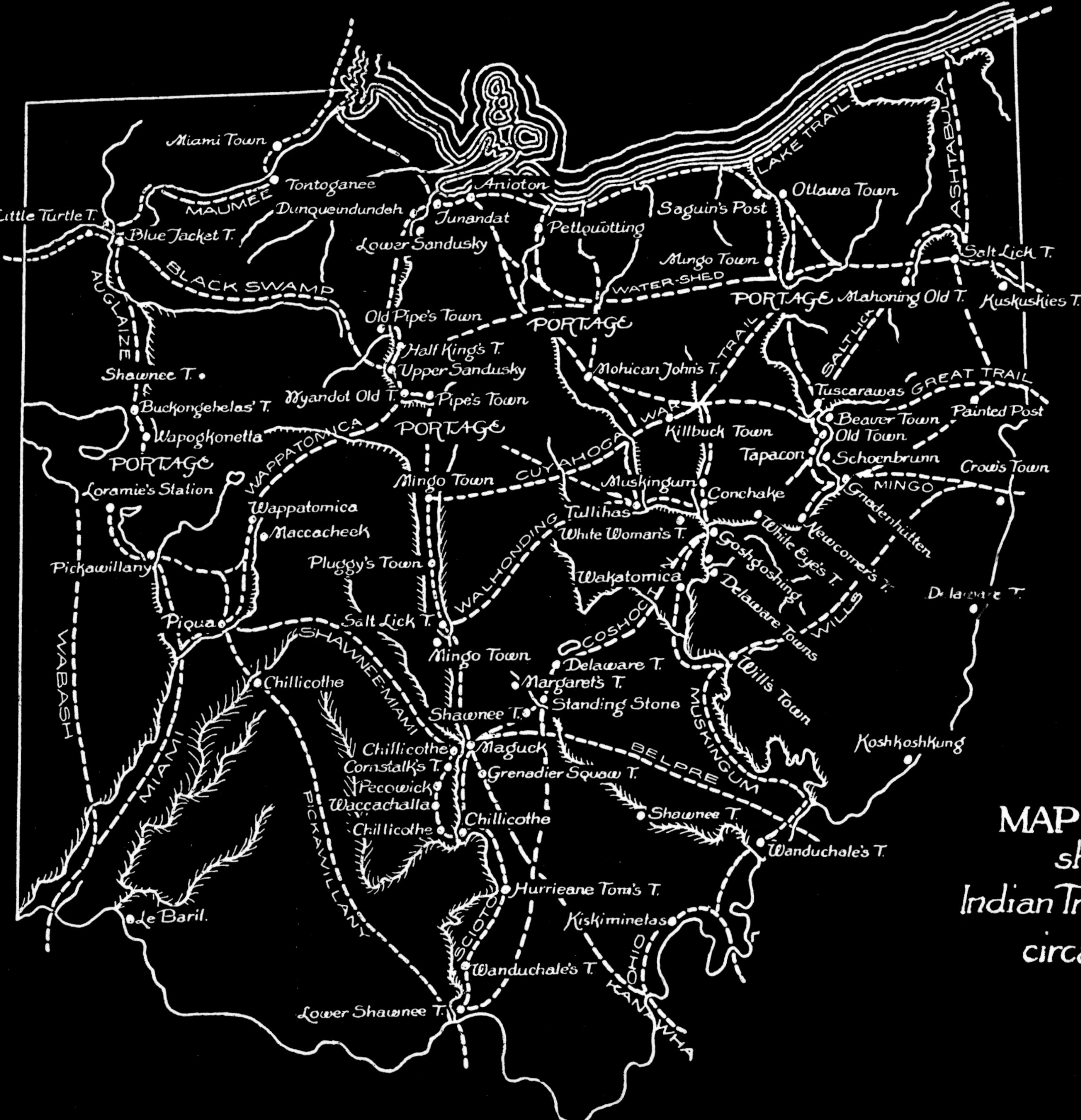

MAP of OHIO
showing
Indian Trails & Towns
circa 1776

OHIO INDIAN TRAILS

Third Edition

Frank Wilcox

EDITED BY WILLIAM A. McGILL

WITH A NEW INTRODUCTION BY RICHARD S. GRIMES

pictorial survey of the Indian trails of Ohio arranged from the works of Frank Wilcox

THE KENT STATE UNIVERSITY PRESS

Kent, Ohio

ISBN 978-1-60635-259-5
Manufactured in the United States

Library of Congress Cataloging-in-Publication Data

Wilcox, Frank N. (Frank Nelson), 1887-1964.
Ohio Indian trails / Frank Wilcox ; edited by William A. McGill ; with a new introduction by Richard S. Grimes. -- Third edition.
pages cm
"A pictorial survey of the Indian trails of Ohio arranged from the works of Frank Wilcox."
ISBN 978-1-60635-259-5 (paperback : alkaline paper)
1. Indian trails--Ohio. 2. Ohio--History, Local. I. McGill, William A. II. Title.
E98.T7W6 2015
917.71--dc23
2014045354

Third edition 2015

29 28 27 26 25 5 4 3 2

This book is dedicated

TO THOSE KINDRED SOULS

whose wholehearted interest and cheerful helpfulness

are more apparent today than Indian trails

Preface

This second edition of Frank Wilcox's *Ohio Indian Trails* is intended not only to satisfy a continuing demand for the long out-of-print limited edition of 1933–34, but also, to expand the visual material to include a greater variety of heretofore unpublished drawings and paintings made by Mr. Wilcox over a period of thirty years.

All but one of the reproductions in this volume were graciously loaned by Mrs. Florence Wilcox from her extensive collection, as also was *Dispossessed* (facing page 113) from the collection of Mr. and Mrs. Robert Backston.

Intermittently during this period Frank Wilcox revived his interest in the Ohio Indians. At one time he enlarged his concept of thirty-six black-and-white pen drawings to include larger full-page works in the same style. Another essay saw the development of a series of wash drawings treating specific historical subjects, while yet another produced a succession of small and charming watercolors. Included in this edition are selected examples, many in full-color, from each of these groups. Together they comprise a remarkable insight into the manner in which an accomplished artist can work with sustained interest over a number of years, enlarging and maturing an original concept of his fertile imagination.

Naturally, recent scholarship has unearthed new discoveries dealing with the archeological aspects of this study. However, Mr. Wilcox deals chiefly with the historic Indians in Ohio. The romance and the lore of the time in the Old Northwest Territory from the earliest European expeditions, during the reign of Louis XV of France, until the end of the War of 1812; lives vividly and with increasing validity in this book.

Alone, the visual material would constitute a commendable pictorial essay of the period, the territory and the never-ending battles in swamp and forest. Together with the text, it serves to enhance our imagined journey as we carefully trace the Indian paths throughout a state whose industrial, agricultural and economic growth has all but obliterated every vestige of its primitive history.

Were it not for the pen and brush of Frank Wilcox, we would suffer immensely in any attempt to reconstruct the spirit of this most important aspect of our heritage—the Ohio Indians.

William A. McGill

Contents

Illustrations xi
Introduction to the Third Edition xiii
Introduction to the Second Edition xix
Prologue 1
Physical Geography of Ohio 3
Brief History of the Indian and Indian Warfare in Ohio . 7
The Classification of Indian Trails 18
The Reconstruction of Indian Trails 23
The Lake Trail 27
The Mahoning Trail 33
The Watershed Trail 39
The Great Trail 43
The Muskingum Trail 49
The Moravian Trail 55
The Tuscarawas Trail 58
The Salt Springs Trail 59
The Ashtabula Trail 60
Trails in the Western Reserve 61
The Mingo Trail 65
The Scioto Trail or Warriors' Trail 69
The Cuyahoga War Trail 75
The Walhonding Trail 78
The Killbuck Trail 81

The Owl River Trail 82
The Mohican Trail 84
The Huron Trail 87
The Coshocton Trail 89
The Standing Stone Trail 93
The Ohio Trail 95
The Belpré Trail 99
The Kanawha Trail 101
The Shawnee-Miami Trail 103
The Pickawillany Trail 105
The Wappatomica Trail 110
The Miami Trail 113
The Wabash Trail 117
The Auglaize Trail 120
The Black Swamp Trail 123
The Maumee Trail 125
Conclusion 129
Bibliography 131
Ohio Rivers and Associated Trails 133
Ohio Towns and Villages Related to Trails . . . 136
Historic Indian Towns in Ohio 141
Topical Index 143

Illustrations

White Man and Red xx
An Old Trail Today xxi
Ancestral Mound xxii
Then and Now 4
The Eroded Plateau 5
Wayne's March to Fort Recovery 8

Color section following page 10
Col. Robert Rogers Discovers the Blue Hole at Castalia
Johnny Appleseed Refuses to Intrude upon a Sleeping Bear
An Indian Ridge Trail of Southeastern Ohio
Ogontz
The Fort Builders
Trader McCormick Befriends Zeisberger at Upper Sandusky
The Gnaddenhutten Massacre
The Death of Leatherlips

A Pioneer Outpost 11
Hamilton the 'Hair Buyer' at Detroit 15
State Archeologists Explore Tuttle's Hill at Willow 22
The Ridge Trail 25
Injured Surveyor 26

Color section following page 26
Habitation Site; Auglaize and Grand
Union Lane, Chippewa Camp
Cuyahoga Portage, Onandaga George's Lookout
Big Bottom
Marietta; Big Rock
Standing Stone Near Lancaster
Old Town; Birthplace of Tecumseh
Wappatomica Between Zanesville and Maccocheek

Wreck of Bradstreet's Expedition at Rocky River 29
Pontiac 30

The Lake of the Eries 32
Daniel Brady's Leap at Kent 35
The Salt Kettle 36
Celeron de Bienville Claims the Ohio Tributaries 38
Sign Language 41
Indian Attack at Fort Laurens 42
Friend or Foe? 45
The De Lery Portage; Fort Junandat to Port Clinton 46
Nicholas Cresswell Visits Heckewelder at Schonbrunn 48
The River Trail 51
The Missionary 52
Heckewelder Preaching to the Delaware at Coshocton . . . 54
The Pioneer's Progress 57
Ambuscade on the Chagrin River 62
Crawford's Forces Occupy 'Butte Island' 64
The Trail of Revenge 67
The Ultimatum of Chief Logan 68
Shattered Silence 71
The White Captive 72
Awaiting the Hunter 73
The Last of the Eries 76
The Lookout 80
The Indian Trader 85
The Huron Portage 88
The Old Northwest Forest 90

Color section following page 90
Col. George Groghan
Murder of Cornstalk at Point Pleasant
Simon Kenton
Spemica Lawba (High Horn) at Defiance
Old Britain Declares for the British at Pickawillany
Little Turtle Refused a Chair at Conference
Josiah Hunt Employs Camouflage During Wayne's Campaign
Simon Girty Refused the Protection of Fort Miami After Fallen Timbers

The Black Hand Gorge 91
The Trail Makers 94
Perils of the Ohio from the Indian Shore 96
La Belle Riviere 97
Unhappy Incident Among the French Engineers at . . . 98
The Forest Invaded 100
The Red Captive 102
Shawnees Attack a Frontier Settlement 104
The War Party 106

Color section following page 106
Prehistoric Flint Quarry, Newark
George Croghan and Christopher Gist on the Walhonding
The Smoke Signal
Col. Bouquet's Exchange of Prisoners at Coshocton
The Standing Stone Trail
The Treaty of Greenville
The Battle of the Wilderness
Dispossessed

Legendary Sacrifices at the Serpent Mound 107
Dispossessed 108
The Intercession 111
Little Turtle Has His Portrait Painted 115
William Wells Takes Leave of His Foster Father 116
The Marksman 118
The Prairie Portage. 121
Blackswamp Mutiny 122
Forest Voices 124
Miami of the Lakes. 126
Finding the Arrowhead 128
The Spirit of the Red Man 130

Introduction to the Third Edition

A "Remarkable Feeling for the Spirit of the Time"

Richard S. Grimes

The Kent State University Press is proud to rerelease *Ohio Indian Trails,* the classic work of Cleveland's Frank Wilcox (1887–1964). Originally published in 1933 and republished in 1970, Wilcox's *Ohio Indian Trails* brought to the American public the story of the thirty-one Indian trails that ranged throughout Ohio during the eighteenth century. These trails, mostly west of the Ohio River, dotted all over the Ohio backcountry and intertwined throughout the reaches of the Muskingum-Tuscarawas country in the east, south to the Scioto River valley, northeast to the Ashtabula-Sandusky region, and as far west as the Wabash, Auglaize, and Maumee areas. The trails served as conduits that allowed for cultural interaction among Delawares, Shawnees, Miamis, Wyandots, and other tribes of Ohio. They also operated as avenues for cultural interchange among Indians, frontiersmen, white settlers, and traders. These passageways had a rich and dynamic history. The Lake Trail (Cleveland area) served as the war trail taken by Iroquois warriors on their way to raid the Erie Indians to the north. The Mahoning Trail—an offshoot of the Beaver River—was used by Moravian missionary John Heckewelder and his Delaware Indian converts during the late 1760s as they fled the Allegheny country of western Pennsylvania and entered Ohio to start their mission towns along the Muskingum River. The Wappatomica Trail was used as a "line of communication" among the Shawnees, Wyandots, and Miamis and stretched from the Mad River valley to its "northern extremity" of the Sandusky Plains.

The trails presented in *Ohio Indian Trails* became meeting points for commerce and diplomacy, as well as backcountry paths taken by Indian war parties in their traditional raids against tribal enemies and early U.S. military during the 1790s in the conflict known as George Washington's War. Many of these trails had become obscured by the 1930s when Wilcox described the region's "rail fences, barbed wire, and tangled underbrush." In twenty-first-century Ohio the Indian trials have been thoroughly covered over with national and state highways, towns, public parks, schools, and shopping malls. Wilcox's thoughtful commentary on the history of these trails and his lament of their passing reveal that the physical geography of Ohio was the first American West of the new United States republic.

While *Ohio Indian Trails* offers a meticulous geographic description of trail locations and places them in their eighteenth-century historical context, it is Wilcox's artwork that augments the story of the trails with superb watercolors, ink, and pencil drawings. Wilcox, as a young aspiring artist, gained an impressive education. He attended the prestigious Cleveland School of Art from 1906 to 1910, studying under such art masters as Horace Potter, Frederick Gottwald, and Henry Keller. Wilcox thrived in the Cleveland area, which by the turn of the twentieth century had gained a national reputation for its artists, art schools, and commercial painters. From 1910 to 1914 Wilcox, seeking greater inspiration, painted in Paris, Europe's greatest cultural center. According to Case Western Reserve University art professor Henry Adams, Wilcox was most productive during these years and "savored Paris," absorbing the city scenes and its people with "intensity and eagerness as a cultural outsider," or, as Adams called Wilcox, a "Buckeye Abroad." His stay in Paris was interrupted by the First World War, and he returned to Cleveland where he taught at the Cleveland School of Art for forty years. While in Paris, Wilcox had honed his art skills, enhanced his sensitivity to the ambiance of the landscape, and, with this, developed his ability to extract meaning from his "subject matter."[1]

His Paris experience no doubt improved his naturalist style in what was known as the American Scene or Regionalist tradition. He used this understanding of natural themes to resurrect eighteenth-century Ohio history—with its wilderness landscapes, backcountry trails, Indian peoples, forts, trading posts, and white pioneers—from the distant memory of America's past. With its release in 1933, Wilcox's *Ohio Indian Trails* stirred a general interest in the past days of the early American western experience. Accompanying the story of the trails, Wilcox, the modern artist and master of watercolor, presented to 1930s America his pen and ink set pieces, as well as his pencil and ink wash drawings—all creatively drawn to show frontier life and historic events in a panorama of visual history. His art invoked a nostalgia and warmth for a long-past era in American history.

The 1930s were not a particularly good time in which to idealize the American western experience. The term *frontier,* especially, was being reassessed by academia. Living in the shadow of a Great Depression, many academics were not receptive to the adoration of Frederick Jackson Turner's Frontier Thesis, written and presented at the Chicago Exposition in 1893, and his veneration of the western frontier epoch that Turner believed spawned a distinct American identity, shaped American Democracy, and solidified the idea of American exceptionalism. As American studies historian Richard Slotkin explains, the "crisis

[1] Lecture by Henry Adams from Tregoning & Company Art Galleries, Cleveland, www.tregoningandco.com.

of the Depression" made the "heroic age of American expansion and the dream of limitless growth," fueled by the myth of the Great American Frontier, an outdated and invalid apparition.[2] This challenge to the romantic frontier was voiced in 1933 by Louis M. Hacker, then a prominent American history professor at Columbia University. Hacker disdained the views of Turner and others who gloried in the pioneer spirit, which, he argued, resulted in the Unites States' eventually embracing anti-Democratic characteristics of "monopolistic capitalism and imperialism." He saw those who romanticized the narrative of the American frontier as "fabricators of a tradition which is not only fictitious but also to a very large extent positively harmful."[3]

In presenting *Ohio Indian Trails* to a Great Depression–American public, Frank Wilcox went against the grain of the then current scholarship. His art and historical narratives were a return to espousing the positive aspects of the frontier experience and how it shaped a courageous and admirable American character. He also brought national attention to the role played by Ohio in the foundation of the United States. Ellen Lew Buell, in her *New York Times* book review of January 21, 1934, favorably noted that Wilcox contributed a "unique study which will nevertheless hold much interest for students of Ohio history. . . ." Buell praised Wilcox's efforts as a specialized study of nature and landscape that would "lend color and interest in [the] exploration of the past."[4]

[2] Richard Slotkin, *Gunfighter Nation: The Myth of the Frontier in Twentieth-Century America* (Norman: University of Oklahoma Press, 1992), 256.

[3] Louis M. Hacker, "Sections or Classes?," in *The Turner Thesis Concerning the Role of the Frontier in American History*, ed. George Rogers Taylor (Boston: D. C. Heath and Company, 1956), 40–41.

[4] Ellen Lew Buell, "The Trails of the Ohio Frontier," review of *Ohio Indian Trails*, by Frank Wilcox, *New York Times* (January 21, 1934): 9.

Leland D. Baldwin, Pennsylvania's preeminent historian at that time, admired Wilcox's "appreciation of the beautiful in nature [which] has made him [Wilcox] see Ohio as it must have existed in Indian days and this has led to the scattering here and there of admirable gems of description." More importantly, Baldwin acknowledged that Wilcox's artwork contributed to early American history and expressed a "remarkable feeling for the spirit of the time."[5]

Within the artwork and narrative provided in *Ohio Indian Trails*, Wilcox introduces readers to the many facets of eighteenth-century life in Ohio backcountry as well as to the historic events and noteworthy persons who shaped the times. Landscapes come to life with such titles as *La Belle Rivière, The Old Northwest Forest, The Big Bottom,* and *Marietta; Big Rock.* Wilcox chronicles the settlers, traders, and missionaries who interacted with Ohio's Native Americans to establish a "middle ground" of cultural accommodation between the races, with such titles as *The Indian Trader, Sign Language, Friend or Foe?,* and *The Missionary.*[6] Wilcox also brings to life the many historical figures who stamped the unique and distinct flavor of Ohio history: the French explorer Celeron de Bienville laying claim to the Ohio in 1749; the prolific Indian leaders Cornstalk, Pontiac, and Little Turtle; the Moravian missionaries John Heckewelder and David Zeisberger and their dedicated mission among the Delawares; the infamous renegade Simon Girty and his intercession

[5] Leland D. Baldwin, review of *Ohio Indian Trails*, by Frank Wilcox, *Western Pennsylvania Historical Magazine* 17 (March 1934): 60–61.

[6] For historical application of the term *middle ground*, see Richard White, *The Middle Ground: Indians, Empires, and Republics in the Great Lakes Region, 1650–1815* (New York: Cambridge University Press, 1992).

on behalf of the captured Colonel Crawford as he faced torture at the hands of the Delawares; General Anthony Wayne and his victorious army known as the Legion; and the legendary Ohio figure Johnny Appleseed on his wilderness adventures. Wilcox's art and narrative not only reflect regional history but, in the larger sense, articulate the dramatic account of European America's movement westward.

Wilcox presented his *Ohio Indian Trails* for a general audience—many of whom, as nonacademics, were less inclined to question the negative aspects of America's westward expansion. They were receptive to Wilcox's thoughtful work on Ohio history. Wilcox, in his romantic storyline, enthusiastically presented the advance and progress of American settlers through the Ohio country. This admiration for development can be found in his black-and-white drawings of Heckewelder, preaching the gospel to western Delawares at their Coshocton town on the Muskingum, and *The Pioneer's Progress,* which shows a hardy and determined frontiersman, ax in hand, clearing a path on the Moravian Trail for his family's Conestoga wagon and perhaps their new beginning in Ohio.

There were also touches of the heroic epic in Wilcox's art. In his brilliant watercolor *Col. Bouquet's Exchange of Prisoners at Coshocton,* he shows the British officer Colonel Henry Bouquet who, in the aftermath of defeating Delawares and Shawnees at the Battle of Bushy Run (in western Pennsylvania), marched his victorious army to the Muskingum to demand that Indian leaders return white captives to their families. Many of these captives were adopted into Indian families and were not inclined to return to white society. In this watercolor, Wilcox demonstrates that the Ohio Indians, with the end of Pontiac's War, faced a new world order of British authority in the West. In *The Treaty of Greenville,* Wilcox displays another transformative moment in Indian-white relationships, when General Anthony Wayne, fresh from his victory over a coalition of Northwest Indian nations (Ottawas, Delawares, Shawnees, Wyandots, Miamis, and Chippewas) at Fallen Timbers in the summer of 1794, together with American commissioners dictated a peace settlement that removed Indians from most of Ohio. The Northwest Confederation Indian nations agreed to cede to the United States the southern and northeastern part of the Northwest Territory. The resulting treaty forever ended any hopes that the Ohio River would remain the geographical and racial boundary between Indian lands and the United States.

Wilcox, in his portrayal of the western advance, was at times caught up in the moment of American triumph at the expense of Indian defeat. In reference to Native Americans, he at times reverted to such prejudiced and stilted descriptions as "lurking," "warlike," the "red man," and "temper of the savages." However, his art also demonstrates a sense of sorrow and remorse for the plight of American Indians and their fate. In his *The Gnadenhutten Massacre,* Wilcox depicts the dramatic moment when Pennsylvania militia from Washington County, cooper's mallets in hand, enter a cabin of Christian Delaware Indians. Over ninety Delawares were executed and scalped by the Pennsylvania militia at the mission town of Gnadenhutten in 1782—a prime example of both white savagery on the frontier and the callousness of territorial expansion. Wilcox's watercolor *Dispossessed* is a sad reminder of the relocation of Ohio's Indians, in the aftermath of Greenville, as they look back one last time at their beloved homeland and face an uncertain future as migrants in Indiana Territory. The motif of *Dispossessed* is tragically reminiscent of the final scene of James Fenimore Cooper's *The Last of the Mohicans* when Chingachgook mourns the death of his son Uncas and laments the passing of an age as his people fade away and accept the harsh reality that the white race will become "masters of the earth."[7] Another example—Wilcox's *Last of the Eries*—refers to a tribe that faced annihilation during the various Indian wars. This piece expresses a tone of poignant finality similar to the classic bronze-plaster sculpture of James Earle Fraser's *End of the Trail.*

Notwithstanding its Eurocentric lens, *Ohio Indian Trails* is as relevant today as when it first reached the attention of readers and viewers over eighty years ago. In Wilcox's nostalgic artwork and reflective narrative, the reader will once again experience Indian life in Ohio with Indian warriors taking the war trail, Indian women making salt while awaiting the return of the hunters, and native communities forging new beginnings by taking the paths of migration westward. Readers will once again experience the "pioneer spirit" that captivated America's popular literary and visual imagination during the distressing period of the Great Depression. Wilcox contrasts the stark reality with the lavish drama, which shaped the depth and richness of the Ohio story. In *Ohio Indian Trails,* Frank Wilcox re-acquaints us with our American frontier past, with its Indian trails, cultural middle grounds, violent racial conflict, and, sadly from the Indian perspective, with its conquest, relocation, and memory of the tragic.

[7] James Fenimore Cooper, *The Leatherstocking Tales* vol. 1, bk. 2, *The Last of the Mohicans: A Narrative of 1757* (New York: The Library of America, 1985), 877–78.

Introduction to the Second Edition

This account of the aboriginal trails of Ohio is offered with apology for probable errors.

The general routes are those determined by the research of the Ohio State Archæological and Historical Society, the works of Henry Howe, and by reference to the published journals of colonial military commanders and to other more fragmentary sources.

Some references are found to be contradictory and, with the hope of achieving an approximately correct statement, careful reference has been made to the topographical charts of the United States Geological Survey; established landmarks have been located, such as lakes, springs, Indian towns and military posts. The terrain between has been studied with a view to determining the original nature of the ground, and thus, the gaps have been filled in with the hope that the paths so laid out are reasonably correct.

Since a knowledge of the old Indian routes serves no practical purpose today, attention has been called to the natural beauties of the country and to the names and places recalling the life of the Indian. His is now a shadowy, romantic world that lies all but hidden under our practical civilization. For this reason, then, I trust the reader will pardon any statements that he may be able to correct with more accurate information.

Wherever possible, national and state highways are mentioned whenever they cover exactly or approximately the historic trails. The less traveled roads are found usually within short distances of them, but since the trails tend to run diagonally to the township byroads, such roads usually cross the trails, sometimes at several points.

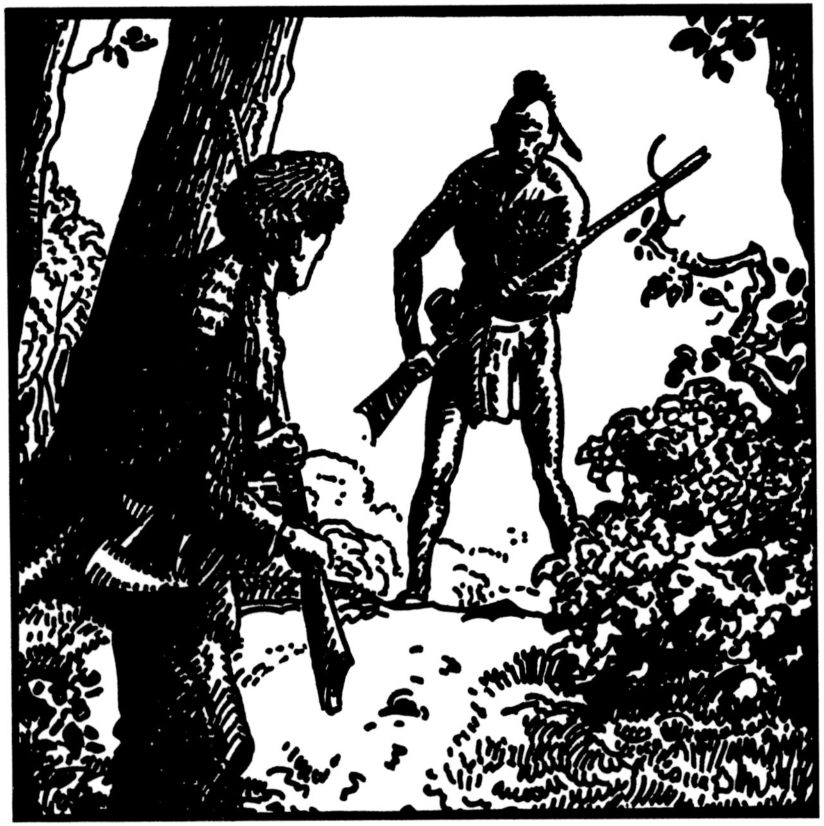

White Man and Red

There is practically no place in the state where the actual course of the trails is not visible from the highway, but there is a certain satisfaction in viewing the country from the historic viewpoint. All highway numbers are quoted as of the road maps of 1970.

Occasionally it is possible to trace comfortably by automobile long stretches of highway with the assurance that one is following an actual Indian trail. At other times the roads are practicable but unimproved. In some places the roads are of such a nature that only by saddle horse or on foot can one follow the actual path. The mere effort to trace in its full extent today one of the old trails or military roads is the best means of realizing the Spartan courage of the pioneer and the woods knowledge of the Indian, even though there is a great difference today between the pasture and wood lot of the peaceful Ohio farmer and the almost trackless wilderness of the Indian.

Perhaps the best policy for one living in this effete age would be to follow in a comfortable, or at least rough and ready, automobile the recognizable sections of trail to the point where, at some fork of the road, the actual trail leads under a fence or at best turns into a rutted track according to its alleged trend; then, to consult the route map for the next point where it again emerges upon brick, concrete or gravel.

Today, rail fences, barbed wire, and tangled underbrush offer obstacles sufficient to test the hardihood of the trail blazer; while an occasional bellowing bull or even an irate landowner may replace some of the dangers of the old trail. On the other hand, we have so many dangers on our own paved trails today that there is a feeling of freedom and safety, if one has the time in this rushing age to stroll leisurely over some section of the old trails in the quiet of the fields or woods.

We know today that ahead lies no trackless wilderness. We do not find it necessary to maintain our communications, but know that it could be accomplished very easily. There is no danger of starvation with money in pocket. The "Indians" of today do not lurk along the lanes, but on the highways and among the cities where once stood the bark huts of the Delaware, Shawnee or Wyandot.

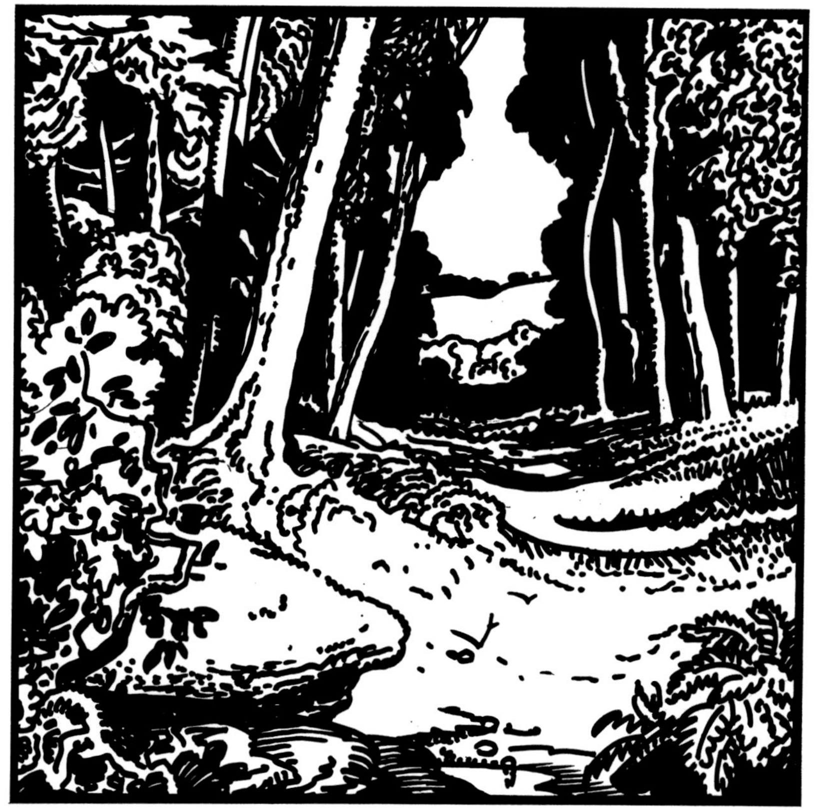

An Old Trail Today

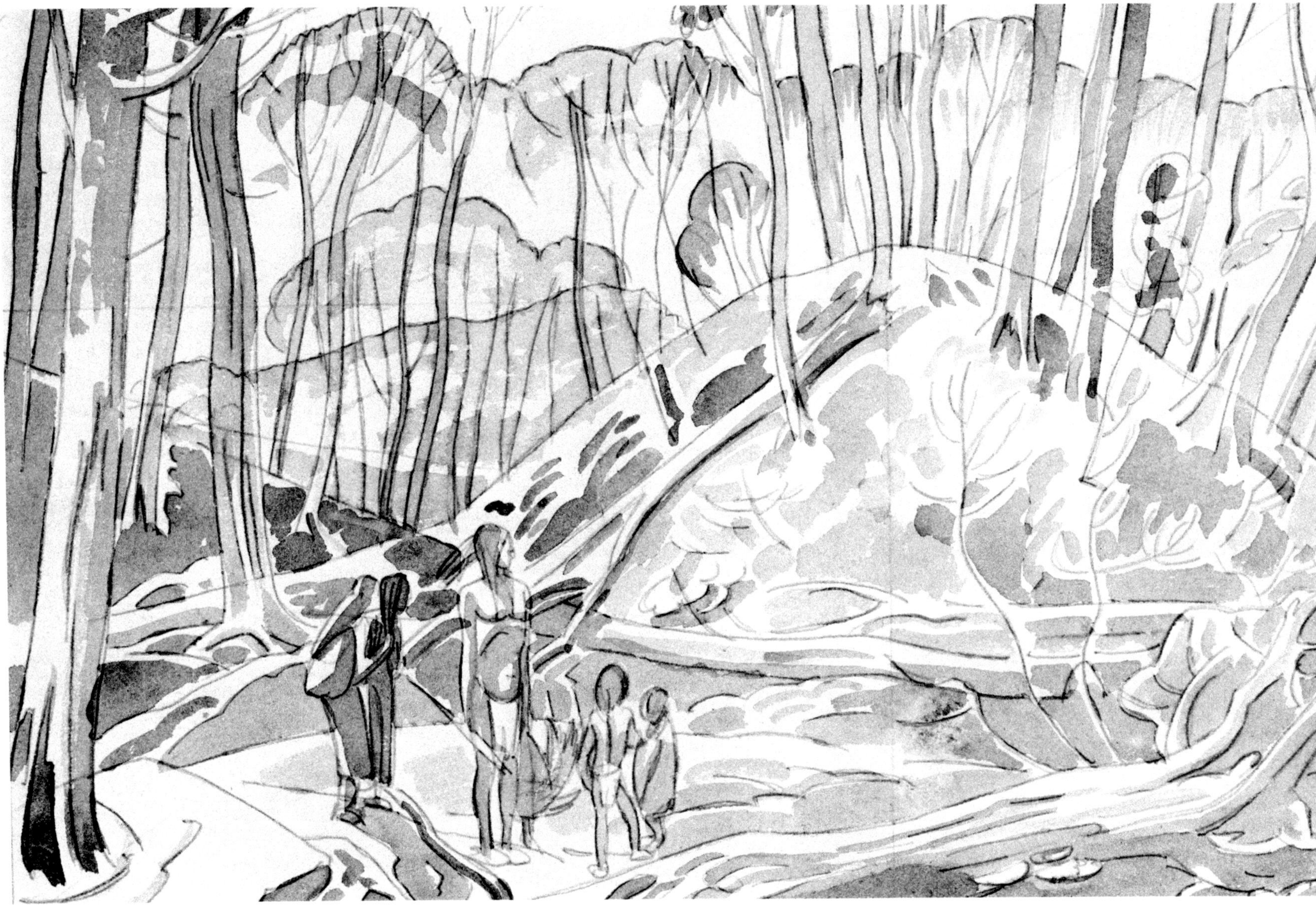

Ancestral Mound

Prologue

At the head of a shallow ravine, a spring flows from under a low ledge of rock. The old stone skillet was found right in the basin of the spring and the old trail, now scarcely more than a vague depression in the forest floor, passed by the spring, and, crossing the field above, now shows as a notch on the sky-line. It is cool and still by the spring, and the scattered sunlight shows a vague shape here and there, suggesting the half-hidden form of dark savage or lurching top of Conestoga wagon.

At one time the old trail, made by moccasined feet, was only a foot or two wide and cut deeply into the leafy floor of a lofty forest. Later it was widened by the hoofs of the traders' pack trains and the wheels of the settlers' wagons. Now it is a wide, shallow depression, hardly distinguishable where, within its bed, the second growth has almost reached again to primæval impressiveness.

If it is difficult today to trace this old Moravian road, how much more difficult would it be to follow the purely aboriginal trail through the plowed fields or the thick underbrush of modern timber where once the path led clearly through lofty aisles, hindered only by the fall of some gigantic tree column. On some few narrow ridges, where cultivation has never been attempted, and where the activities of lumbering have been too difficult, you may still see where the feet of the red man wore the ledge rock bare; and although the plowed lands, and the rivers yellow with silt, appear below, here at least the moss, wintergreen and pigeon berries still grow in the rusty needles of the hemlocks.

The aborigine did not blaze the trees along his highway, nor could the frosts of winter or the lush growth of summer hide the path from him. He did not trouble to straighten or improve a pathway blocked by fallen timbers or cut by freshets and landslips. When he traveled for days without meeting one of his own kind, how immense the land must have seemed and how futile the labor of road building must have appeared.

It has been said that the Indian trusted to the instinct of the wild creatures to lead him over the easy grades and down to the spring heads of the watercourses. Doubtless the mighty buffalo and elk led him over the watersheds, and the path of deer led him surely to the springs and salt licks. He felt his kinship with the creatures of the forest and learned from them wisdom. Who knows today where the plum thickets and cranberry bogs lay, and where hid the great wild turkey? It is only given to us to reflect upon the names he left behind him, and upon the dim suggestions that remain of the one time appearance of his country.

Over the wild grass lands of the river bottoms fell the shadow of the passenger pigeons; in the marshes the cries of water-fowl were seldom raised in fear of attack. The then broader and clearer waters of the streams were broken by the silver flash of leaping fish, and in a few favorable corners of the flat the squaw tilled her meager crop of maize, beans and pumpkin. The Indian towns, seldom more than temporary huts of bark, lay where the trails crossed the riffles, and around them for a season or two lay the rude gardens. These communities would appear pitiful indeed today, yet they were relatively important in their time, and have at least left their names to many a thriving city.

Much may still be discovered about Indian life in Ohio in spite of meager records and the obliterating effect of progress. Knowing eyes can read the vague depressions or ridges of the levels where path, earthwork or dance ring still show. The dark places in plowed land may reveal a camp site, or the peculiar erosion of a hillside may have originated in the Indian track.

To the practical and unimaginative mind it may be sufficient to cast a careless glance at a crossroads where over some roadside stand or gas station appears the sign "Old Trail Garage," but this purely geographic identification has an appeal to romantic sentiment in spite of its utilitarian nature. It is difficult, however, to conceive the glamor of the past where all evidences of it are concealed under concrete, and where adjacent landscapes are hidden by the glaring lights and colors of modern commerce. Rather let us journey on to where, at an abrupt turn of the concrete, an old road disappears into some vague and seldom trodden wood lot, and there seek out evidences to reconstruct the primitive.

Among certain lonely hills near the old trail by the spring, there stood a cabin where, on a night long ago, savages brought terror to the invaders of their solitude. Hated as they were then, the Indians appear today merely as a pathetic and romantic memory. Should one risk a trip over bad roads merely to see the spot whence they are gone? There is now no cabin, but only a little grove of trees with half-forgotten mossy slabs of stone. The slabs of stone are our heritage from the past, and the black woods to the west, where lurking shadows seem to move, recall the red man.

The Physical Geography of Ohio

To comprehend properly the vague pattern of trails that crossed the Ohio wilderness, we must consider the original character of the country.

The first to venture down the blue reaches of the Ohio saw only a dense and forbidding forest covering the semi-mountainous slopes of the Indian Country. Until the Muskingum was reached there was no clear glimpse into the dark and dangerous interior. To venture up the small streams that were closely overhung with trees and vines was to invite an ambush.

The valley of the Muskingum afforded a wider entrance into the region, but the tributaries, although they carried more water than they do today, were choked with driftwood, and the shores of the larger rivers afforded few good landings. The Scioto and Miami were similar approaches to the interior. They had wider bottom-lands and were probably less densely forested, but were occupied by the most hostile savages. The more daring of the traders and explorers ascended the various streams below Fort Pitt in turn: first the Beaver, then Yellow Creek and Cross Creek and others, until the water-shed was crossed in various places. This was a high and hilly region, cut by conflicting ravines that led down into the Muskingum-Tuscarawas Valley. Fort Laurens was built in the Revolutionary period as a protection against the red allies of England. It stood at Bolivar where the greatest of these Allegheny trails crossed the Tuscarawas. It was untenable in the face of the dark valleys that led westward into still more savage-haunted hills.

The height of land between the Ohio and the Muskingum system follows the line of Alliance, Lisbon, Carrollton and

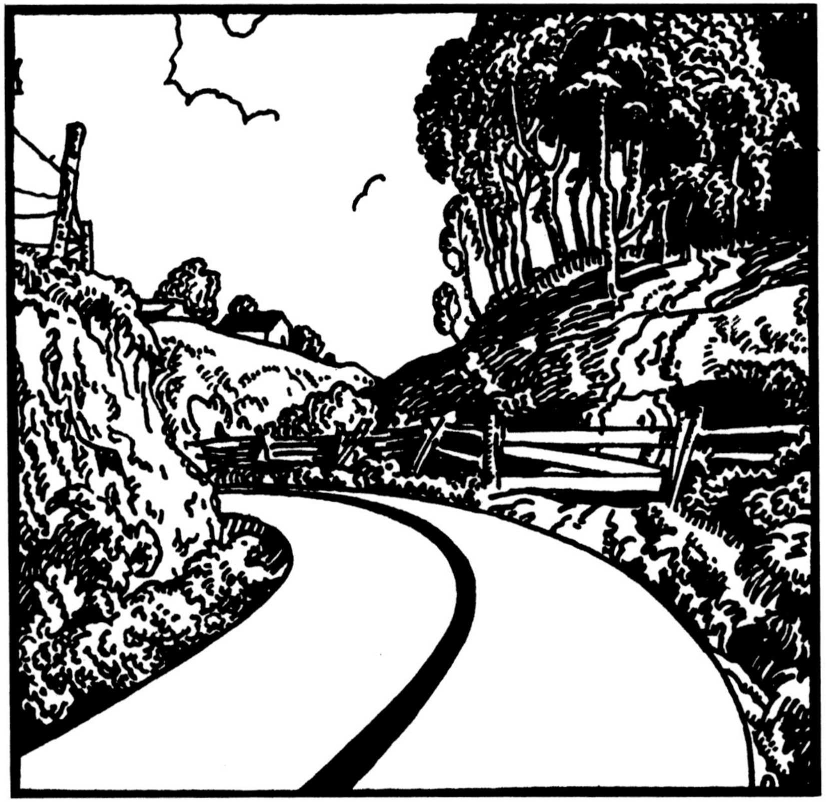

Then and Now

Cadiz and from these places a definite idea may be gained of the difficulties of early exploration. Apart from the danger of lurking savages, the endless blue ridges showed corresponding misty valleys, which are difficult to cross today when one is off the beaten track.

Below the Muskingum, the Hocking enters a region less lofty, but definitely broken by narrow valleys and gorges that must have seemed to lead nowhere. The Scioto Valley opened like a great highway between rounder and smoother hills, but the fertile flats above were guarded by warlike and hostile Shawnees. The mouth of the Scioto was a dangerous point to pass for many years.

Below the Scioto the streams entered more hilly and impenetrable ravines until the Little Miami was reached. This valley, after entering the back country, soon became invested by close-clinging woods. The Miami, however, aside from the hostility of the tribe of that name, afforded an easy approach to the interior except at high-water when it was swift and dangerous.

Since the white man was prone to depend upon the canoe in fear of ambuscades, these rivers mark the chapters in the history of the settlement of Ohio. The trails were used as warpaths from river to river in the attempts of the savage to frustrate the advances of civilization. It was only after the country was fairly well-known that military expeditions attempted to follow the trails or to blaze by the compass independent routes to the Indian settlements.

Northeastern Ohio, with its short streams, was not entered from the Lake. The Sandusky-Maumee territory, though easy of penetration, was held by England and her savage allies, the Wyandots and Ottawas.

Standing on the height of land just east of Bellefontaine we can look down upon this old region, the ancient bed of Lake Erie. To the north and west lie the lakes around the portages at the heads of the Miami, Auglaize and Wabash. To the northeast lies the portage from the Sandusky to the Scioto. To the east the ground descends rapidly to the head of the Mad River; southward extends the long dividing ridge between the Scioto and Miami systems.

From the height of Bellefontaine the watershed leads northeastward through the Cuyahoga Portage to Little Mountain, where the northern drainage is only a few miles wide and the streams are short and rocky. This line, which conforms roughly with the Greenville Treaty line, separates the northern and southern valleys. The most lofty points on this line are the heights of Bellefontaine, Big Springs at the head of the Mad River Basin, and the extent across the high prairies around Marion, south of the Sandusky Plains; another abrupt elevation is found east of the Scioto Portage around Mansfield, and so on northeastward through Barberton, Akron and Chardon. This great ridge is cut into on its southern slopes by the Miami, Scioto and Mahoning, and on the north by the Sandusky, Cuyahoga and Grand Rivers.

Another point where the topography of Ohio is realized is on the slope of the high land southwest of Mount Vernon where we come upon the steep descent into the Scioto Valley levels. At Gambier we look eastward down to the distant blue Walhonding and Muskingum Valley hills. On the high

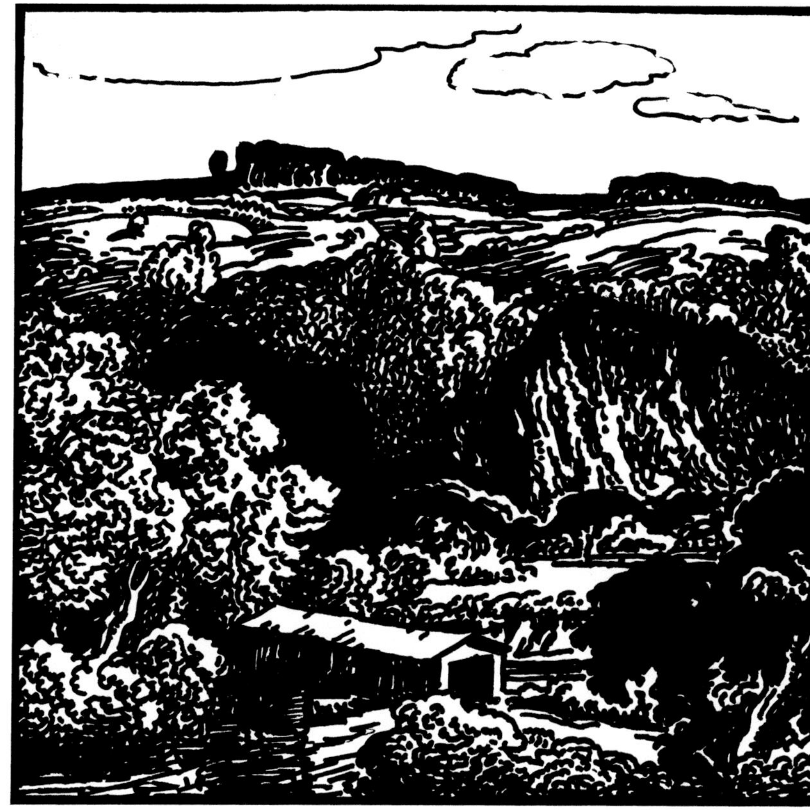

The Eroded Plateau

broken plateau around Canton are the descending radii of streams, and at Little Mountain the steeper eastern shores of Old Lake Erie are visible. The Killbuck leads southward from Wooster to the Walhonding, showing a long north and south cleft in the glaciated plateau.

Evidences of high land isolated by erosion show at several places. One of these is a cluster of hills east of Flint Ridge, surrounded by the flats of the Muskingum, Licking and Wappatomica; another is the series of long parallel ridges between the tributaries of the Scioto, running principally north and south between them, such as the Olentangy and Walnut Creek. These ridges disappear around Columbus, and the Pickaway Plains appear in the wide basin below.

Water gaps are seen just south of Chillicothe where the Scioto cuts the hills of Pike County, and in the long north and south reach of the lower Muskingum.

Descending from hilly Vinton County, the land south of the Pickaway Plains is studded with the isolated hills around Mount Logan and the many knobs of which Rattlesnake Knob is the most conspicuous. A distant view of this region is a mountain landscape in miniature, the haze of the plains seeming to magnify the blue ridges.

Southwest of Paint Creek is the region of flat topped hills between the Scioto and the Little Miami, of which Fort Hill is typical.

It might be said that each county has a distinct physiognomy. Physical conditions of the country have contributed to the forming of political divisions in the past, and this is true with the possible exception of the counties in the "black swamp" region to the northwest. At the present day there is sufficient difference in situation and soil to afford a recognizable diversity in vegetation. The solid groves of the Sandusky Plains resemble the description of the "Battle Island" at the time of Crawford's Defeat, although the prairie grass is gone. The ragged forests of the eastern coal hills differ radically from the high meadow trees of the moorland from Bellefontaine to Hillsboro.

With this conception of the surface of Ohio, we can easily see that the Indian Trails were bound to vary in character, situation and purpose.

Brief History of the Indian and Indian Warfare in Ohio

Four major river systems are found in Ohio. These river basins were occupied early in our history by four major tribal divisions of the red man. In the Muskingum Valley dwelt the Delawares who had entered Ohio territory soon after the first settlement of the seaboard. The Shawnees occupied the fertile prairie bottom-lands of the Scioto River, and the Miami Basin was inhabited by Indians of that name. In the Maumee Valley, then called the Miami of the Lakes, were found Ottawas and Hurons or Wyandots who seem to have entered that territory after the invasion of Ontario by the Iroquois. Certain sub-tribal divisions also existed in definite places, such as the Mingos, a group of Iroquois clans near Steubenville, at Mingo Bottom and elsewhere, and the Mohican colony in Ashland County.

As the white man disturbed their solitudes they were scattered and became allied with other tribes to the west and north, and fought their last battles in the northwestern part of the state. The Western Reserve was at that time largely untenanted, probably on account of its proximity to the Iroquois confederacy in New York, but was visited by hunting parties and had at least temporary settlements.

Very early in our history the Frenchman had fixed trading posts at the Cuyahoga, the Sandusky and the Maumee. Loramie's Station at the present Loramie Reservoir on the Miami, Wabash and Auglaize portage was known at an early date and Pickawillany especially, above modern Piqua, figured largely in French and English dealings with the Indian at the time of the French and Indian War, when Ohio first engaged the attention of the English.

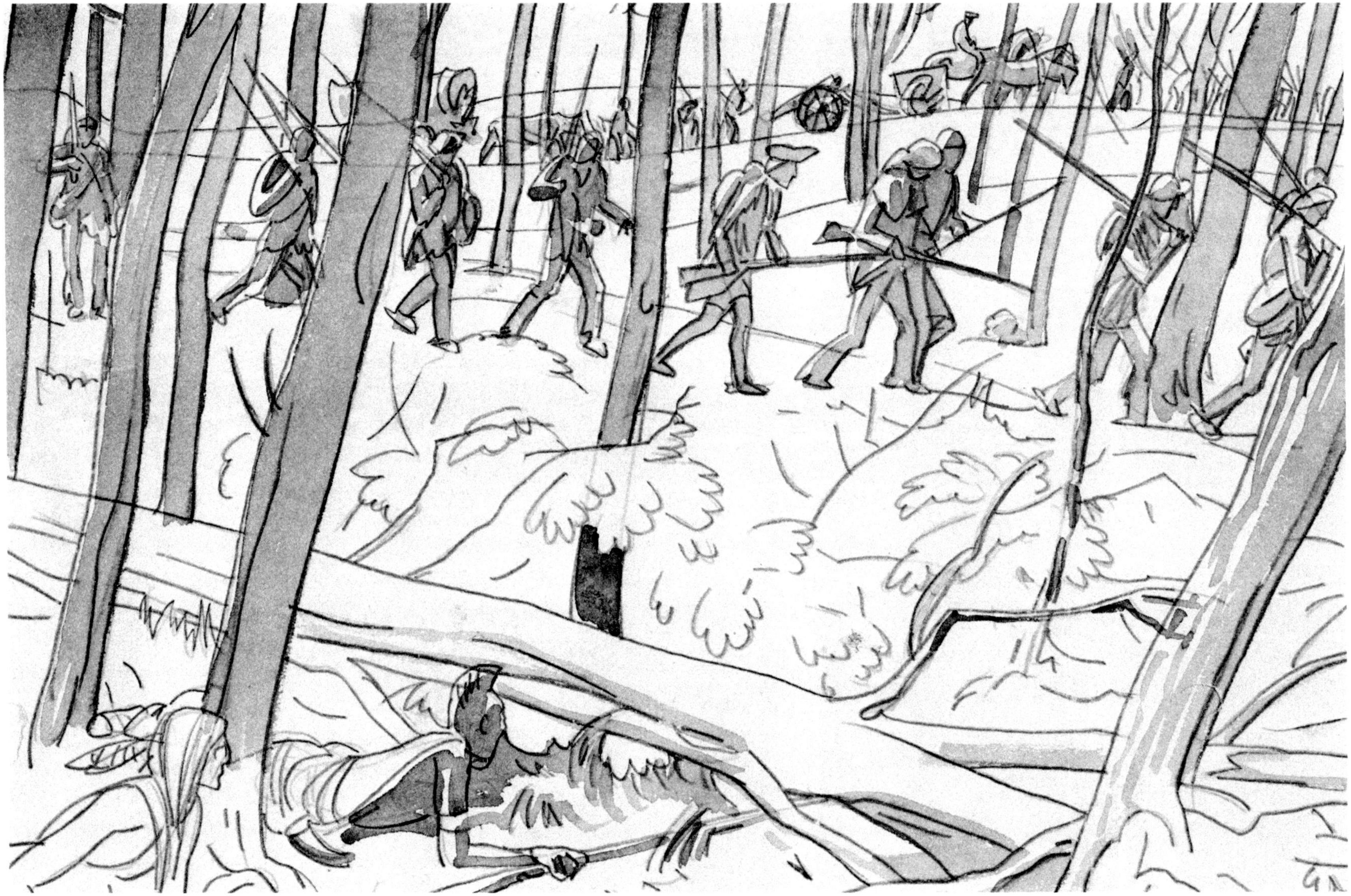

Wayne's March to Fort Recovery

Pickawillany, far as it is from the Alleghenies, was visited by the scout and emissary of the colonial government, George Croghan, where the friendly chief "Old Britain" defied French authority in that region. It became the policy of both nations in the French and Indian War to try to control the Ohio country and to establish forts throughout the region.

Christopher Gist, the agent for the Ohio Company and associate of Washington, was sent in 1750 to study the Indian country now known as Ohio. His explorations cast much light on the nature of that little-known territory and on the temper of the savages who were largely loyal to France on account of the tact of French traders and their disinclination to take up land or settle in the region. The Moravian Missionaries to the Delawares, Post and Weiser, were followed by Heckewelder who made the first map of the region later known as the Western Reserve.

Another explorer and diplomat of the period following the conquest of Canada by the English was Robert Rogers of New Hampshire who had gained fame in the region of Lake George in the French and Indian War. He was sent by the British government into Ohio from Montreal and visited Detroit and Sandusky, returning by the Great Trail to Fort Pitt. On this trip he discovered the famous Blue Hole Spring at present Castalia.

The English, after the fall of Quebec and the cession of Canada, took over all French posts and Indian agencies, but failed in many cases to win the loyalty of the Indians, probably on account of their immediate programme of settlement and exploitation. Chief among the Indian leaders in the west was Pontiac who was born at Piqua on the Miami.[1] He succeeded in organizing a masterly attack on all posts almost simultaneously from Michilimackinac to the Ohio and almost succeeded in winning his campaign. The expedition of Bradstreet from Albany, in co-operation with Bouquet from Fort Pitt, was designed to win over the loyalty of the Indians prior to this insurrection. Bradstreet failed in gaining any ground and his expedition was wrecked at the mouth of Rocky River on the return. Bouquet, however, effected such a show of force on the Great Trail to Coshocton that he succeeded in rescuing many hostages seized by the Indians up to that time.

After the failure of Pontiac the settlers from the east mustered for the invasion of the Ohio country and there were desultory attempts on the part of the Indians to frustrate them. Minor wars of retaliation on both sides occurred. The family of Logan, the Mingo chief, was massacred by white men opposite Yellow Creek on the Ohio during what is known as Cresap's War. This provoked another definite Indian insurrection.

Against this uprising was organized the campaign under Lord Dunmore, Governor of Virginia, and Colonel Lewis of the colonial rangers. Dunmore with his regulars moved down the Ohio and Lewis down the Kanawha with a plan to meet Dunmore at the mouth of that river. Since at this time the coming Revolution was already in the air, much comment has been made on Dunmore's ascent of the Hocking to the

[1] The Ottawas were driven by the Iroquois to Green Bay, Wisconsin, and a fragment later settled on the Maumee. They had a reputation for cowardice, but produced the great Pontiac.

Shawnee towns, leaving Lewis to fight Cornstalk, the Shawnee chief, at Point Pleasant. Although Lewis had won a signal victory, his forces resented the independent action of Dunmore, and it was this victory rather than any diplomacy on the part of Dunmore which ended the uprising. The peace treaty was signed under the no longer standing Logan Elm where that famous chief was said to have delivered his eloquent speech rebuking the white man.

In this campaign served many borderers whose names are famous in the history of Ohio; George Rogers Clark, Simon Kenton and the notorious Girtys were among them. The impending War of the Revolution tested their loyalty. To some, Point Pleasant appeared to be entirely a colonial victory and the conduct of Dunmore was considered evasive; by some, it is still considered the first battle of the Revolution. Some of these borderers, like the Girtys, went to Detroit to serve under Hamilton, the "Hair Buyer," whose activities during the Revolution provoked many depredations on the part of the Indians.

During the nominal peace which followed Dunmore's Treaty, Cornstalk, the Shawnee chief, was cold-bloodedly murdered at Point Pleasant, and the troubles continued along the border. The colonial government after the outbreak of hostilities with England felt it necessary to establish an outpost between Pittsburgh and Detroit, and Fort Laurens was built where Bolivar now stands on the Great Trail crossing of the Tuscarawas. This lay above the settlements of the loyal Christian Delawares, but was untenable in the face of strong Indian attacks prompted at Detroit.

The settlers thronging into West Virginia and Kentucky felt themselves too aloof from international war to trust to the protection of the colonial government and took it upon themselves to deal with the Indians in their own way. For this reason they were not always amenable to discipline when official expeditions were sent out. The scout Kenton, like Daniel Boone, was a free agent who lived through many thrilling adventures at Wappatomica on the Mad River, at Chillicothe and elsewhere. He scouted for the colonial commander Logan on the Mad River Expedition during the Revolution.

Another famous scout of the day was Brady who, escaping from the stake at Sandusky, was pursued to the Cuyahoga at Kent where he leaped over the gorge and hid in the lake now bearing his name, thus escaping his pursuers.

George Rogers Clark had achieved his famous victory at Vincennes and had overcome the Englishman Hamilton when in 1780 he made his successful attack on the Indians at Piqua and Old Town or Chillicothe in the Mad River Valley. The British commander Bird, accompanied by the Girtys, had at about the same time attacked posts in the Miami Valley.

In 1781 an expedition under the American Brodhead destroyed the Indian towns around Coshocton on the Muskingum. The Christian Indians had for some time lived in several towns above this point on the Tuscarawas. In this troubled period the inhabitants burned and abandoned Schoenbrunn, but many Indians from Gnadenhutten, including their missionaries, were led as hostages to Detroit under

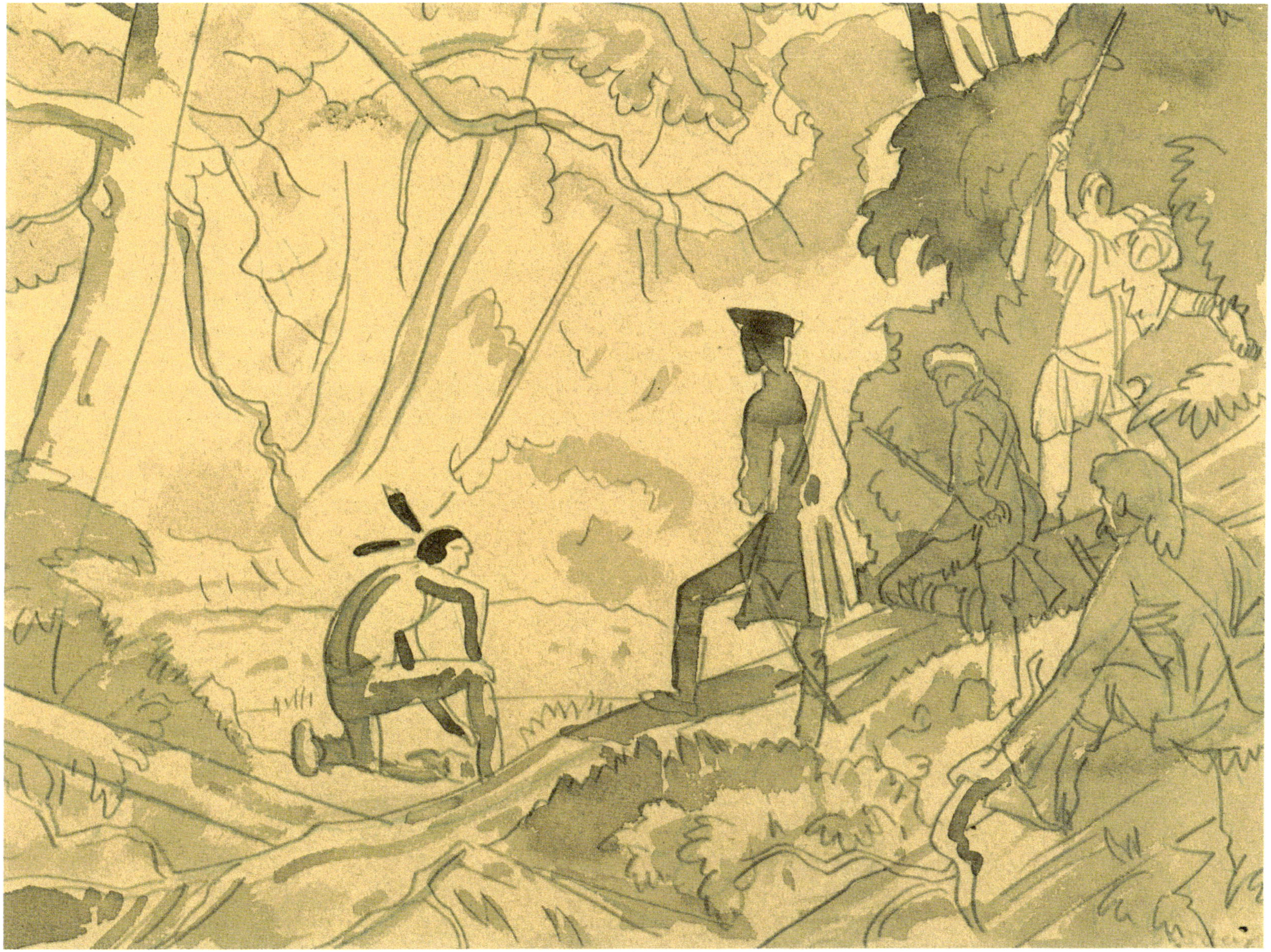

Col. Robert Rogers Discovers the Blue Hole at Castalia

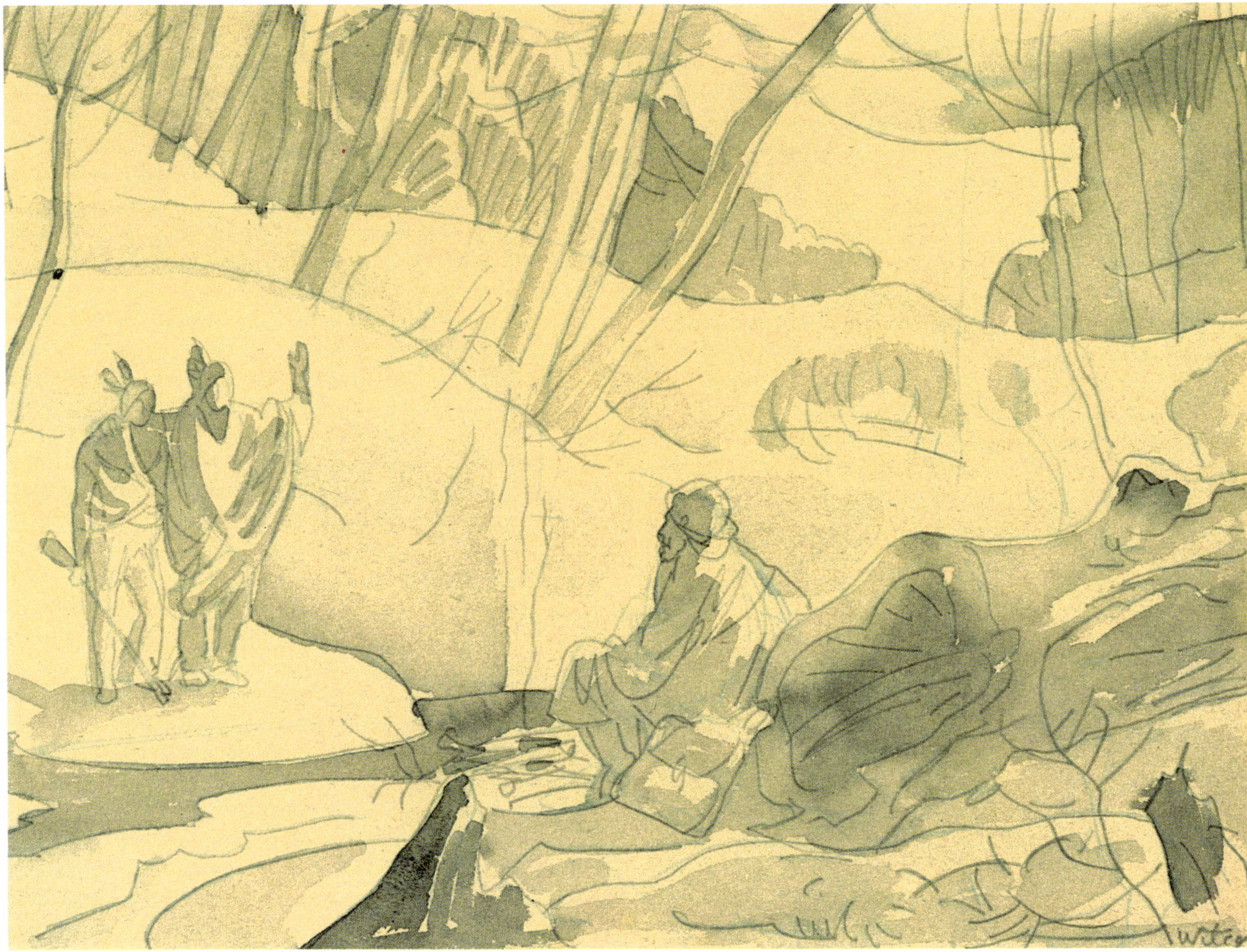

Johnny Appleseed Refuses to Intrude upon a Sleeping Bear

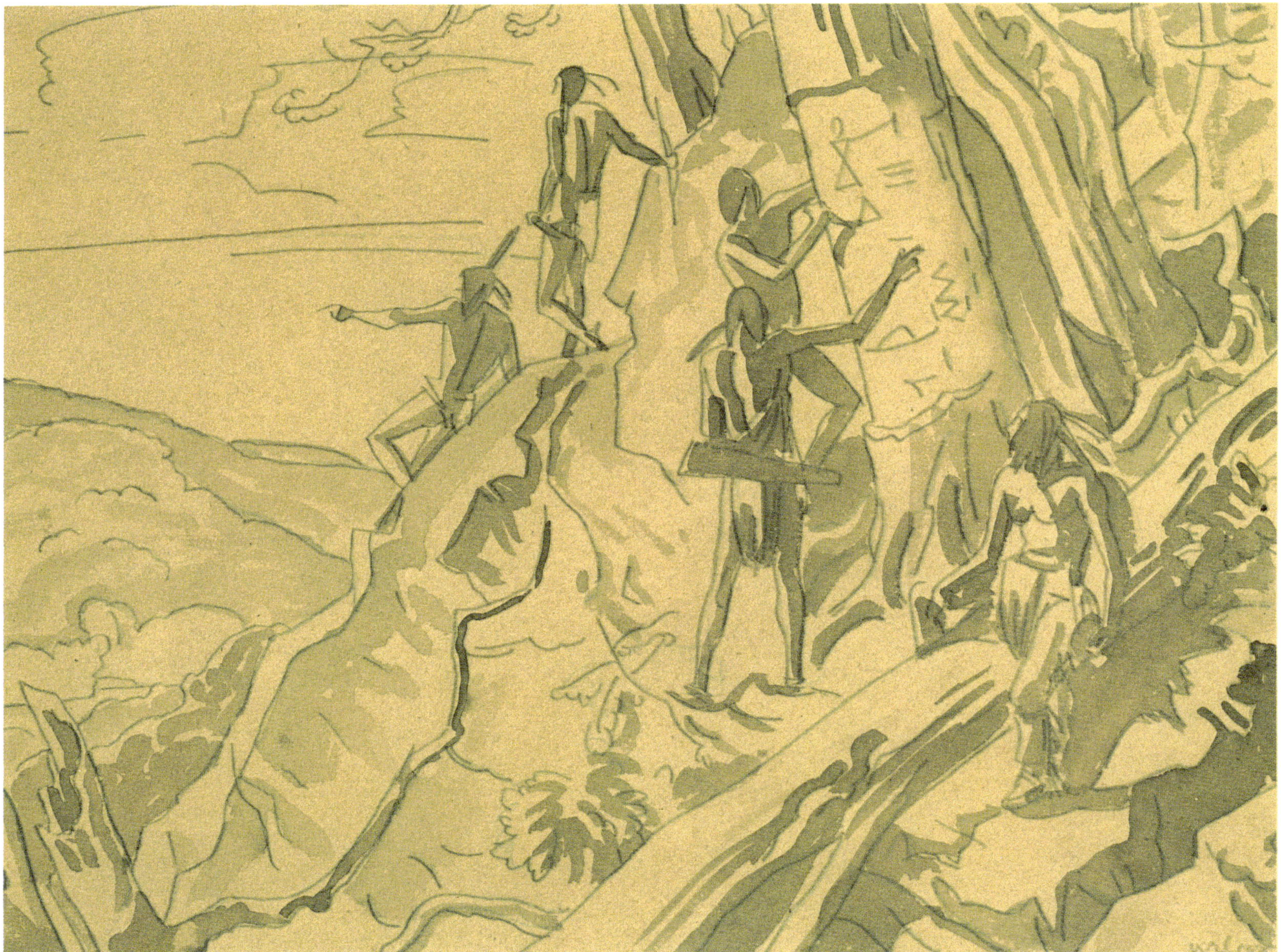

An Indian Ridge Trail of Southeastern Ohio

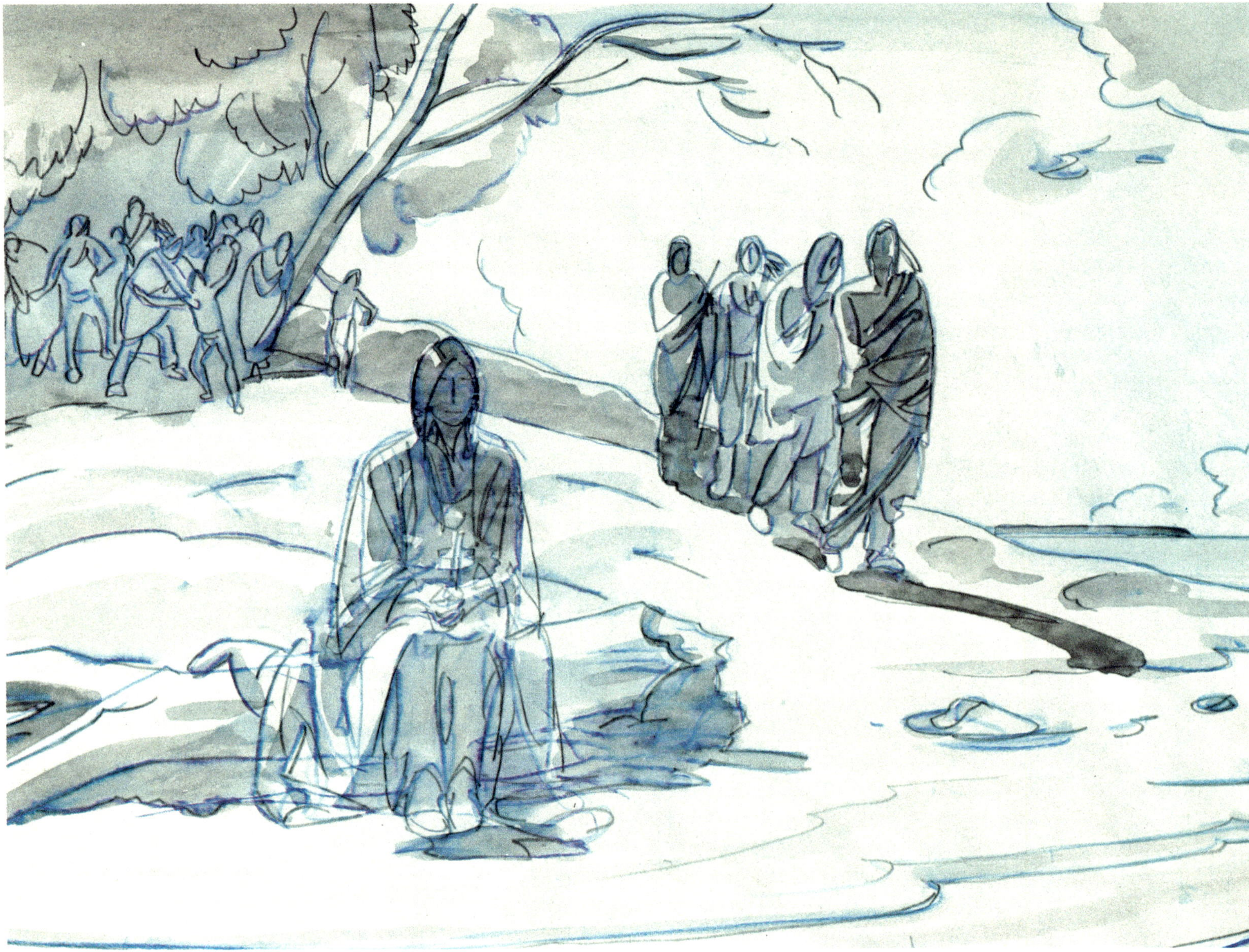

Ogontz

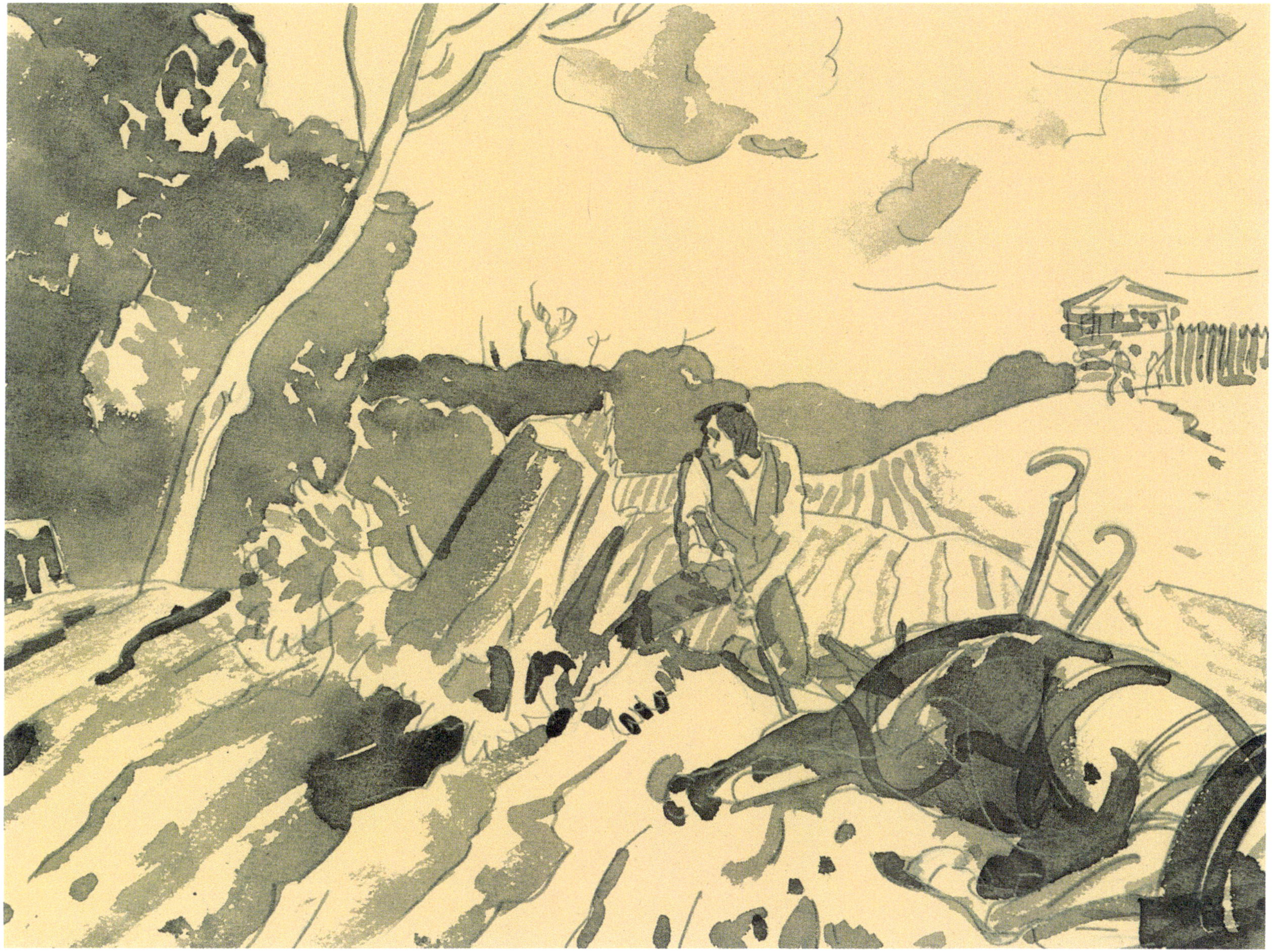

The Fort Builders

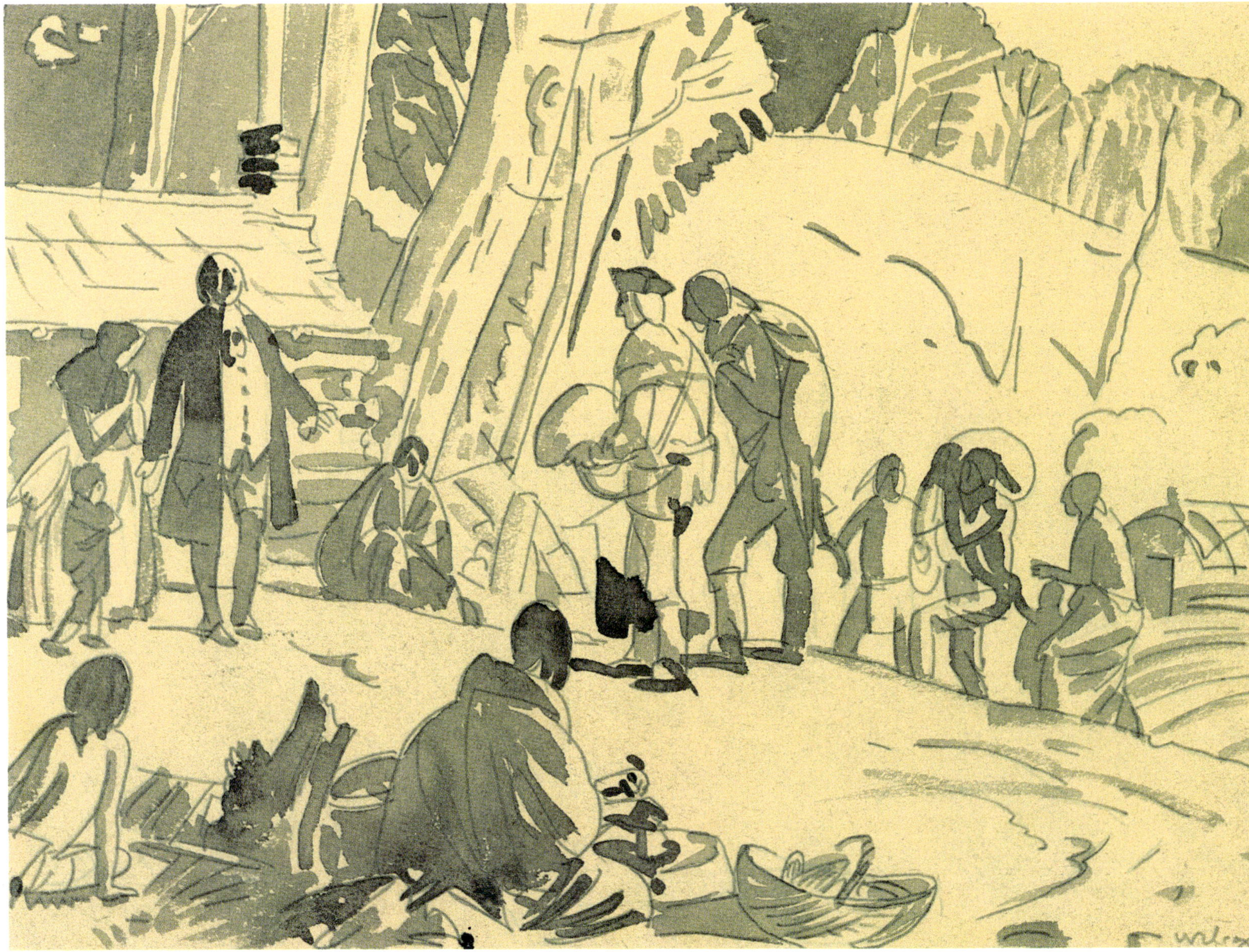

Trader McCormick Befriends Zeisberger at Upper Sandusky

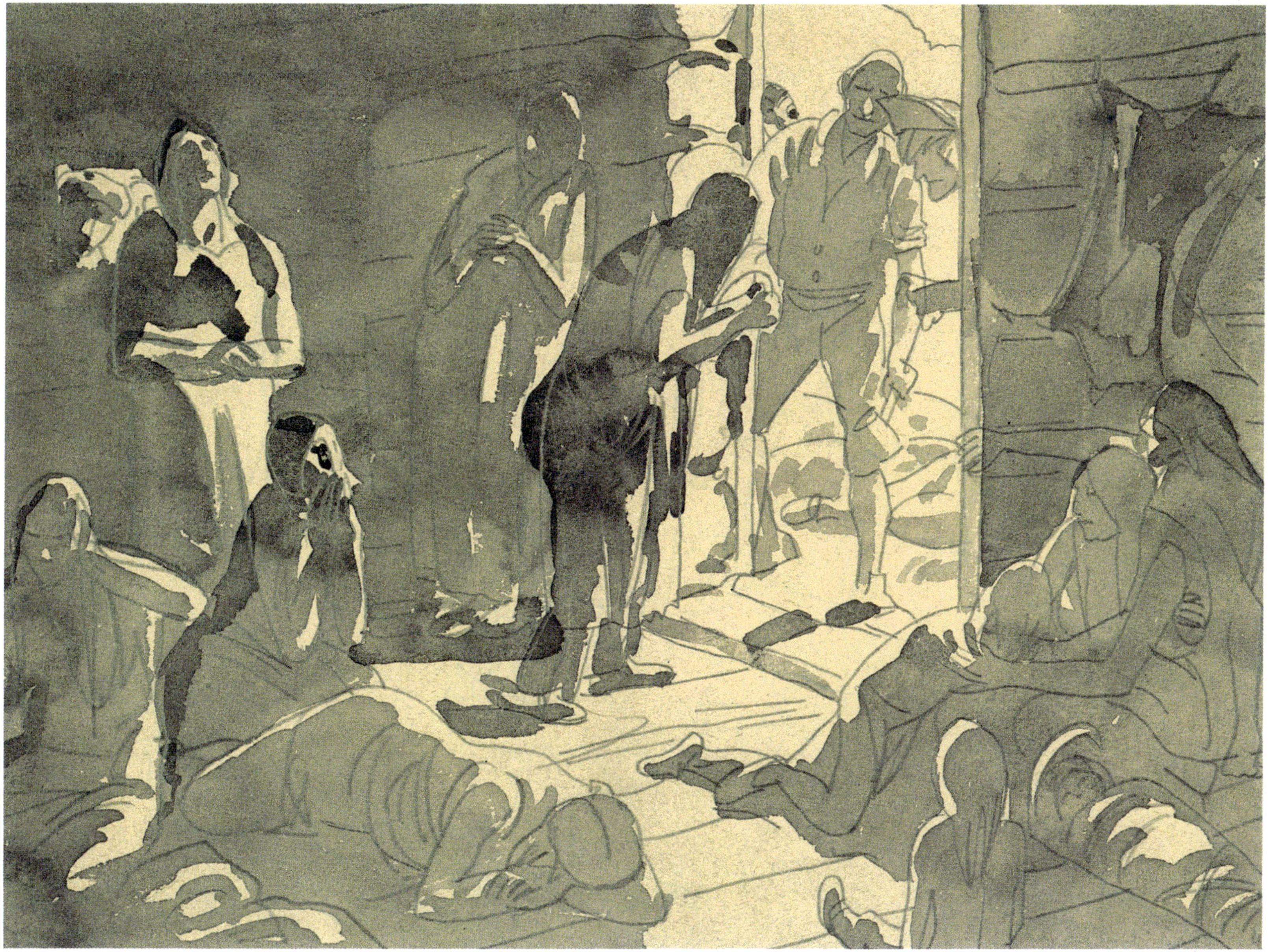

The Gnaddenhutten Massacre

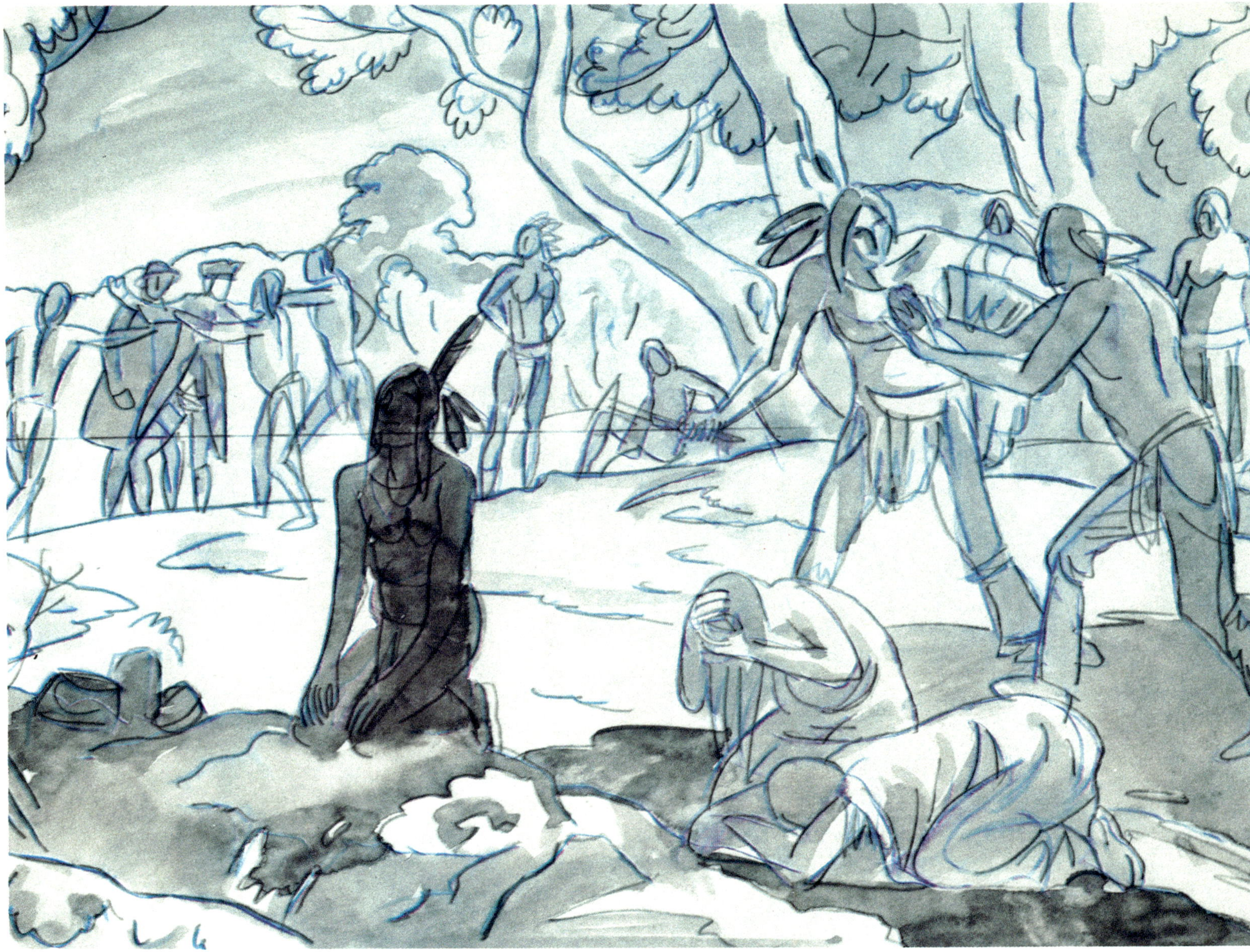

The Death of Leatherlips

the Wyandot, Half King, and the Tory scouts, McKee and Elliott, owing to the belief that they might bear arms against England. They spent an unhappy winter at Upper Sandusky Old Town and some of them were allowed to return to Gnadenhutten to harvest the former year's corn. While here they were attacked and murdered by American borderers under Williamson in 1782, having played a tragic neutral part in the war.

In 1782 it was decided to settle the Indian problem definitely with a well-organized expedition against Sandusky. Colonel William Crawford, an associate of Washington, was defeated at Upper Sandusky and was seized by the Wyandots on the retreat and burned as the perpetrator of the Gnadenhutten massacre though he had played no part in it, nor had the Wyandots been particularly hospitable hosts to the Delawares.

Although the Indians continued to menace the eastern part of Ohio, Marietta, the first town, was founded in 1782, and the land was opened to settlement. Harmar launched an ineffective attack against the Maumee and later in 1791 General Arthur St. Clair gathered forces for the purpose of building a strong fort on the Maumee to protect Ohio from the powerful confederacy forming between the Indians of Ohio and Indiana. He was disastrously defeated where Fort Recovery now stands, but General Anthony Wayne succeeded in defeating the great Indian leaders, Little Turtle and Tecumseh, at the Battle of Fallen Timbers. Wayne built several forts, including Fort Recovery and Fort Wayne, and thereafter no serious difficulty with the Indians was experienced in Ohio.

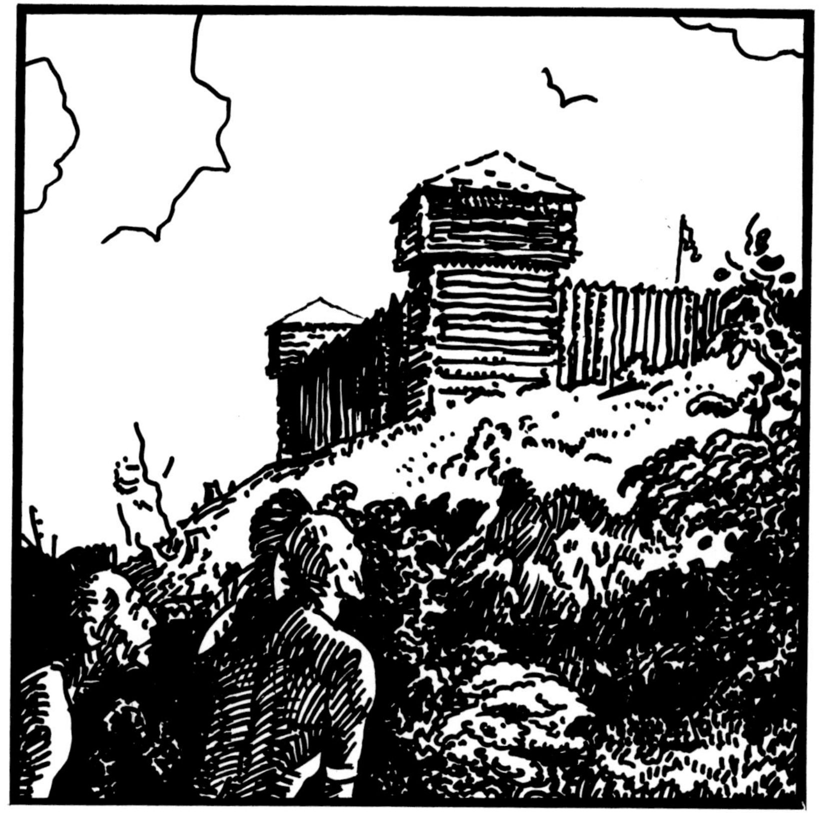

A Pioneer Outpost

At the treaty of Greenville the frontier of the United States in Ohio became the Greenville Treaty Line to the Cuyahoga Portage. This line extended from a point opposite the mouth of the Kentucky River to Fort Recovery; thence to Fort Loramie and northeastward to Fort Laurens. Northward it followed the route to the Cuyahoga Portage and Lake Erie, via the Cuyahoga. Early in the nineteenth century the last Indians who had dwelt northwest of this line retired from Ohio entirely. Many served the United States in the War of 1812, but did not remain much longer in the state. The Indian mission still stands at Upper Sandusky, as do the house and Indian Agency of Johnson, the American Agent, near modern Piqua.

Kenton and Zanesfield, at the head of the Mad River, recall Ohio's two great borderers and these places exhibit much to remind one of their times. The Zane Trace still remains in memory of Ohio's first trail blazer in the period of colonization.[1]

[1] Lewis Wetzel was one of the sworn enemies of the Indian in Ohio. On a promontory west of Moundsville, West Virginia, members of his family were lured to their death by the Indians, by means of a simulated turkey call. His activities against his enemies took place largely in Belmont County in southeastern Ohio. A spring near St. Clairsville bears his name.

One of the first of the travelers of Ohio roads and trails was Johnny Appleseed. The Indians believed him to have been touched by the Great Spirit, and thus he was enabled to travel in safety throughout the state where he went about planting orchards in advance of settlement. His real name was John Chapman and he was born at Springfield, Massachusetts, in 1775.

Famous Indians and Indian Towns

Early accounts of Indian warfare mention a few outstanding Indian leaders. In the Muskingum Valley are mentioned names that reappear in the Scioto and Maumee Valleys. We gather that the period of the Revolution saw a rapid retreat of the Indian across Ohio. Many served in both armies during the Revolution and we are surprised at their capacity to travel long distances from their tribal towns, many having fought on far eastern battlefields such as Saratoga.

Chief of the Indians in the Muskingum Valley appears to have been Captain White Eyes. Logan, the Mingo, was prominent near Steubenville, and Cornstalk appears to have been the great leader of the Shawnees. Captain Pipe, Tarhe (the Crane) and Blue Jacket figure prominently among the Wyandots, but Tecumseh and Little Turtle are prominent throughout the period. Pontiac has assumed almost legendary dignity since he figured largely before much was known of Ohio.

Of the Indian towns in Ohio, Coshocton claims the great Delawares, the territory around Circleville the Shawnees, and Old Piqua near Springfield claims Tecumseh. Pontiac was born among the Ottawas of the Maumee, but Little Turtle was born out of our territory at Fort Wayne.

By the time of the second war with England in 1812 most of the Indian trails had become the white man's property. Many Indians remained about Sandusky Bay and the Maumee and they fought as usual on one side or the other, but they were then definitely leaving our territory. Tecumseh fell at the battle of the Thames in 1813.

The White Man's Use of Indian Trails

Considering the known Indian trails of Ohio from the standpoint of the white man's history, they may be summarized as follows:

The Lake Trail

This trail was traversed in the neighborhood of Sandusky Bay by Colonel Robert Rogers in 1760. He discovered the Blue Hole Spring and noted many present day landmarks. When on his mission he is said to have met Pontiac at the mouth of one of the northern rivers and to have received from the Chief definite warning of opposition to intrusion by the English.

The survivors of Bradstreet's and Amherst's expeditions utilized the Lake Trail to Fort Niagara after the shipwrecks near Rocky River.

The Mahoning Trail

This trail was used by Heckewelder, the associate of Zeisberger, the Moravian Missionary to the Delawares. His manuscript map of the region traversed by it may be seen in the museum of the Western Reserve Historical Society.

The Mahoning Trail became one of the first roads of the Reserve when early settlers used it to reach the seat of government in Warren.

The Great Trail

The Great Trail is well described by Colonel Robert Rogers who followed it from Sandusky to Fort Pitt. It was first recorded by Christopher Gist, the associate of Washington, and was used by Bouquet in 1764 on his expedition to Coshocton for the exchange of hostages of the border wars. It was also used by Lachan McIntosh on a punitive expedition in 1778.

The Moravian Trail

The Moravian Trail, the Salt Springs Route, the Tuscarawas, and, if authentic, the Ashtabula Trail, were probably subsidiary Indian paths utilized later by early settlers of Ohio after the Revolutionary Period.

The Muskingum Trail

The Muskingum Trail was traversed in part by Gist from Bolivar to Coshocton, by Bouquet over the same route, and by Rogers and Crawford in the portions near Schoenbrunn. Fort Laurens was built to guard its junction with the Great Trail.

The Mingo Trail

This trail was also known as "Williamson's Route" since it was utilized in the attack on Gnadenhutten. It was followed by Crawford as far as the height of land west of the Ohio. He then directed his course for Schoenbrunn.

The Scioto Trail

The Scioto Trail was followed first by Gist from Circleville to the Ohio. It was utilized by Crawford from the mouth of the Little Sandusky to his battle-field north of Upper Sandusky. It was much used by militant free lances from Kentucky, particularly Simon Kenton.

In the War of 1812 it was followed by General Harrison

to Port Clinton where he embarked for the battle of the Thames.

The Cuyahoga Trail

No accounts mention military use of the Cuyahoga War Trail but the location of Indian villages seems to establish it.

The Coshocton Trail

This trail was adopted by Ebenezer Zane northeast of Lancaster as part of his trace from Wheeling to Maysville.

The Huron Trail

Colonel William Crawford, after his defeat at Upper Sandusky, followed this trail eastward from the present Indian Mill and then directed his course to Leesville where he was captured.

The Walhonding Trail

This trail is well described in the accounts of Indian traders. It is mentioned in the Diary of Nicholas Cresswell, a young English adventurer of the Revolutionary Period, and was traversed in part by Christopher Gist and George Croghan.

The Mohican Trail

The Mohican Trail branched from the Walhonding to traverse the Mohican villages in present Ashland County and to reach the headwaters of streams leading into Lake Erie.

The Belpré Trail

This was the trail followed by Lord Dunmore of Virginia to reach Camp Charlotte on the edge of the Pickaway Plains east of Circleville, where he awaited the arrival of Colonel Lewis from Point Pleasant at the mouth of the Kanawha.

The Kanawha Trail

This trail was followed by Colonel Lewis, after the battle of Point Pleasant, to join Lord Dunmore at the famous conference beneath the Logan Elm on Congo Creek.

The Standing Stone Trail

This is an exceedingly scenic route, traversing difficult country, and was not used by military expeditions.

The Ohio Trail

This trail connected the bottom lands opposite the two Kanawhas and was probably an Indian short cut.

The Shawnee-Miami Trail

This trail was doubtless an Indian highway, connecting two confederacies, but was visited in the Mad River section by Bowman, Logan, Clark and Harmar who led military expeditions during the Revolution against Old Chillicothe, Wappatomica and Maccocheek.

The Wappatomica Trail

This trail was traversed as a northeast extension of the Miami Trail from the site of Cincinnati by the above military commanders from 1779 to 1786 as far as Zanesfield; by Hull as far as West Liberty to Detroit in 1812; and also by Shelby, via Kenton, to Upper Sandusky and Fremont in 1813. It was also the route from Upper Sandusky to Wappatomica by which Dr. Knight, the friend of Crawford, was led captive

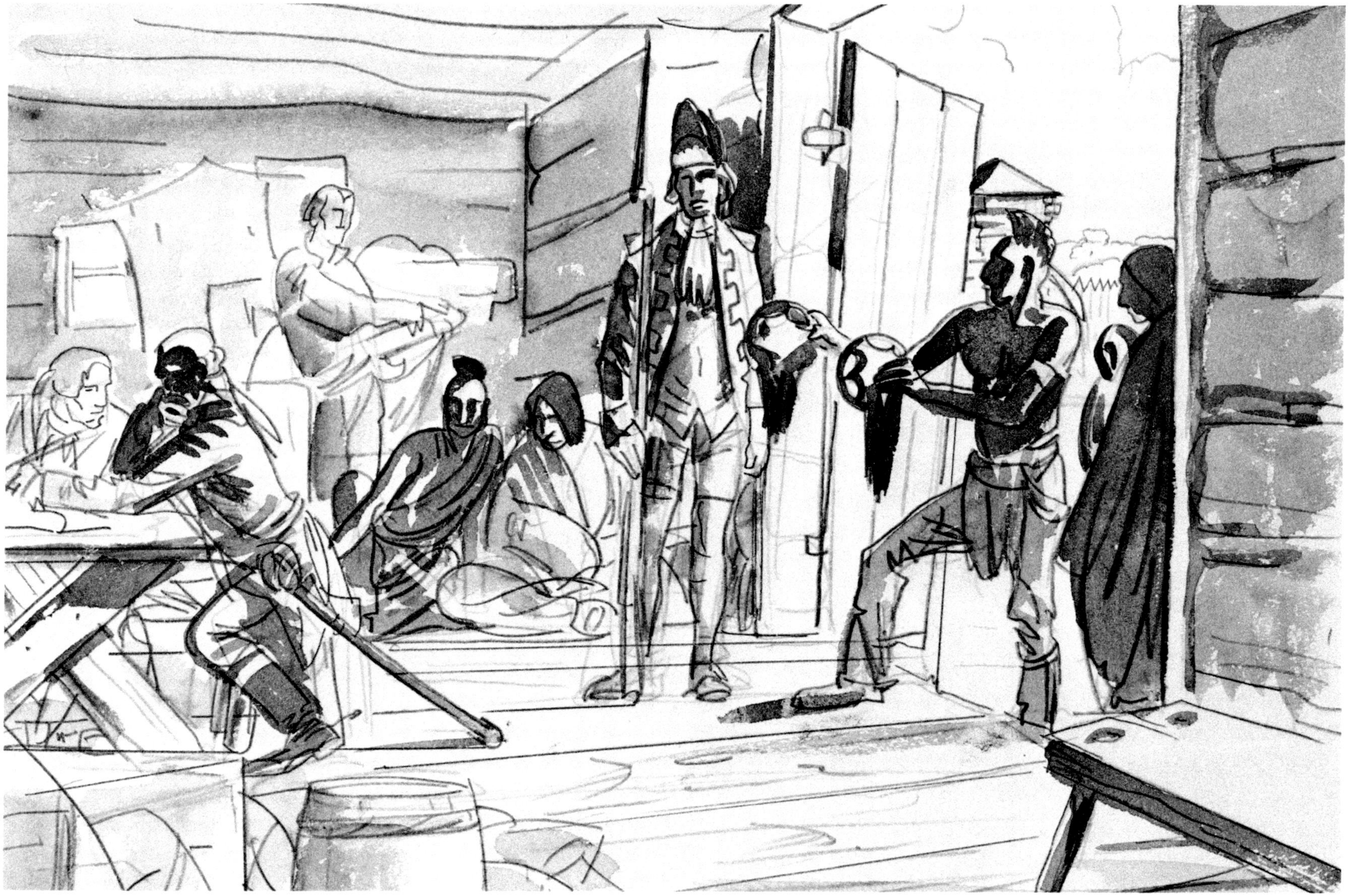

Hamilton the 'Hair Buyer' at Detroit

and upon which journey he escaped his captors. The site of Wappatomica still shows the depression made by Indian feet around the stake, where the monument now stands. Here Kenton was rescued by Girty. Many other interesting spots lie on this trail.

The Black Swamp Trail

This trail was traversed from Upper Sandusky to Findlay by Harrison in 1812 on his way to Fort Meigs. Crawford was also led along this trail as far as Tymochtee Creek and the place of his death, where stands the village named after him.

The Pickawillany Trail

This trail, largely an Indian road, crossed the courses of the military expeditions to Old Chillicothe and the route of George Rogers Clark in 1782 to Pickawillany and Loramie.

It was followed also by Anthony Wayne in 1794 from the Mad River towns in his expedition against Little Turtle.

The Miami Trail

This route was followed by Revolutionary expeditions against Piqua and Wappatomica, from the mouth of the Licking opposite Cincinnati, under Bowman, Clark, Logan and Harmar, and by Harrison, Shelby and Clay to the north in 1812.

The Wabash Trail

This is the famous route of General Arthur St. Clair to his defeat, and the route of Wayne to Fort Recovery and against Little Turtle and Tecumseh at Fort Wayne and to Fallen Timbers on the Maumee. This is the trail associated with the signing of the Greenville Treaty.

The Auglaize Trail

This trail was used by Commander Bird of Detroit in 1780 against the Miami country. It was also used by Harrison from Cincinnati, via Loramie, to Fort Meigs in 1812.

The Maumee Trail

This was the great route of General Anthony Wayne from Fallen Timbers to Defiance and Fort Wayne, the route of Bird and Harrison, and the route by which the white man for many years had entered Ohio prior to the crossing of the Alleghenies.

Trails as Military Roads

The first expeditions of British regulars and American militia in eastern Ohio found the trails over that hilly region well beaten by the warrior and trader. These routes followed ridges, and did not necessitate change of course on account of high water, unless we may except the prairie crossings in the flats of the Muskingum and Tuscarawas. No mention is made in the records of any material difficulty in the transport of goods and artillery.

In contrast to this, much difficulty was experienced by St. Clair in the heavy swamps and forests of the flatter Miami Basin in the later western campaigns. George Rogers Clark had profited by his experiences in the swamps around Vincennes, and Wayne also had St. Clair's unfortunate experience as a warning.

The portages are said to have varied in length according to season by many miles and, whenever possible, the military expeditions were accompanied by flotillas for the transport of baggage. The French voyageurs, traders and missionaries seem to have preferred the bateau and canoe to foot or horse, and were able to reach practically all Indian towns which usually lay upon streams navigable to light craft.

In contrast to the present day, streams were definitely navigable where now it would seem impossible. There are records, of course, that tell of difficulties of navigation, but this was largely due to driftwood. There are so many "riffles" or shallows today, even in the larger rivers during dry weather, that it is difficult to determine where ancient fords existed.

When we consider the thin and barely increasing population of the Indian under savage conditions, it is remarkable that any definite roads could continue to be traceable from season to season.

It might be said that there were three types of military operations in Ohio: first, the frank use of Indian trails as in the Muskingum and Mad River campaigns; second, the cross-country wandering under the guidance of backwoodsmen, as in Crawford's campaign against Sandusky; and third, by costly pioneering and engineering, as in the larger operations of St. Clair and Wayne.

It was such operations that started the development of highroads and towns across the forested and trail-less areas. Along the rivers, the present towns practically coincide with the old Indian villages of history.

Ohio is today dotted with towns which have grown up around railroad crossings and about growing industrial centers. Many of the old canal towns have developed and decayed, but some of the original Indian villages and their connecting trails, although dim and faint, remain much as in the early decades of settlement.

Occasionally historic significance is attributed to certain roads or highways that has no foundation in fact, but is believed by local residents. Word-of-mouth tradition is easily misinterpreted, and a road may have developed, not through, but in consequence of, some military operation such as the various roads built after the Greenville treaty line was drawn. This line today has no significance whatever. One such road exists in northern Ohio, attributed to Wayne on his march to Fort Wayne, but the origin of the myth is completely lost. It was probably a road developed immediately after the opening of the Firelands to settlement and the abandonment of the Greenville treaty. That treaty was the result of Wayne's campaign.

The Classification of Indian Trails

Generally speaking, the greater part of the trails of Ohio have been obliterated by national or state highways, railroads and canals, which have utilized and made practical for commerce the well-chosen paths of the Indian. The later county and township surveys introduced arbitrary boundary roads, which were laid out by compass. These roads in some cases may have included trails, but usually they were graded and filled to be made practicable, and the earlier traces were abandoned and forgotten. The long state roads, extending sometimes diagonally across the pattern of townships, especially when connecting the sites of former Indian towns such as Delaware and Wooster, may be said to conform to Indian routes. This is especially true if no obvious grading has been necessary.

The scenic beauty of these routes may be said to lie in the fact that the trails, especially war trails, followed ridges to avoid snow and marshy ground and to have as far as possible a comprehensive view of the country and thus avoid ambuscades.

Railways and canals usually run parallel to trails when not lying directly on their courses.

The Indian was indifferent to minor configurations of the ground, although he took the easiest route in the long run. In this sense he may occasionally have climbed the abrupt termination of a ridge, if not too high, or have veered around some marsh now drained and crossed by a modern road.

Modern real estate operations may have determined the course of some county and township roads, but there were no arbitrary barriers to the Indian and his trails do not respect modern property rights. Modern draining and grading may have left the original Indian path upon a hillside or have cut it down to a lower level.

The nature of the country tended to vary the character of trails. Along the shore of Lake Erie they seem to have followed the upper old lake bench below the high plateau, or, where no lowland existed, the immediate bluff of the Lake, as along the Lakewood Cliffs. In the case of rivers with wide flood plains, such as the Scioto and Miami, they followed the banks closely; but along the Tuscarawas and Muskingum the trails are said to have lain far back and high above the stream, where, avoiding the marshes, the ridges were perhaps somewhat bare and windswept, and hence free from deep snow in winter. There, a long view could be had of valley bottom and river confluence.

In the Scioto Valley the wide flood plains show a shelf, or second bottom, similar to the lake benches, where lay many of the Scioto villages safe from flood water. There were few evidences of trails along the Ohio on account of the precipitous slopes cut by deep ravines. The narrow bottoms are said to have been choked with a half-mile strip of impenetrable driftwood knit together by vines and river vegetation. In the flat northwestern country the trails were not enforced by the topography unless the one-time swamps were in the course. Sometimes the roads and main streets of the "Black Swamp" towns indicate the influence of Indian trails in pioneer days.

It is interesting to note that the most scenic points in the state lie upon ancient paths. The great rock shelters lie close to trails, such as those in Hocking and Licking Counties; and while the savage may not have taken any conscious delight in their beauty, he at least found in their shadows pools favorable for fishing, and at their springs the deer were likely to come at evening.

The great masses of untraversed and level land now so suitable for agriculture were perhaps seldom visited by the Indian. His numbers were few; he possessed no horses except in later days, and few of his trails encouraged the use of vehicles.

The narrow bottom lands at the crossings were sufficient for his meager crops; the grassy prairies he burned over in hunting and his semi-permanent habitations lay along the river trails. The cross-country trails were usually warpaths which led by the easiest if not the most direct way to the point of attack.

The Delaware center of occupation lay in the Upper Muskingum Valley which includes the modern Tuscarawas; the Shawnees lived in the Lower Scioto around the Pickaway Plains; a few Mingos inhabited the Mingo Bottom below Steubenville; while the Miamis centered in the Miami and Mad River district. In the Maumee and Sandusky region lived the Wyandots or Hurons and the Ottawas. A little settlement of the Mohican tribe lived around the forks of the Mohican and Walhonding in Richland and Ashland Counties.

In the later colonial period these tribes were scattered so that adjacent towns were unrelated, and many of the names were applied to successive towns in the westward retreat, such as Wappatomica on the Muskingum or the Mad River, and Piqua on the Scioto or the Miami. Flint Ridge, where today the flints still lie thick around the quarries, was apparently a neutral spot dedicated to the necessary hunt for arrowhead material. No war points have been found there. The Western Reserve was apparently little inhabited and the trails there were hunting trails, unless we are to regard the Great Lake or the Cuyahoga War Trail as the route of the neighboring and dreaded Iroquois.

There is romance in the study of the old trails. Sometimes in a spot where nature is unspoiled one senses something of the one-time, remote mystery of Ohio, a feeling which must have been familiar to the first pioneers. This quality is felt in the early landscape painting of America, an impression of wide misty rivers leading into forbidding mystery; dark forests with sharp giant tree tops hiding some unknown terror; but over all a feeling of immediate joy in the natural and perfect beauty of the scene. It is difficult to reconstruct this picture now, inasmuch as the smooth concrete, so easily followed, belies the remoteness of the hills and the signs of direction that indicate definite distances and destinations; not to mention the garish wayside stands that so complacently shatter the natural beauty of the scene.

Even the sought-for beauty along the highway cannot give back the thrill of mystery inspired by the eighteen-inch path that led into tall dark forests or down the reaches of a mist-hung river—something that led the soul of the woodsman on into the hypnotic solitudes of what was once the Indian Country.

It is already too late to learn from old men the origin of those names that cling to places on the old trails. The men who named the streams, ridges, hollows, and flats were gone generations ago. They were practical and unimaginative souls who followed the path of the more venturesome woodsman and prophetic trail blazer. They had no ability or desire to leave records that could give us a satisfactory idea of their thoughts or their times.

There are bottom lands along the Ohio that suggest the memory of famous men of another day, and tributaries to large rivers that bear the names of plants, trees or fish formerly flourishing there, such as Laurel, Kinnikinnic or Sunfish; or, on account of the ocherous soil, Paint Creek. These names, not in themselves poetic, are clues to an imperfect reconstruction of their time. Wherever the plowman turns up the now seldom found war point or skinning stone, there is possibility of extended knowledge. Wherever a firestone is found there may have been a camp or village site.

In the refuse pits of the village sites are found the bones of black bear, deer, elk and buffalo. To see the expert archæologist excavate a dark circle exposed upon the surface of a sandy promontory, and there, within the limits of a modern city with its many smokestacks, take from it the antler of a giant elk, not to mention a broken Iroquois cooking pot, is to look with new interest upon the commonplace present. The smokestacks turn then to towering forests; the railroad by the river converts into a dim track among waving ferns, and the murky river is again a green mirror to the silver fish; the idly curious passer-by becomes a mourner for the poor savage whose pathetic bones lie exposed in such an unhappy hunting ground.

Some say that the forest Indian was only a filthy savage, with no culture or impressiveness, and that his relics suggest no dignity; but a study of the trails and military roads shows the difficulty with which he was conquered. Most of his battles were relative victories, and his effigy stands in marble to testify to the unconscious respect that has been paid to him. His paths lead us to points of sheerest beauty, though he himself has left us little of the work of his hand.

The known trails of the Indian leave untouched great areas of country once inhabited by a higher culture and whose roads have been lost to us; but it is interesting to note that in most cases we have preserved in situation and name the towns of the red man in Ohio.

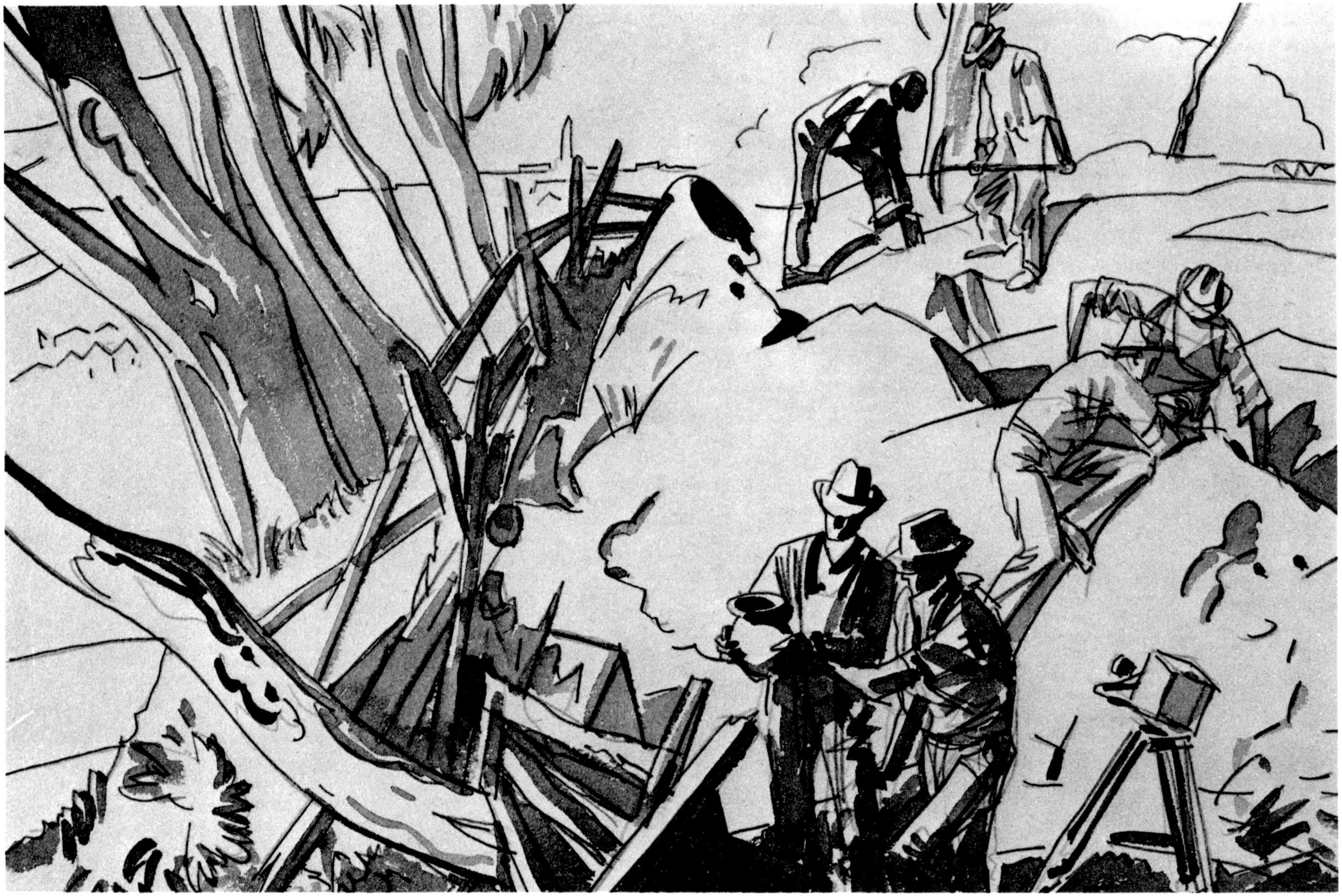

State Archeologists Explore Tuttle's Hill at Willow

The Reconstruction of Indian Trails

Those British or American military officers who utilized in whole or in part the various Indian trails of the state gave us a fairly clear idea of the start and destination of these roads. As to certain points along the route they are also usually clear, but frequently there are gaps where it is difficult to trace the course with a modern map. They were then traversing practically unknown territory, and they were too harassed by the difficulties and dangers to give careful attention to distances and directions or to note all significant landmarks.

The general course of the main trails is well known and is clearly explained in the publications of the Ohio State Archæological Society. The journals of the military leaders of early days, together with the diaries of their aides, and also many works on general Ohio history, give space to the subject of Indian paths.

Naturally, to attempt to give an absolutely authentic report of a trail today would be to attribute to the Indian a tendency to follow beaten paths. Knowing his nature for what it was, we may assume that at no time were all the trails in service; nor were they constant in their courses. As the Indian retreated westward many of his paths were overgrown and forgotten, while others were preserved where the white man found them useful.

One must be pardoned for using a bit of hopeful imagination in reconstructing a trail, although the possibilities and probabilities may be balanced by determining the original physical characteristics of the country. A study of the governmental topographical charts is most helpful if one can cancel out all roads leading to modern bridges or over graded ridges; the contours, considered in this light, prove that the longest way round would once have been the shortest way home.

Ohio is primarily an eroded plateau, and to go anywhere in a straight line necessitates much crossing of steep ravines, marshes and hillcrests. In the days of heavy forestation, none of the ravines were filled or graded; they held a more continuous head of water owing to the humus of the forest. This made river crossings difficult and fallen timbers made portages arduous. Even canoeing was difficult on account of the tangle of driftwood projecting from the changeable beds of the streams.

Since the Indian possessed no steel axes, we can pardon him for seeking a new path if some huge tree-top fell upon the trail. This may have on occasion deflected his path to a considerable degree; or a freshet cutting into a bank may have persuaded him to ascend some new river fork to the trunk trail upon the watershed.

Taboos of one sort or another may have been laid upon portions of certain trails; some traces now existent may be but the preservation of an unusual variation in the route.

The study of fords and riffles is today unsatisfactory, for rivers change their courses frequently; also, the modern streams of Ohio run bank-full only at flood season; thus the crossing of rivers by the Indians is difficult to determine except where authenticated by record.

It is a common tendency for those of us with a romantic taste in history to exaggerate evidence, or even to conceive evidence where it does not exist. How many arrow-heads and other objects interesting to the archæologist have been dropped carelessly by the farmer's boy miles from where he found them! In the heart of an oak there has been sealed by the tree's growth a cache of war points that no Indian put there, but which some day will probably be used as evidence to prove the great age of the tree.

Traditional accounts are susceptible to misinterpretation and even official records of the early period were pardonably inexact as to place names that were sometimes used interchangeably or differently interpreted; also, places bore different names at different times. The best means to a proper grasp of the subject of Indian trails should be a proper conception of the physical difficulties of the region in early days. Then, banks were steeper and rivers deeper and swifter; forests, though perhaps more open, did not permit long range views of guiding landmarks. A descent from a ridge in those days meant to flounder in circles in the six-foot brakes of the bottom lands. Tree climbing for a lookout was common practice with the early scouts. It was by following the ridges that the best judgment could be had of the eventual destination of stream or river.

One should, in imagination, study the map in the mood of a heavily laden and weary pedestrian, avoiding unnecessary physical difficulties in the way, such as steep descents and marshy ground, and keeping as much as possible to the ridges even though the way be longer. This the earlier railroads did, before the days of power excavation, and on the levels they are good trail indicators today.

Such lakes as are not of modern origin were undoubtedly

included in the long Indian routes. There is record of periodic migrations for fishing, hunting, berrying and sugar-making. The prairies were visited for ring hunting, and timber was burned over for the fungus that would follow. All this lore, if traces were available, could cast light on the courses of the trails.

In this work much faith has been placed in the topographic charts of the state. The drainage and general conditions of the country have not been so altered that the descriptions of the trails to follow are impossible, nor are they improbable in the light of the original conditions of the ground. All the trails may have varied from a fixed line like a string vibrating between fixed points, at which points fallen timbers, high water, or the discovery of not too distant food supplies may have tempted the travel-worn aborigine to digress from the beaten track.

It is interesting to note how the white man, on his early expeditions against the Indian, utilized the trails when they tended to follow his compass bearings; and how, when in his impatience he struck across country, he became bogged and mired and spent his strength in the marshy bottoms and steep ravines.

When in his ignorance he fell upon a cross trail, he usually met an ambuscade where he seldom emerged with dignity or success. He seems to have been unable to adapt himself to the eighteen-inch path where his carts and pack horses could not easily travel, and where, when attacked, he could not form his instinctive solid front to the enemy. It was only at Point Pleasant with his back to the rivers that he was not flanked, but at Fallen Timbers he had learned the lesson, and for the first time proved himself the equal of the red man on his own ground.

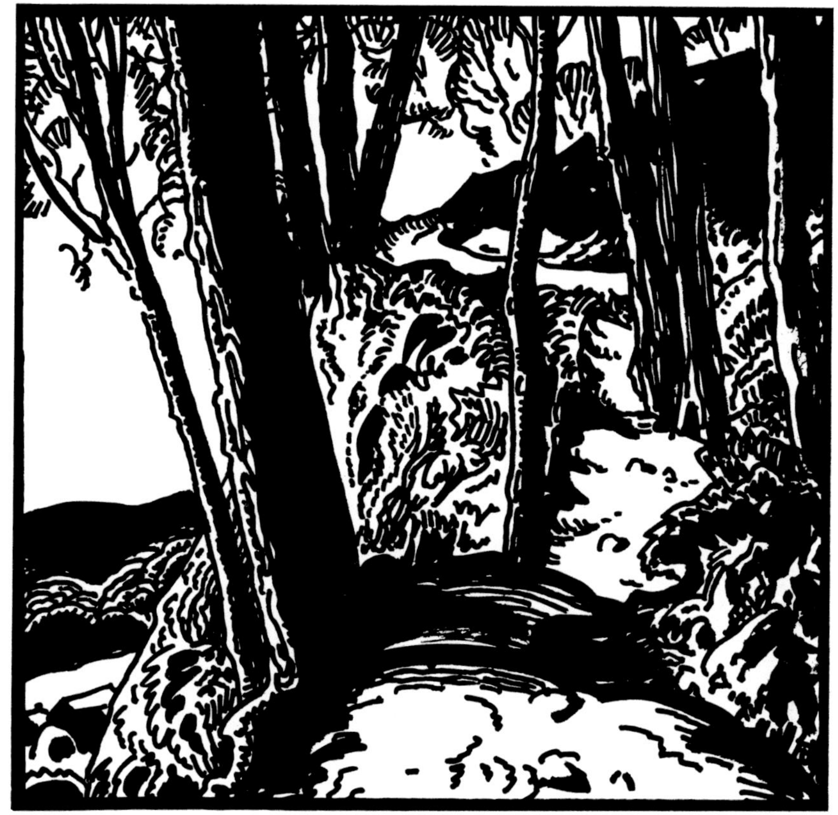

The Ridge Trail

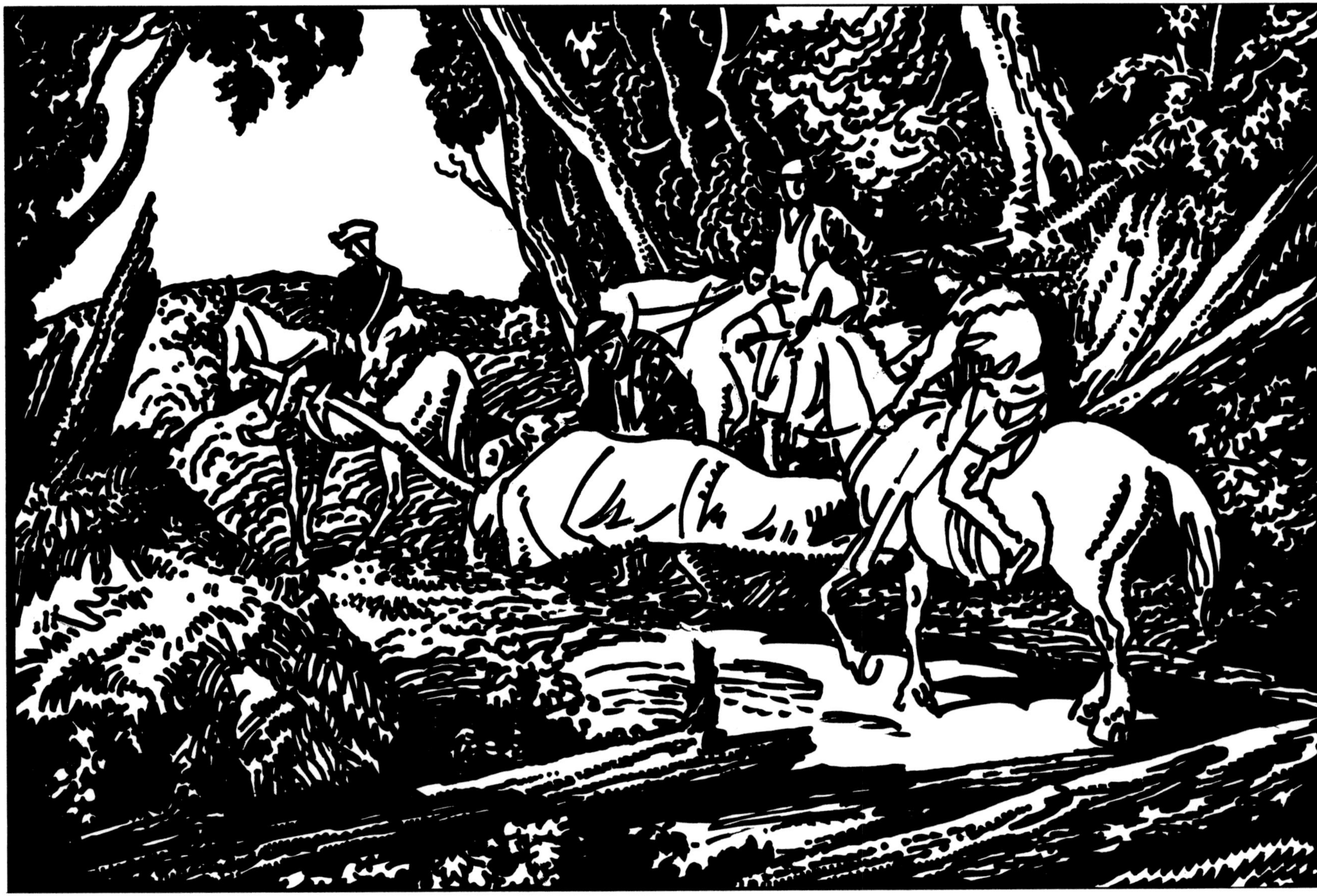

Injured Surveyor; Cleaveland's Survey of the Western Reserve

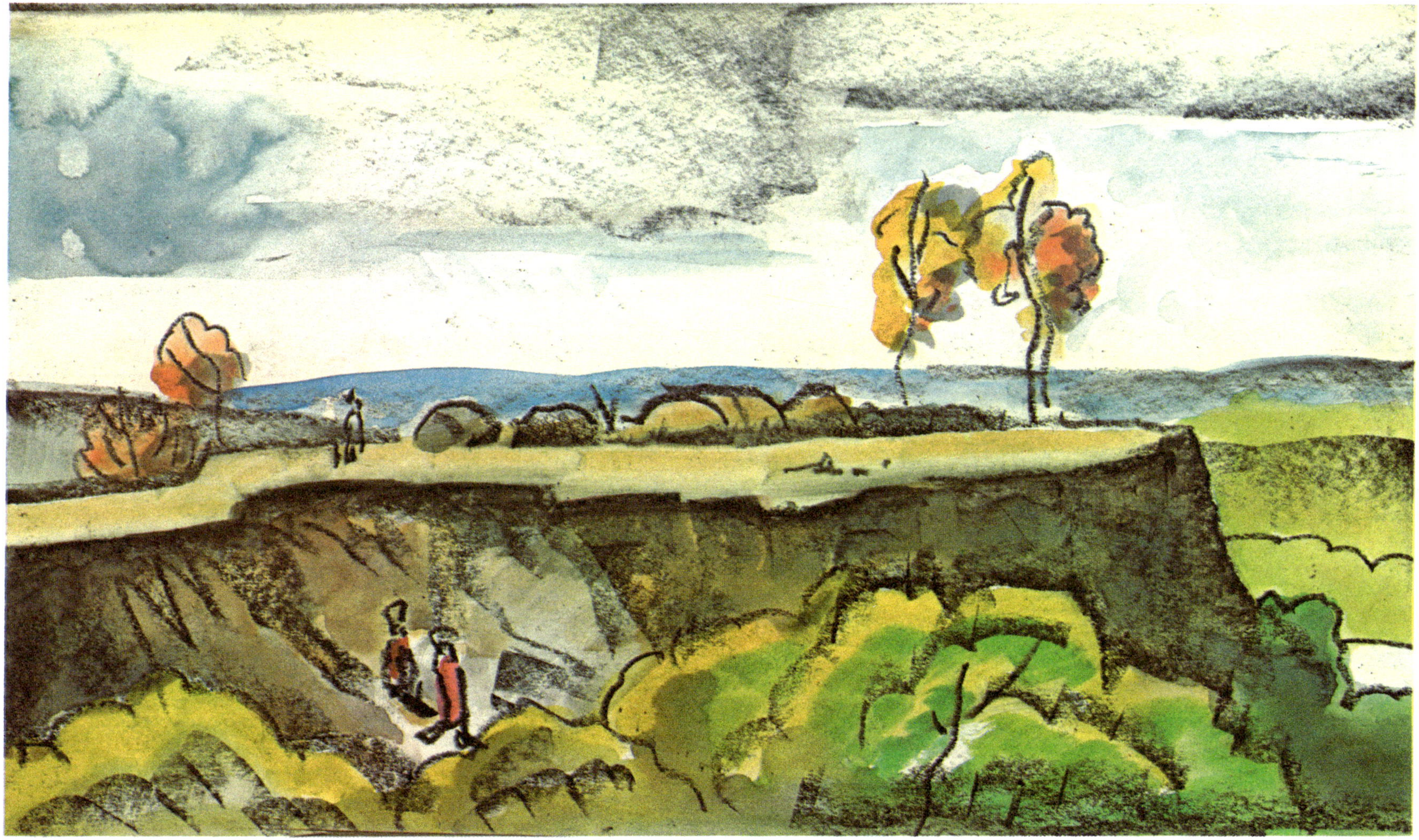

Habitation Site; Auglaize and Grand

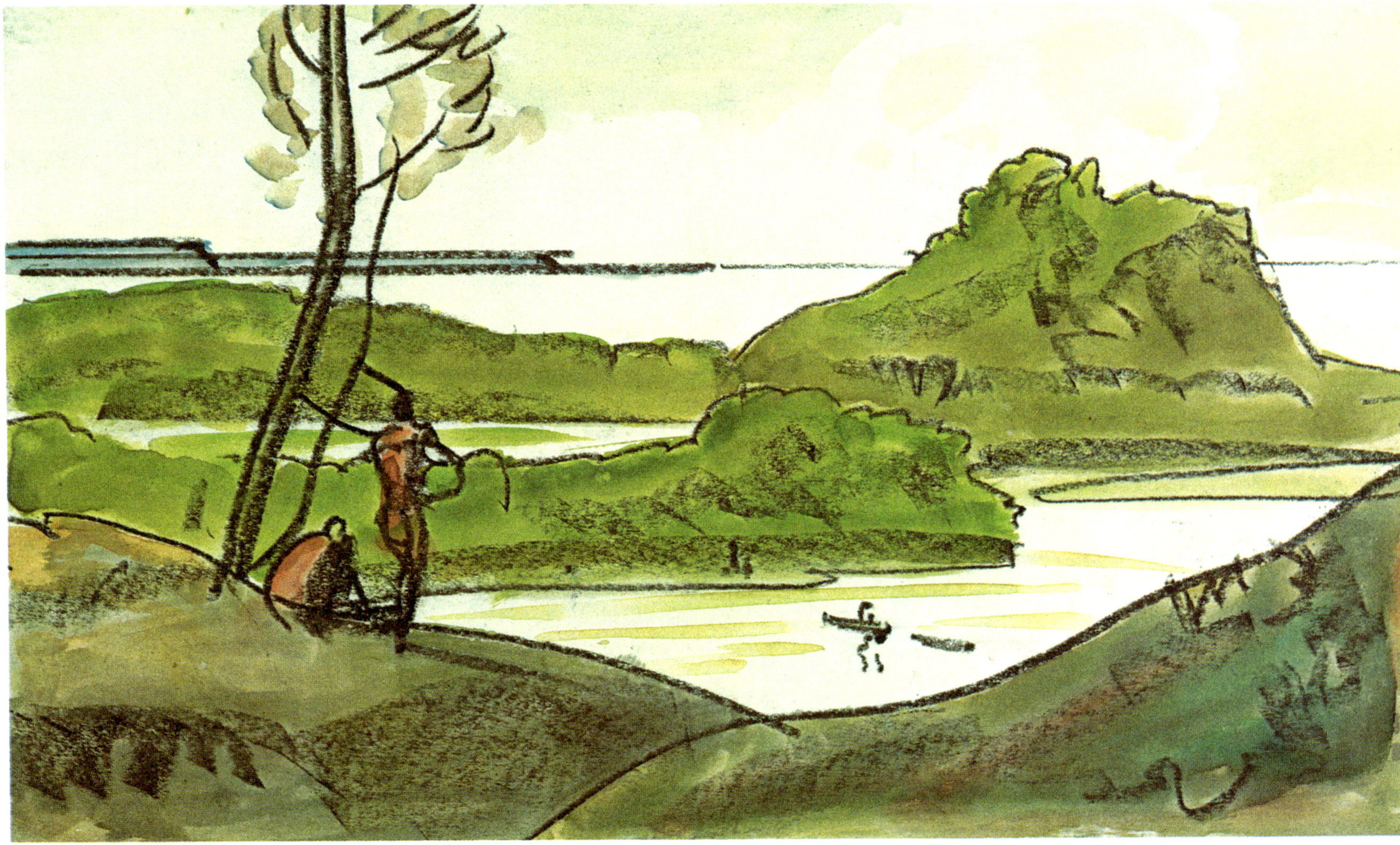

Union Lane, Chippewa Camp

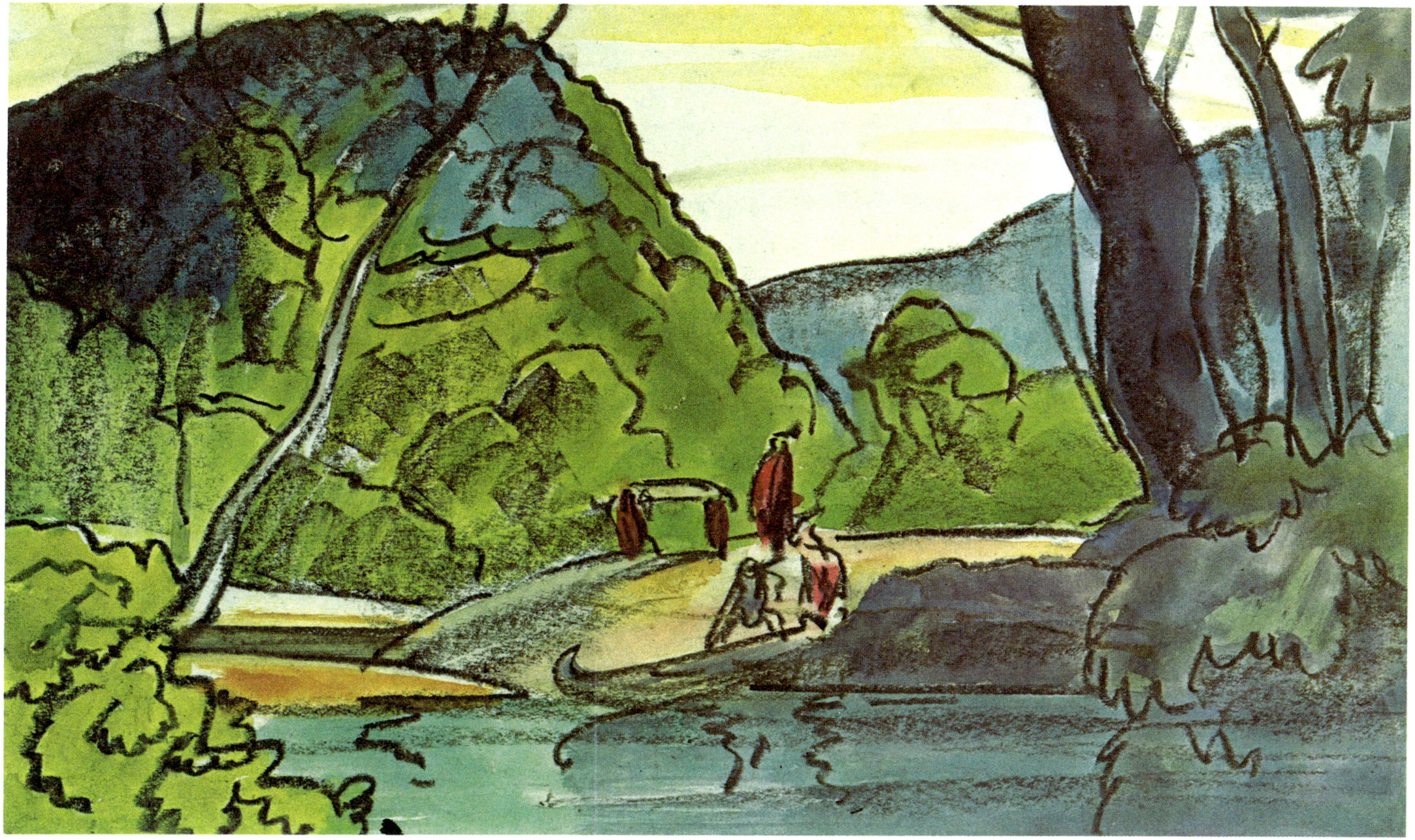

Cuyahoga Portage, Onandaga George's Lookout

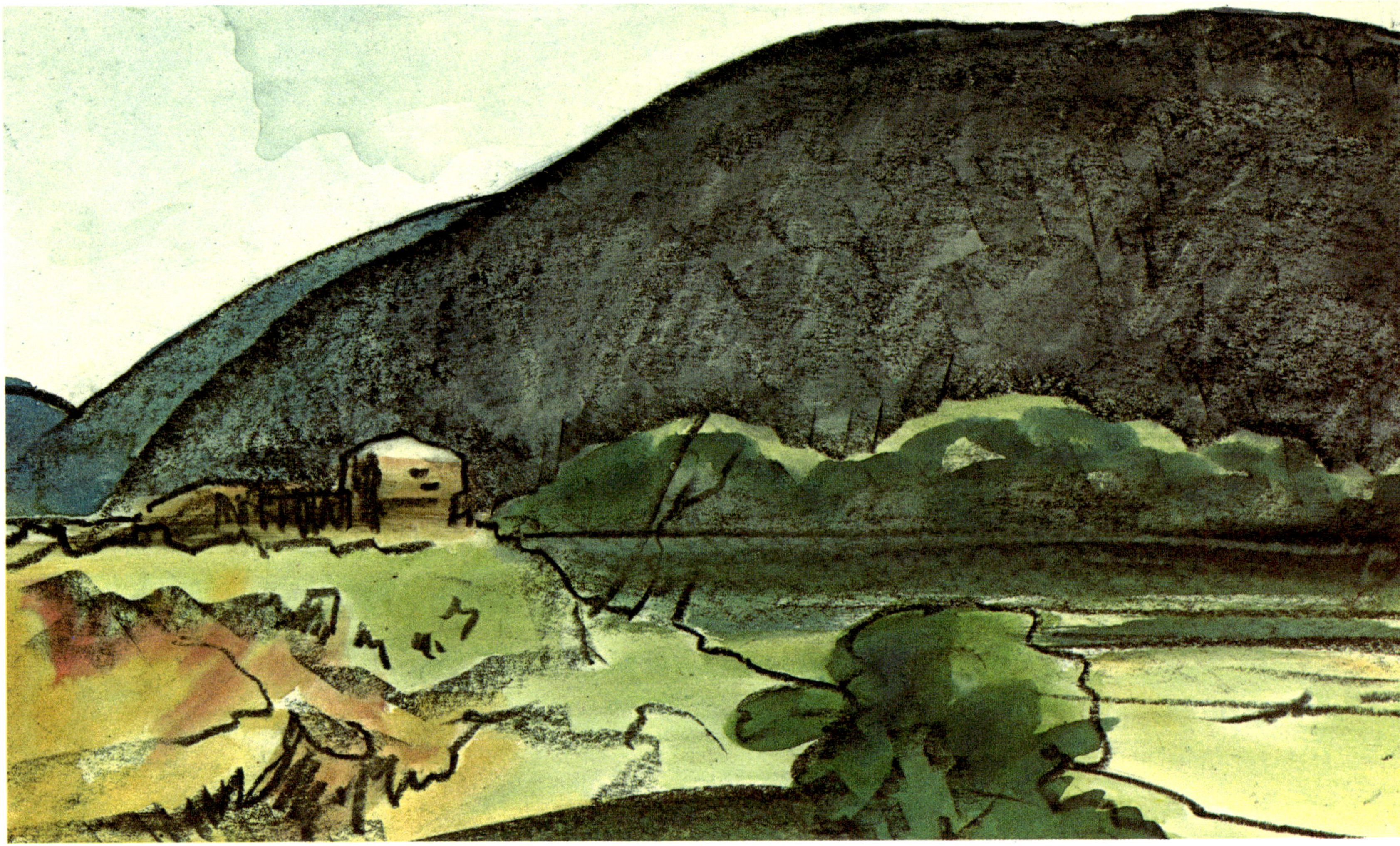

Big Bottom

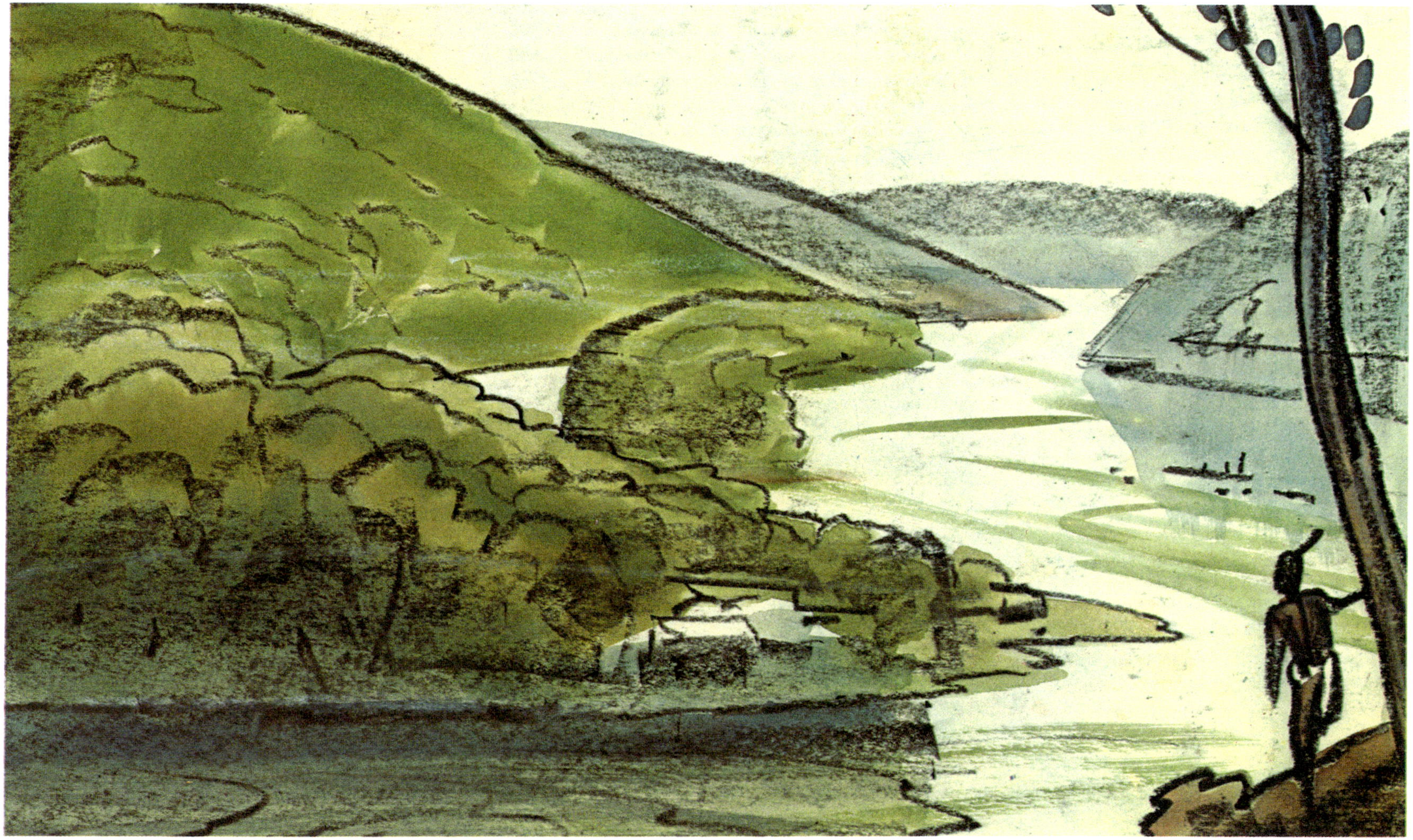

Marietta ; Big Rock

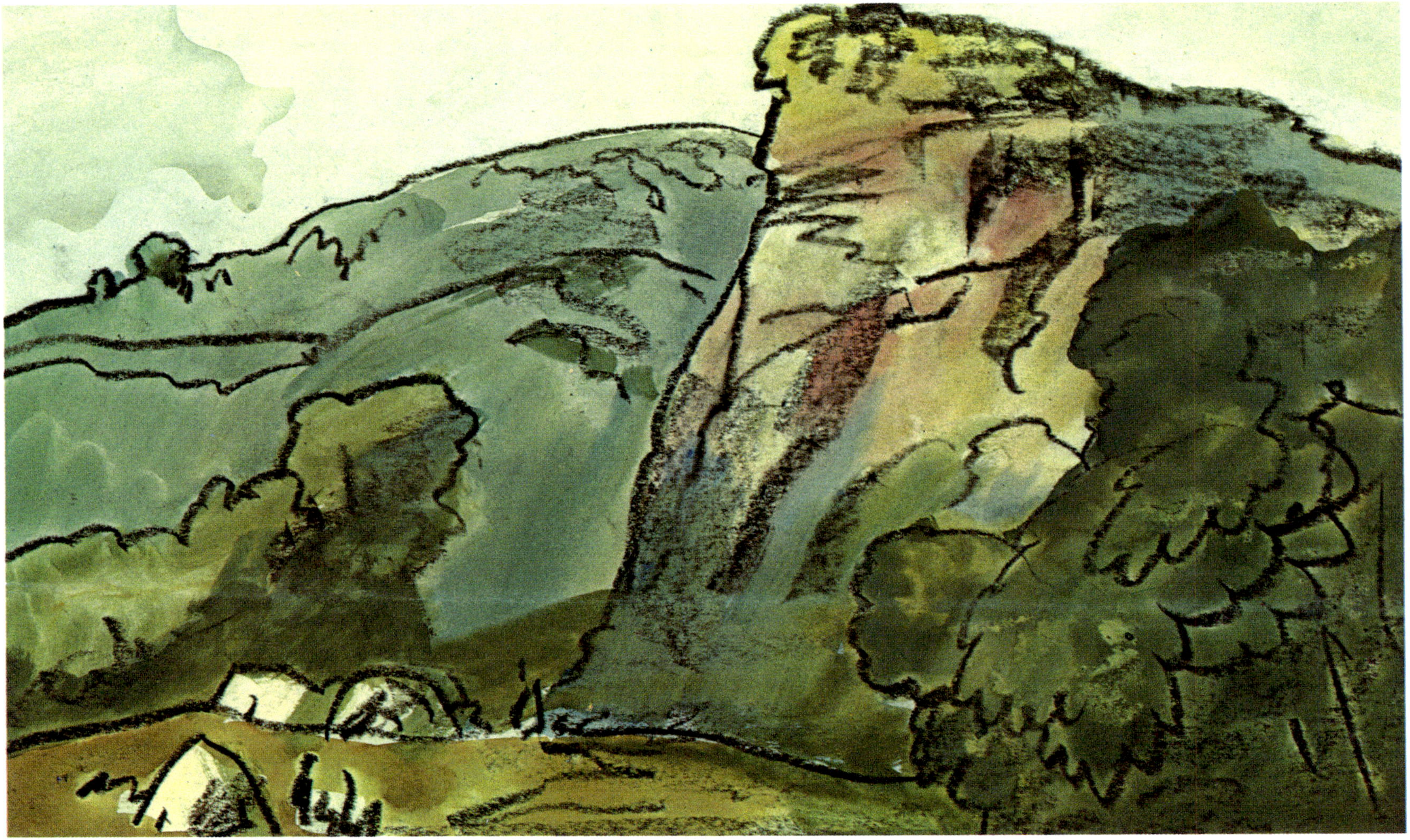

Standing Stone Near Lancaster

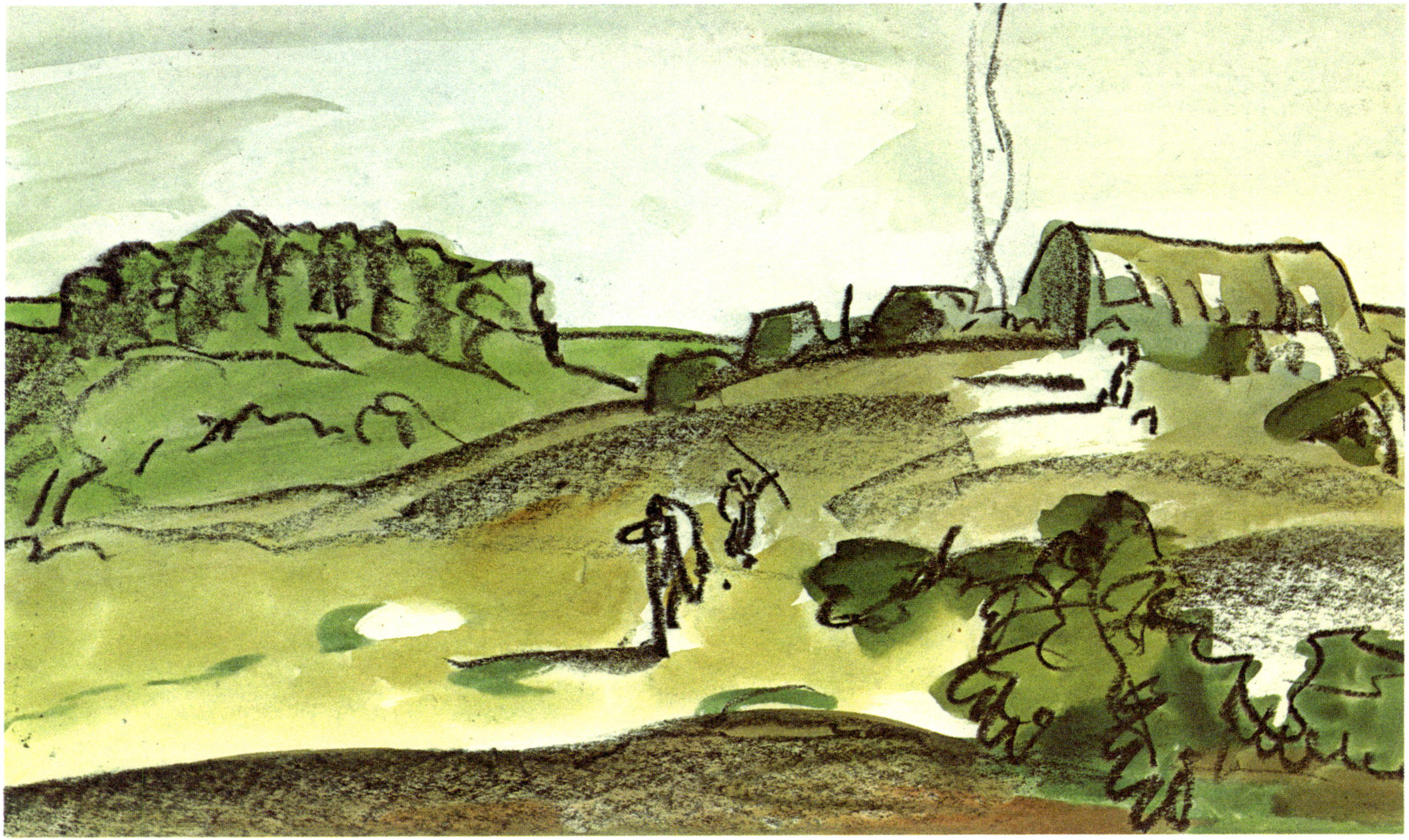

Old Town; Birthplace of Tecumseh

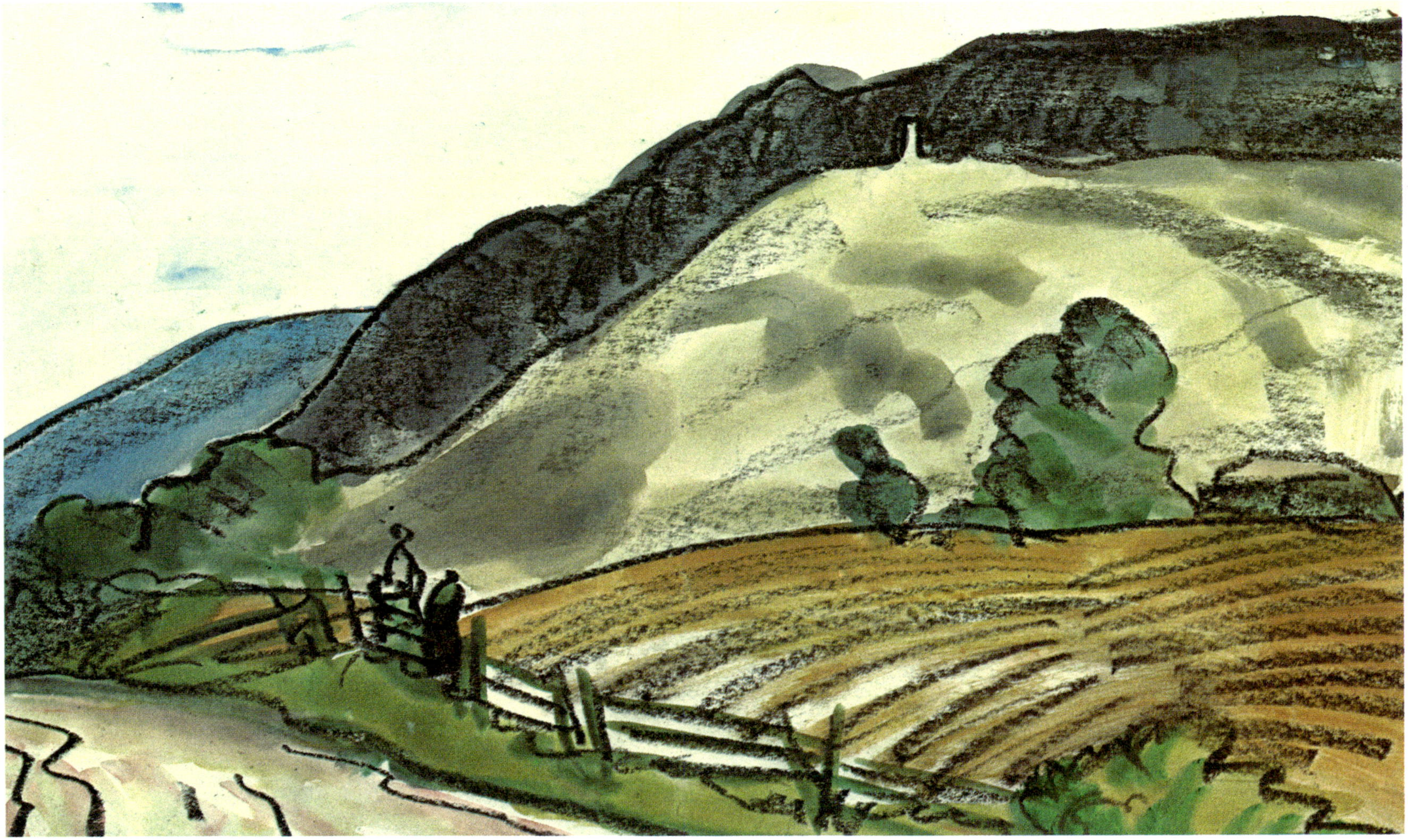

Wappatomica Between Zanesville and Maccocheek

The Lake Trail

This aboriginal highway was destined to become a principal thoroughfare of the State of Ohio. Running parallel as it does to the chief rail link between New York and Chicago, it follows the easiest grade across the northern part of the State, the edge of an old bench of an earlier Lake Erie, as far as Rocky River west of Cleveland (U.S. 20).

Euclid Avenue lies nearly upon this old trail within the limits of Cuyahoga County. From Painesville as far east as Buffalo we may imagine Euclid Avenue as continued along what is known as the South Ridge, the third bench of the old lake just below the plateau that is visible a short distance to the south.[1]

In imagination we can see the Iroquois wending westward against the Eries, following this gentle slope of land that overlooks on the north a wide area of marshes, bogs and tangled woodland varying in width, but with the distant blue lake frequently visible through scattered gaps in the forest.

On the left rises a continuous slope of dense timber, broken

[1] To be exact, Euclid Avenue does in many places conform to the Lake Trail. In all probability a path lay close to the lake in favorable weather, but the prevalence of numerous small brooks rising from springs and washes from the heights, now controlled, suggests that the level of Euclid Avenue was the nearest practical ground for a permanent trail. It doubtless followed Terrace Road and Forest Hill Avenue in East Cleveland for the same reason, and a reputed beaver dam in Lakeview Cemetery would have afforded a crossing to the brook there.

Euclid Avenue as extended eastward through Lake and Ashtabula Counties is not, strictly speaking, a preservation of the Lake Trail. In many places, as in Wickliffe and Willoughby, it appears to lie much to the north. The best guide is the bench level that begins at Euclid Village immediately below the bluff. At that place it lies closest to the old route and is there identical with Euclid Avenue.

Detroit Avenue, across the Cuyahoga, bears a resemblance to Euclid Avenue in regard to the lowland north of it.

at intervals by the sharply cut ravines of the Chagrin River or Euclid Creek, where the yellow shale banks appear as scars on the hillsides and the bottom lands are filled with sycamores and willows.

Passing what is now the Lakeview district, numerous small brooks cut the trail; a beaver dam is visible where now stands the Wade Memorial Chapel in the cemetery. Doan Brook formed a wide and depressed flat across which cut the stream on the site of the Circle and the Wade Park Lake, and at the intersection of Euclid Avenue and East 55th Street was a tree-shaded bog.[2]

The heights have now become invisible on the left, and all is a level solid forest where uprooted trees reveal a thin yellow sandy soil, for this is the delta of the ancient Cuyahoga River.

It was not long since that the remains of a mastodon were found but a few feet below the surface, just to the north of the old trail on present East 40th Street. The former Millionaires' Row was once a narrow track worn deep in the sand and leaf mould of the ancient forest.

Cleveland Public Square, as we now know it, is seen to slope gently to the north from the old lake bench just before it is cut down by the younger river to form the bluff where now stands the Union Terminal. At this point the valley of the Cuyahoga was discernible ahead, and the trail fell diagonally across the slope to approach the mouth of the river.

[2] An interesting work casting much light on the physical aspects of early Euclid Avenue is "Doan's Corners and the City Four Miles West" by Mr. Chas. A. Post, a life-long resident of that district, whose recollections of the early day are invaluable.

Following the line of Superior Street it diverged again, and by way of Union Lane,[3] crossed the river, probably on a sand bar to the opposite shore and the south side of the old river bed, which existed then as now, except that its eastern end was silted up and it was shallow and marshy. Just north of its eastern mouth stood an isolated, sandy dune-like hill, long since graded away.[4]

The trail then led westward up Main Street to modern Detroit Avenue, which, situated upon the lake bench, led west to Rocky River. The heights are now miles to the south, and the trail, gradually rising, passes through heavy oak forest firmly rooted in a heavy blue clay, and in the gaps to the north the steep shale cliffs of the shore are seen to reach out, one behind the other, to the far west.

Soon the track approaches a gap of light in the dark woods, and there is an abrupt zigzag descent into a narrow, shaly gorge overhung with trees and vines; across the river is a dark bluff crowned by tall trees to the very edge, and on the right a long bar of white sand extends out into the lake.[5]

The river crossed, the path divides near the edge of the

[3] On Union Lane, about half way between Superior Avenue hill and the river, a tablet marks the site of the cabin of Lorenzo Carter, Cleveland's first permanent resident. It stood above the Indian ferry. The land across the river was used as an Indian camp.

[4] The Moravian Indians who returned from Detroit with a view to settling on the Cuyahoga found the mouth of the river too shallow for boats and blocked with sand bars. They were warned of the danger of passing the cliffs west of Cleveland in canoes.

[5] Bradstreet's Expedition was wrecked upon the sand bar at the mouth of Rocky River. Amherst's Expedition met its fate a few miles westward where a small stream cuts down the steep cliff.

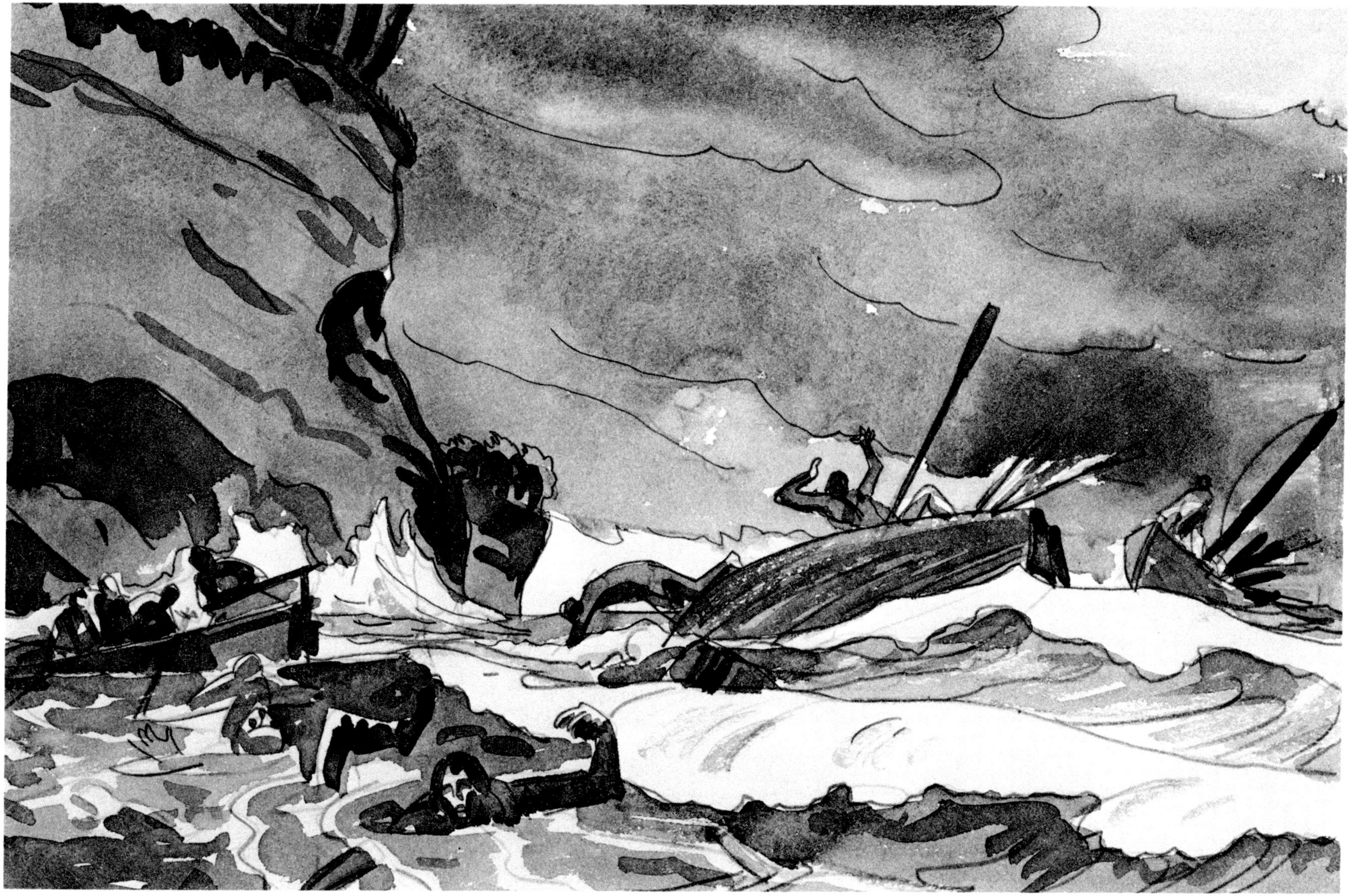

Wreck of Bradstreet's Expedition at Rocky River

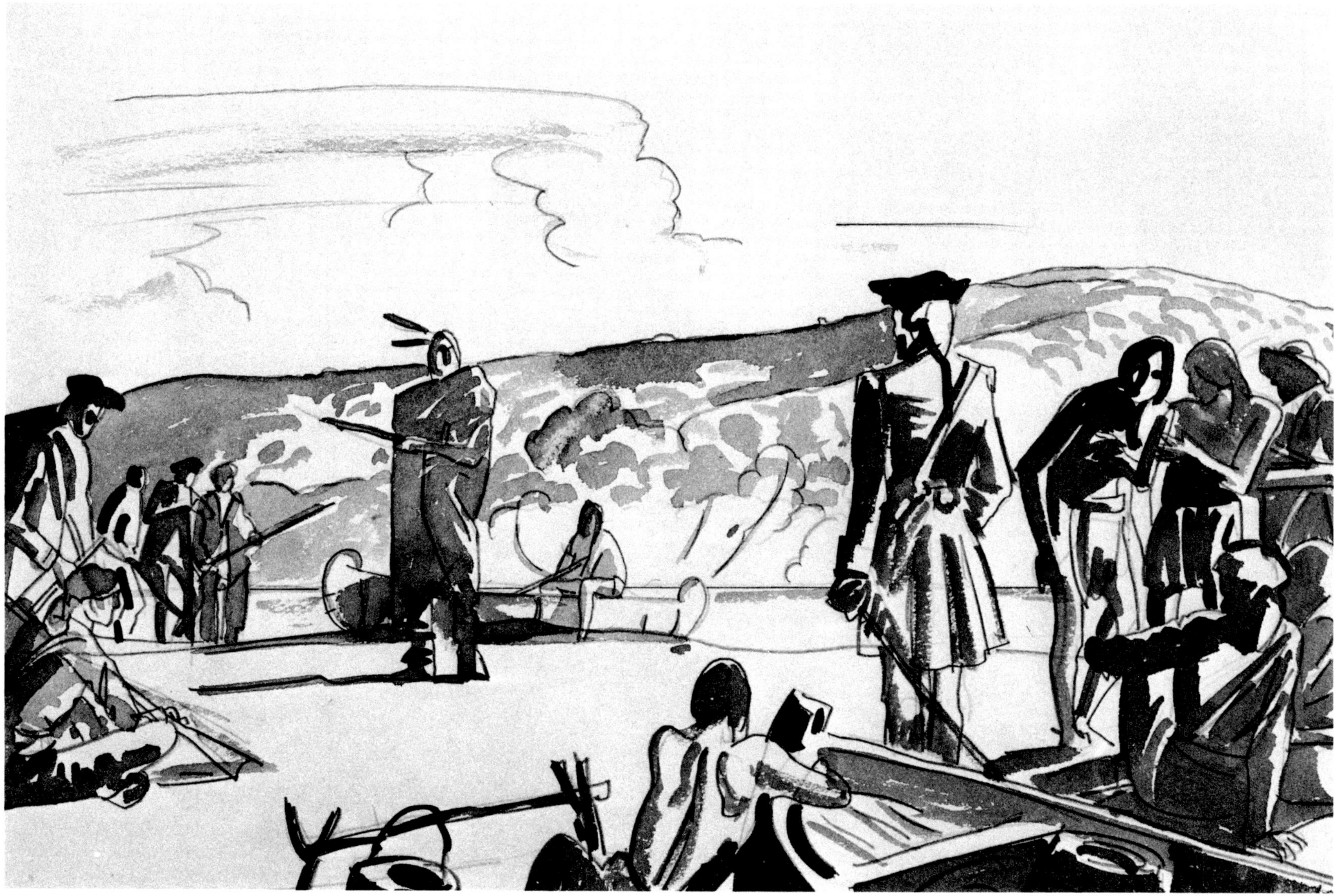

Pontiac

bluff. One dark path follows the line of precipitous and undermined cliffs westward (U.S.6); the other, rising slightly, finds a moderately elevated bench to the southwest from which a distant view of the lake is seen over a dense floor of treetops (U.S.20).[6]

Following this bench, the second path led west through present Amherst, Brownhelm and Rugby, where it crossed the Vermilion River at Rugby and so on to Ogontz, where in the distant northwest are visible the Lake Islands. Here may have stood an Indian town of that name.[7]

The other trail (U.S.6) has followed the lake and may have converged upon this point through Brownhelm Station, for here numerous creeks cut the lowlands from the heights, and below the present Berlin Heights the cranberry bogs extended to the foot of the hills. Passing through Berlin Heights (S. 61) the combined trails may have crossed the Huron at Freese's Landing (Pettquotting) where the riffles begin and where later the grain schooners entered the canal;[8] and so on to Avery and Bloomingville on the high ground at the stream-heads south of modern Sandusky, where, tending more northerly, they joined the Great Trail a few miles westward, to descend over broken ground to the Blue Hole of Castalia, most famous of Indian springs (Ohio 12).

At Freese's Landing the Lake Trail connected both with the mouth of the river via Mud Creek, where old mounds are seen, and also with the Ottawa Town of Salem (Ohio 299) on the bluffs just north of Milan.[9]

The point where the Lake Trail joined the Great Trail from Fort Pitt is four miles southeast of the Blue Hole with its turquoise limestone basin; here another branch trail is said to have led to a town where Venice now stands on the bay shore (U.S.6) called Anioton.[10]

From the Blue Hole, the combined trails led over the heads of the streams converging on the bay through Vickery, to the site of the French Fort, where Bark Creek enters the Sandusky. They then ran northwestward over the low land and the Portage River at Oak Harbor to the Maumee Rapids at Toledo (Ohio 19; 163; 120; I280), and so on over the River, and, after crossing many other rivers entering the west shore of the Lake, reached Detroit (U.S.25).

Events of historic significance have transpired in relation to the Lake Trail. It is an ancient Iroquois route for forays

[6] The steep cliffs of the lake throughout Rocky River and Lakewood figure in many a tale of pioneer days. The treacherous and shallow waters were a dangerous, but the only practical, route past those cliffs at one time. The lack of beaches made the passage risky at any season. Wreckage from the Bradstreet and Amherst Expeditions was picked up from time to time for many years. Few visitors of the present day know or can visualize these historic events, but relics of these expeditions are to be seen in the Western Reserve Historical Museum at Cleveland.

[7] Ogontz was educated as a priest at Quebec. He shepherded a mixed flock at the site of modern Sandusky and was known to early settlers of the Firelands Tract, but moved to Canada rather than take up the American cause in 1812.

[8] This canal was built to permit the loading of grain at Milan. In the old canal days Milan is said to have been the most important wheat port on record. The old schooner mast used as a flagpole on the green is a symbol of her former glory.

[9] From Freese's Landing a canal once led up the Huron River to Milan, and schooners once were filled with grain at that point. It is said that in the "Forties" this was the greatest wheat shipping port in the world. The speed of settlement and development of Ohio agriculture, after the passing of the Indian, is remarkable.

[10] James Smith, captive of the Indians, reported a Wyandot town called Sunyendeand about two miles from the present Sandusky.

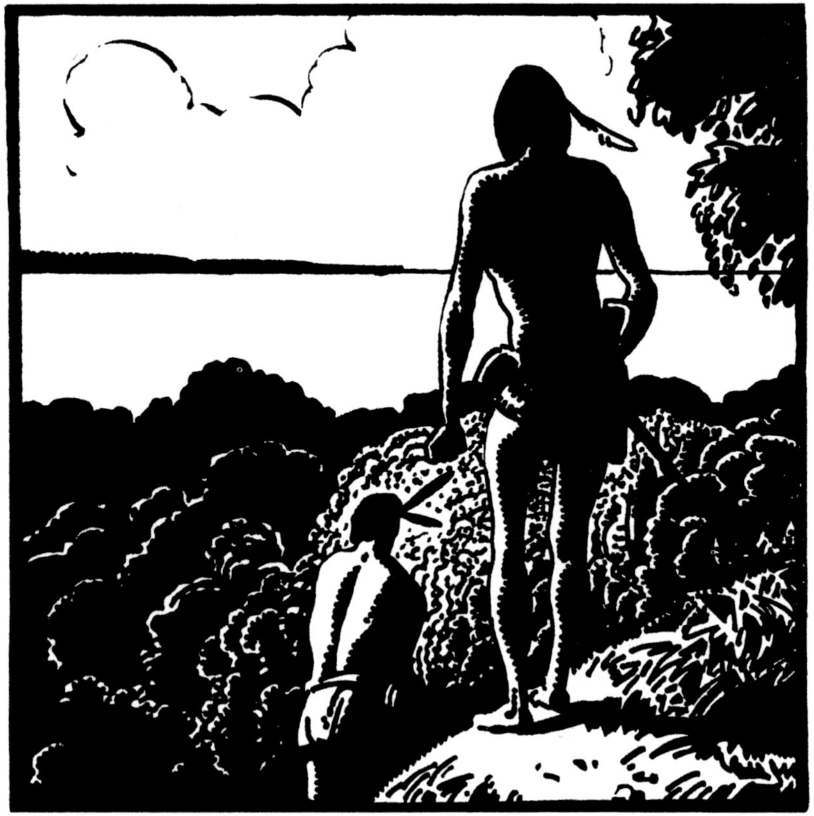

The Lake of the Eries

into the land of the Eries. In 1763, during Pontiac's war, the Expedition of Bradstreet was wrecked on the sand bar at the mouth of Rocky River near present Clifton Park. On the bluff opposite, many of the drowned were buried. Two miles west, the Amherst Expedition was also wrecked under the cliffs of Dover Bay where a brook cuts the bluff. Many of the survivors of these forces used the trail in their retreat eastward.

There must have been a practical path on the immediate shore in many cases, for there is a report that the great Pontiac himself saw fit to warn the invaders in person at one time either at Fairport Harbor or at the mouth of the Cuyahoga. He is also said to have resided in the Cuyahoga Valley on the west side, one-half mile north of Boston Mill, where a fine spring and bottom land give credence to the rumor. This was known in pioneer days as "Ponty's Camp."[11]

The Lake Trail must have been known to the forces of Anthony Wayne, although he himself reached Presque Isle by ship after Fallen Timbers. In 1760 Major Robert Rogers, after sailing up the Lake to Sandusky Bay, returned to Fort Pitt by the Great Trail. His journal gives an interesting account of the points touched by his passage, both up and back. He discovered the Blue Hole at this time. Kenton, the scout, was carried a prisoner over the upper section to Detroit in 1778.

[11] Francis Parkman states that Rogers met Pontiac near the mouth of the Cuyahoga where that great Indian "stood forth distinctly on the page of history."

The Mahoning Trail

Fort Duquesne, Fort Pitt, or Pittsburgh was the first important military and trading post of the French and English in the Ohio Valley. The Frenchman approached it via Lake Chautauqua or Presque Isle (Erie); to the English it was the first important post across the Alleghenies. It was therefore the point of departure for all ventures into the unknown Indian Country.[1]

For the Indian, Fort Pitt was a logical rallying place on account of its position at the confluence of the Allegheny and Monongahela.

The streams emptying into the Allegheny and Ohio served as doors to the wilderness. They were ventured by the whites in the order of their position as time went on and the conditions of the interior became known.[2] It was natural that the Mahoning, a tributary of the Beaver, should be known at an early day. It was followed by Heckewelder, the Moravian missionary, whose manuscript map is to be seen in the museum of the Western Reserve Historical Society. His was the

[1] The chain of French posts from Lake Erie to Fort Duquesne lay along French Creek and the Allegheny just outside of modern Ohio. Among them were Le Boeuf and Venango, visited by Washington as a young man, when he acted as an agent for the government of Virginia and sought to claim the western territory for England.

[2] Prior to the outbreak of hostilities between England and France over the control of the Ohio River and its tributaries, Celeron de Bienville descended the Allegheny and planted, at the mouths of the principal streams emptying into the Ohio, certain plates of lead claiming title in the name of France; many of these have been found. The present territory of Ohio was well known to the French.

The English for a long time found the northeastern approach to Ohio blocked by a chain of forts running south from Erie, or Presque Isle, to Fort Duquesne, or Pittsburg. After the French and Indian war they found a readier access by the streams below Fort Pitt, formerly Fort Duquesne, and they explored these as the scouts and traders gained the confidence of the Indian tribes.

first known map of the unknown country to the north, now the Western Reserve. The Indians used the trail to reach the famous salt lick near Niles. There, approaching the Beaver, with its settlement of Logstown, from Fort Pitt (Penn. 856) they followed up the hills to the east of the Beaver (Penn. 18) to Beaver Falls, where the Great Trail led to Negley (Penn. 251). The Mahoning continued up the Beaver to the confluence (Penn. 288) and following up the east side of the Mahoning past Struthers (Penn. 18), passed through Youngstown to a point about three-fourths of a mile from Girard (U.S. 422) where it crossed the Mahoning between the mouths of two opposing streams. It mounted diagonally the opposite shore through the Wilson Farm and struck west between Mineral Ridge and Niles across the foot of the main street of Mineral Ridge, and, crossing Meander Creek, led west to the Salt Spring about one mile northwest of that point. It then led westward over the headwaters of Duck Creek to Newton Falls where it crossed the Mahoning on its upper reaches, and following somewhat south of Ohio 5 it passed by Crystal and Muddy Lakes, and then through more of the broken and glaciated plateau to the Cuyahoga at Kent (Ohio 59).

To this point, the trail had traversed the rather steep hillsides of the Mahoning, which today, where not disfigured by the many steel mills, shows its willow-grown banks. It then traversed the broken land of the tributaries of the Mahoning, and arrived at a lake-dotted region among the moraines and glacial heaps of the high plateau.

From Kent, it crossed the Cuyahoga in the southern part of the town about a half mile south of the rocks where Brady made his famous leap for life,[3] to Silver Lake where stood two Indian towns, one probably southwest of Silver Lake and the other northwest of Little Silver Lake (Ohio 59). It then followed the line of the old Akron, Bedford & Cleveland Electric Line through the marshy land east of Turtle Lake and past Mud Lake, where a mile to the northwest it met the Cuyahoga War Trail; thence it led to Iron Bridge two miles or so southeast of Northampton where stood an Indian town. Soon the blue valley of the Cuyahoga was visible to the west, over where on its western hills the other Cuyahoga path probably descended to the mouth of the river, or served as an approach to the Lake Trail westward. Those hills today, though cleared of first growth, are cut by deep water-courses and abound in deer licks and other likely signs. We can see today where nature lovers have created an echo of the older Ohio in the more remote fastnesses of the Metropolitan Park.

From the point at Iron Bridge where one branch continued to the Portage, the trail led northwest to Northampton Center (of Ottawa origin) and followed the heads of ravines past

[3] According to Henry Howe, Brady, on the occasion of his famous leap for life, was in pursuit of a band of Indians from the Cuyahoga towns who had attacked a place in Washington County called "Catfish Camp." At Ravenna his party divided; one force pursued a band of Indians to Cuyahoga Falls and his party continued to Northampton where at the Indian village he was overpowered.

He was pursued alone to Kent where he leaped over the 22-foot chasm and caught by his hands. This delayed his pursuers and he was able to lie hidden under a log in the lake which presently bears his name.

Henry Howe states that the Mahoning Trail passed over the Cuyahoga at a point between the modern bridge and a rock in midstream just below "Brady's Leap." This would be north of the main thoroughfare of the town of Kent.

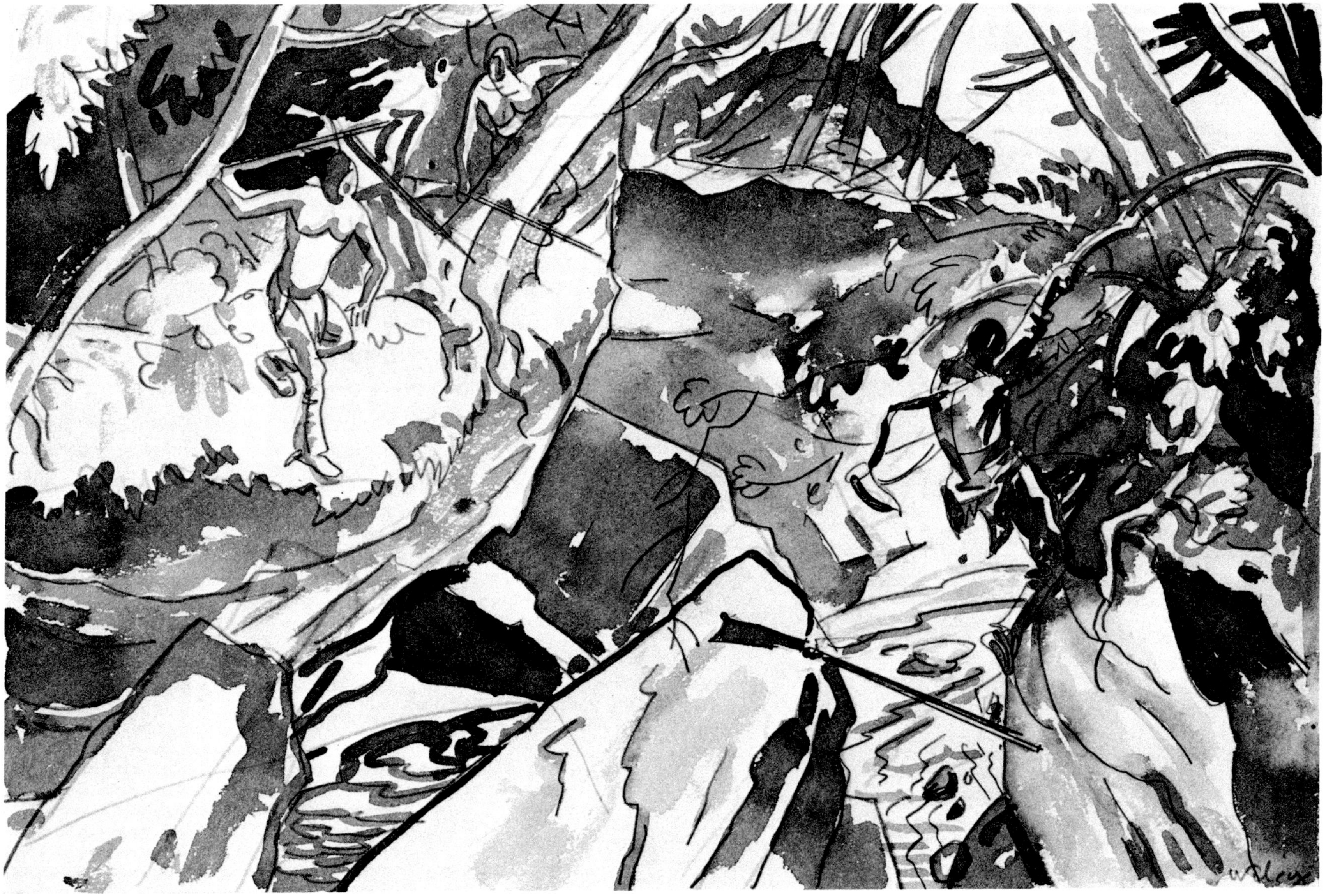

Daniel Brady's Leap at Kent

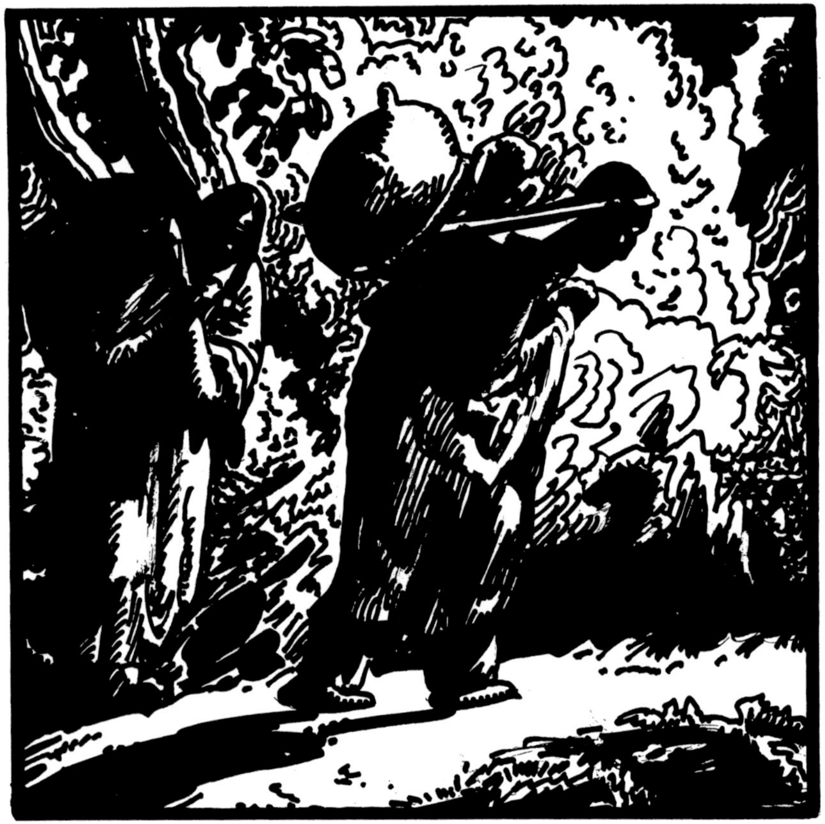

The Salt Kettle

Ritchie or Kendall's Ledges and Boston Ledges,[4] which, like so many others in Ohio, lie on the natural highways of the State (Ohio 8). The white man's railroad has shattered the Boston Ledges, but the Kendall Ledge stands in its savage beauty in the solitude of primeval gray birch and hemlock.

Passing by the head of Brandywine Falls and arriving at Northfield by the southwest road (Ohio 8) it apparently cut west of the town and struck the present byroad past Willow Lake and leading down over Tinker's Creek where Dunham Road Hill mounts the steep northern bank at the foot of Bedford Glens. Descending the abrupt hollow, the trail crossed the flats and climbed the opposite ridge, across the face of which a cart track mounts diagonally.

On the end of this promontory, where many relics have been found, probably stood a French trading post, popularly identified with the Pilgerruh of the liberated Moravian Indians.[5] The trail crossed this ridge and descended into the

[4] Kendall's Ledges, now a park, is one of the typical "pudding stone" or conglomerate outcroppings of northern Ohio. It is one of the few places where the big gray birch tree of the Ohio woods still stands with its neighbor hemlocks.

[5] Pilgerruh or Pilgrim's Rest was the name given to the place upon the Cuyahoga occupied for a short time by a remnant of the Moravian congregation who were converted by Zeisberger on the Tuscarawas. They were held at Upper Sandusky as hostages to the English during the Revolution and occupied this place among others after the Gnadenhutten massacre.

The bluff at the mouth of Tinker's Creek has long been considered the actual site and certainly shows indications of Indian habitation; also a French trading post has been claimed to have existed nearby. The so-called Moravian Treaty Tree, a huge and ancient sycamore, stands to the southwest across the Cuyahoga.

The promontory to the north opposite Rockside Road, however, answers more completely the description in the Moravian records recently examined to determine the point; also, it lies adjacent to the historic ford of the Mahoning Trail.

The Moravian settlement, according to Heckewelder, lay twelve miles from the lake on the east side of the Cuyahoga and across from old Indian cornfields.

cornfields of the possibly genuine Pilgerruh nearly two miles northward. This it crossed diagonally northwestward, or followed around the U-shaped height and crossed the foot of the ravine to the east of the hill. This hill has been identified by representatives of the Moravian Church with a map and reference to springs and cornfields which here answer the description.

Just opposite the promontory is the "Indian Riffle" known to early settlers as the place where the Indians crossed the Cuyahoga.

Here the trail crossed, and moving diagonally up the steep western bluff, passed Mingo Town on the site of which proof of habitation has been found. This would be about half a mile north of the riffle at South Park. It then continued to where the bluff came to a point at Willow, where another village site has been found. This may have been Saguin's Post, else that place lay at Tinker's Creek as mentioned, or even farther north where Big Creek enters the Cuyahoga in the city limits.[6]

Descending the point of the hill or promontory, where some claim to see the original trace, the trail led across the flats and mounted Schaaf Road (to Ohio 176) and leading near the bridge just east of Brookside Park (U.S. 42) (Ohio 3) mounted the shaly bluff of Big Creek and followed Denison Avenue and West Madison Avenue to Rocky River, where it descended to join the Lake Trail for Detroit (U.S. 6).

[6] The exact location of Saguin's Post or "French House" indicated on ancient maps of the period prior to the Revolution may have been at Tinker's Creek. The point is in dispute and certain records claim that it stood in Brooklyn Township where traces of it were found. Since successive "Brooklyns" have grown southward from old Ohio City or the West Side of Cleveland, it may have stood either at Big Creek or even as far north as Walworth Run.

The most picturesque section of the Mahoning Trail lies between Northfield and Willow. Here it conforms to no major highways, but in the Cuyahoga Valley its traces are visible in various places. Elsewhere it passes through industrial and residential districts where nothing suggests its original character, but in the Cuyahoga Valley time has been kind to the old trail, near as it is to the heart of Ohio's greatest city.

Many accounts of pioneering at Cleveland mention use of the Mahoning Trace, over which the citizens traveled to the seat of government at Warren and to the salt lick for a then precious commodity.

A description of the Watershed Route, a branch from Kent, will follow. This led down to the Portage and was used by the army recruited at that point in 1812, in their march against the British around Detroit.

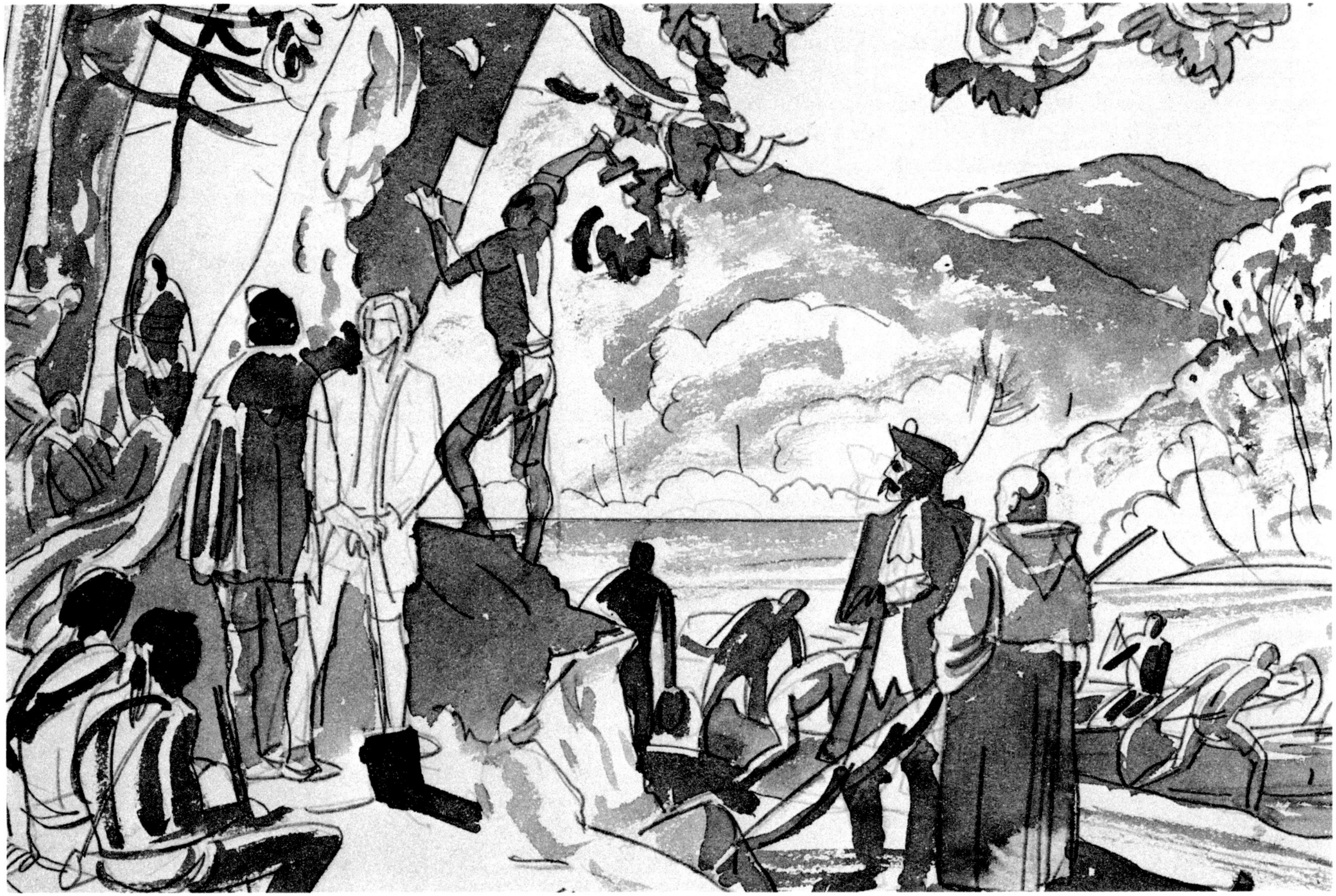

Celeron de Bienville Claims the Ohio Tributaries

The Watershed Trail

The Mahoning Trail, from the point where it crosses the river at Girard to where it reaches its northward trend at Kent, is a true watershed trail, passing as it does along the divide of the glaciated plateau between the lake and the Ohio tributaries. It continued westward from Kent past the falls of the Cuyahoga, and crossing at the Portage, followed the same divide until it struck the Great Trail and joined its northwestward descent into the Sandusky Bay region.[1] The portion previously described, which led down the Cuyahoga, may have been in a sense a branch encouraged by the French traders in the Cuyahoga; and the westward portion may have been developed partly by traders both French and English. It was, at any rate, well known when in 1812 it was used for the transport of supplies and the passage of recruits for Hull's Army.

From Kent it led along the north bank of the Cuyahoga through Munroe Falls, past Silver Lake with its villages, to Cuyahoga Falls where more villages stood, and passing over the "Old Maid's Kitchen," a famous shelter ledge of the Indian and now destroyed by highway grading, it led to the

[1] The Portage Path, marked by a monument at its start, is one of the most interesting trails in Ohio. Passing up from the still more or less primitive valley landscape, it leads through the fashionable residential district of Akron and southwards past the numerous lakes to the headwaters of the Tuscarawas. The Portage Path may be considered as definitely preserved in its entirety by modern thoroughfares.

It has been claimed that the Portage was used for some time as a mobilization point in 1812. When we consider the then lack of highways it is probable that the Indian roads were still in use. It is on record that early residents of the west side of the Cuyahoga Valley frequently drove southwards towards Akron to reach the river and a road to Cleveland. This can be realized today if any attempt is made to traverse the country between the river and U. S. 21 which then did not exist.

old Cuyahoga town, the Ottawa Ostionish in the so-called Indian cornfields at the confluence with the Little Cuyahoga. From Kent to this point it coincides roughly with Ohio 9, Munroe Falls lying to the south on Ohio 91. The Indian cornfields lie thus on the north edge of Akron, a mile southeast of the Portage. It may have led also to Iron Bridge where it met the Cuyahoga War Trail from the Portage, which, continuing, struck the north branch of the Mahoning down the Cuyahoga at a point one mile west of Mud Lake on the former A. B. C. Electric Line.

It probably extended also through the Indian cornfields northwest to the Portage where it crossed the Cuyahoga, and diverging from the Portage Path crossed the flat to the north, passing two brooks on either side of the so-called Onondaga George's Lookout, a high hill where a scout of the mobilizing army is supposed to have been posted at the time of Hull's campaign. Then it mounted the ridge to the north and struck due west to Montrose (Ohio 18) at the north edge of the Copley Swamp.[2]

From Montrose the trail continued westward on the so-called Old Smith Road (Ohio 18) to Medina. At Montrose it crossed the trail running from Pipe's Town on the Tuscarawas to Indian towns at Ghent, Bath and Richfield.

The trail crossed the west branch of Rocky River two miles east of Medina, and passing near that place, probably to the south, continued over Mallet Creek and down the slopes of the East Branch of the Black River; a few miles south of Wellington it approached the Vermilion River probably through New London and Fitchville on that stream (Ohio 162). It then ran northwest past the lake southeast of Norwalk, and descending into the Huron Valley on a ridge southeast of Milan, passed through on the main street (U.S. 250) and, crossing the river, mounted the hill to the north of Milan, the Ottawa town of Salem of Moravian history.[3] Thence it followed the present highway to Avery (U.S. 250), and, turning westward, met the Lake Trail at Bloomingville, and beyond Sand Hill, the Great Trail, at the present crossroads southwest of Wyers on the P.S.&C.R.R. (Ohio 4).

Certain evidences indicate a trail on the northeast diagonal road from Medina to Weymouth (Ohio 3) leading through the intricate shallow valleys of the highlands,[4] passing around Weymouth and over the East Branch of the Rocky River, past Whipps Ledges southeast of Hinckley to Richfield, and down to the trail on the west side of the Cuyahoga at East Richfield (U.S. 21).

[2] Early writers state that the prehistoric earthwork in the midst of the Copley marshes was the scene of the final battle of the Cats against the Iroquois. Early French authorities mention the traditional battle, as told by the Iroquois, in which they exterminated these earliest inhabitants of northeastern Ohio.

The probable truth of the last battle of the Eries is told in the *Jesuit Relations*. The battle is said to have taken place midway between Canandaigua Lake and the Genesee River, which seems likely in view of the fact that the Cats were the attacking party and the Genesee was called the "Western Door of the Long House." The so-called "Erie Fort" in the Copley Marshes may be of much earlier origin than this period.

[3] Salem was one of the towns settled by the unfortunate Moravian Indians after their wanderings following the burning of Schoenbrunn and their captivity at Detroit and Upper Sandusky. The site is authenticated by archæological remains.

[4] Weymouth had at one time traces of earthworks similar to those in the Copley swamps. These were probably occupied prior to the period of French exploration.

The proximity of the Watershed Trail to Chippewa Lake, where stood the Chippewa Town, suggests that the westward trail passed near that spot south of Medina.

The directness of the Watershed Trail and the Old Smith Road suggest that this trail may have been an Indian trace adapted and straightened by the earliest white settlers.

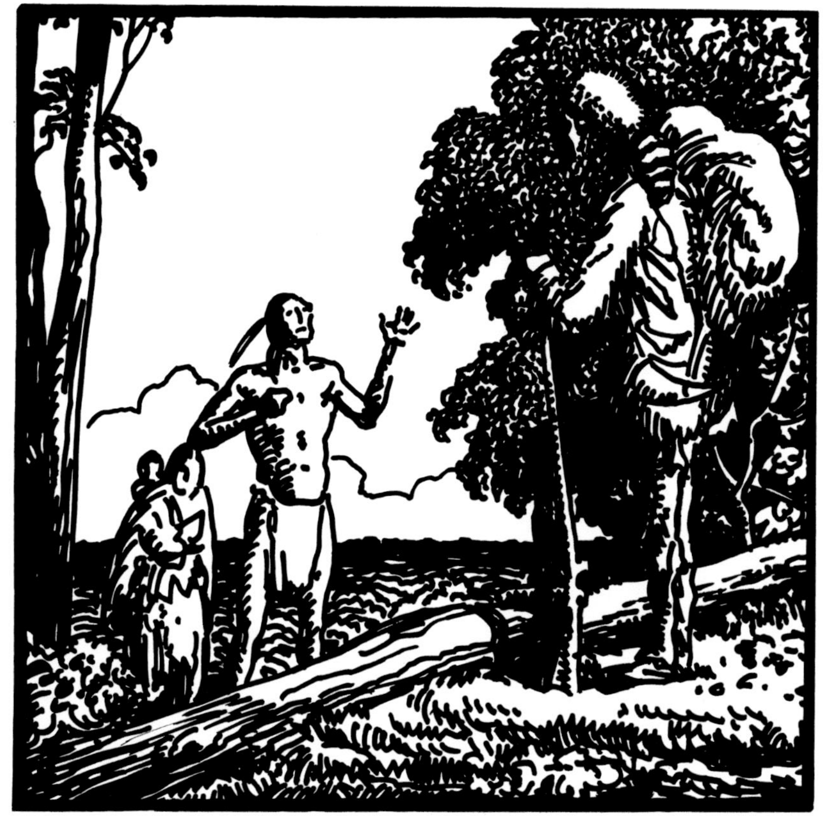

Sign Language

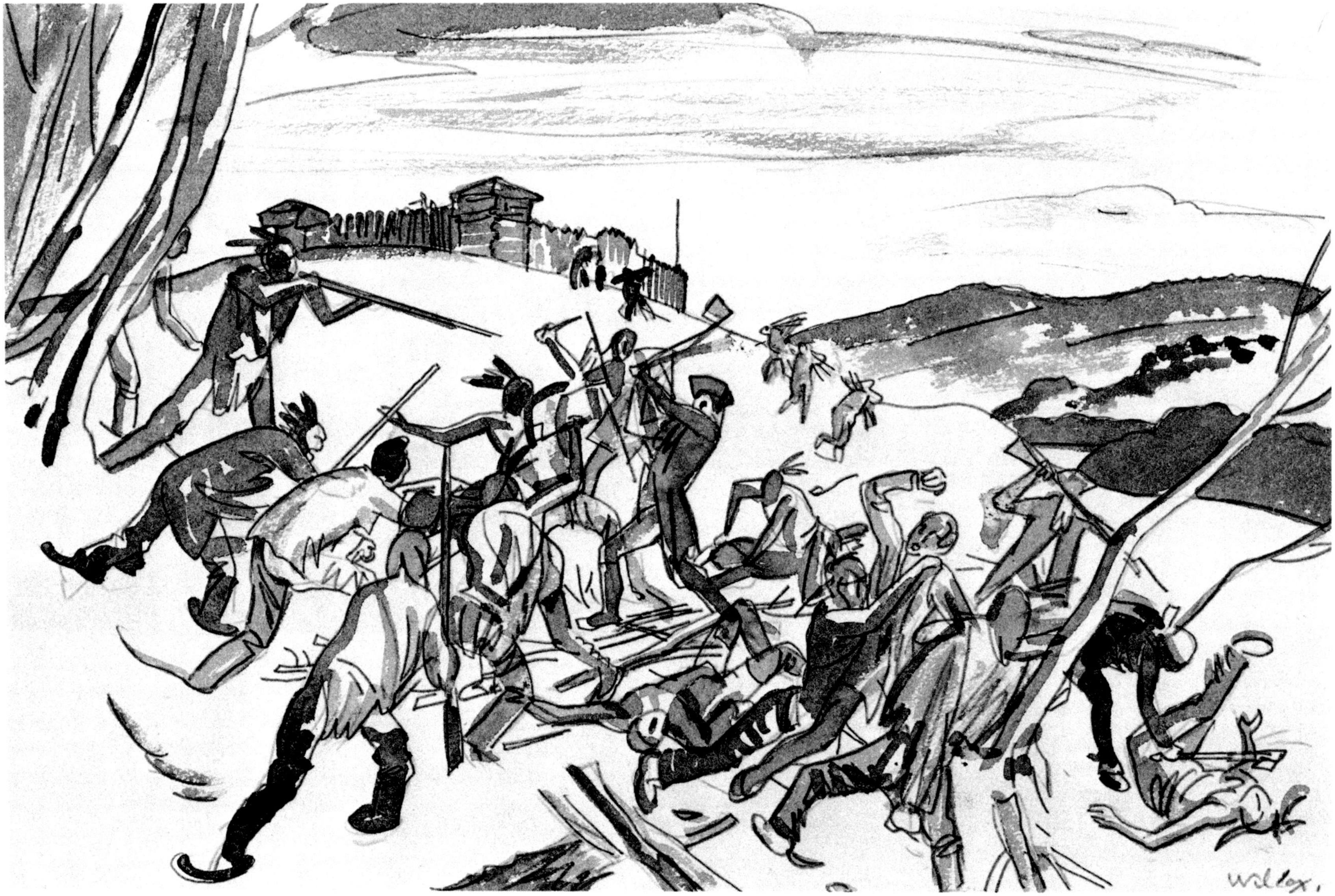

Indian Attack at Fort Laurens

The Great Trail

Logstown was noted in Washington's time as the most advanced post in the Ohio Valley. Situated at the mouth of the Beaver, it served as a base for the Indian traders who traversed the Mahoning and the Great Trail. The Great Trail is said to have led up the eastern ridge of the Beaver and to have followed up to Negley at the forks. This region is semi-mountainous and extremely beautiful. In those times, the ridges of the hills formed the only practical route among the deep and tangled gorges.

At Negley there is a large area of bottom land at the confluence and in the center stands the isolated hill or butte which served as a strong camp for Colonel Bouquet on his expedition to the Indian towns of the Tuscarawas and the Walhonding.[1]

Descending the heights from the south (Penn. 251), (Ohio 154) Bouquet followed the route to the hill and then continued on the trail along Union Ridge to the southwest. From this ridge the hills are a tossing sea of blue, but in the southwest there is the deeper gulf of the Ohio Valley. This region gives an impression of wilderness to this day; the blue hills are surmounted here and there by an isolated knob like an especially high wave. The valleys are misty as if filled with spray. In those days they must have been an impenetrable tangle filled with fallen timbers and overgrown with vines.

[1] From the top of the isolated hill at Negley a worthwhile view of the surrounding country is to be had. The semi-mountainous nature of the ground is evident. There is no indication, at this point, of the prairie country westward that is crossed by the Great Trail.

They harbor today occasional deer, and the rattler and copperhead are seen.[2]

The trail led due west over the ridges until it met Elk Run at Newhouse, about a mile and a half above its confluence with the Little Beaver. It then led westward just north of Lisbon on the ridge above, crossing the Middle Fork of the Little Beaver at McKinley Crossing (Ohio 164), where it led southwest up the West Fork to cross at a point two and a half miles east of the hamlet of Dungannon, and thence to that place.

The little town of Dungannon, lying on a knoll in a basin formed by the junction of several creeks, is now far from major highways. It was once called "Painted Post," from the peeled tree which bore "war marks" at this junction with the Moravian Trail.[3] It was once a spot of major importance, but now sleeps in its pleasant isolation. Lying as it does upon the abandoned Sandy-Beaver Canal, it was also a portage point for canoe travel into the Tuscarawas Valley, and is frequently mentioned in the stories of early Indian traders, particularly the interesting diary of Nicholas Cresswell.

From Painted Post the trail led northwest over the hills to Hanoverton (U.S. 30), west along the north ridge of the Sandy, and thence down Conser Run to Bayard on the north bank of the Sandy. (U.S. 30.) The hills are now less rough as we approach the Tuscarawas Valley and the sandy outcroppings which give the name to the river are evident. The trail led down the Sandy Valley bottoms through Minerva (U.S. 30), Pekin and Malvern (Ohio 43), the valley growing wider and gentler; through Magnolia and Sandyville with views up the Little Sandy, Pleasant Valley and Nimishillen at Sandyville (Ohio 8); then crossing the ridge west of Sandyville it descended what is now a long sandy ridge to the Tuscarawas. The present day sandiness of the hills must have been well masked by heavy foliage in Indian days and the approach to the river consequently more difficult.

The trail crossed the river about a quarter of a mile north of Fort Laurens where the bridge to Zoar now stands. The Sandy enters the Tuscarawas a mile north of the crossing. We find that the trail touched the southern edge of the present town of Bolivar and led northwestward over the hills.[4]

Standing at Fort Laurens one can easily comprehend the importance of this point in frontier history. Here is such a convergence of streams from the northeast and west that one begins to feel the drift of the mighty Muskingum. This is the back door of a very desirable and rich country-side. The hills have here taken on the characteristic sharp-cornered or pointed character of the Tuscarawas country, and the rivers give evidence of their one-time desirability to the early fishermen.

The trail now leads northwest over the rolling hills to Beach City (U.S. 250) (Ohio 93) in the flats of Sugar Creek. Crossing these flats, which we may assume flourished once

[2] Deer escaping from the game preserves of Pennsylvania do not find it difficult to reach this district unmolested on account of the rugged and forested nature of the ground. They have even been reported in the Chagrin Valley recently.

[3] Nicholas Cresswell includes in his diary a sketch of these "war marks" made by boastful savages.

[4] Fort Laurens has been called the western Valley Forge. The large Indian mound to the south was used as an ambush by Indians, to attack foragers for firewood, during the one winter of great privation suffered by the small garrison.

with the rock maple, we approach hilly country to the northwest, passing through Mt. Eaton on the summit of a high plateau with the land falling off in all directions, and so on, gradually descending into the Apple Creek Valley and on to another important trail crossing at Wooster. (U.S. 250.)

The Great Trail met the Killbuck branch of the Muskingum Trail in the fields of the present Ohio State Experimental Farm, a mile south of Wooster, and passed through the old cemetery south of town on the steep eastern slope of the Killbuck. In the flats beyond, it crossed the Cuyahoga War Trail in the vicinity of the fairgrounds, and continuing, led up the western slopes (U.S. 30). Wooster, like Bolivar, is another junction of trails at the head of a valley leading southward into the Walhonding, the main tributary of the Tuscarawas and Muskingum. From the Killbuck Valley, the trail leads westward over high, rolling land with level reaches (U.S. 30), dips into the shallow valley of the Muddy Fork of the Mohican, and then crosses more hills to Jeromesville, once an Indian town on the Jerome Fork, near where Old Town Run enters that stream.[5]

The course is now west up a rolling ridge, and passing a few miles south of present Ashland, the trail runs northwest between the Jerome and Black Fork to the high plateau at Olivesburg (Ohio 96); thence, over levels once heavily wooded, it approaches the steep, dark slopes of the Black Fork at Rome, and tending northward to Plymouth, crosses the watershed (Ohio 61). Here a spring and pond form a

[5] Jeromesville was the trading post of Jean Baptiste Jerome who withdrew to the mouth of the Huron at the outbreak of the Revolution.

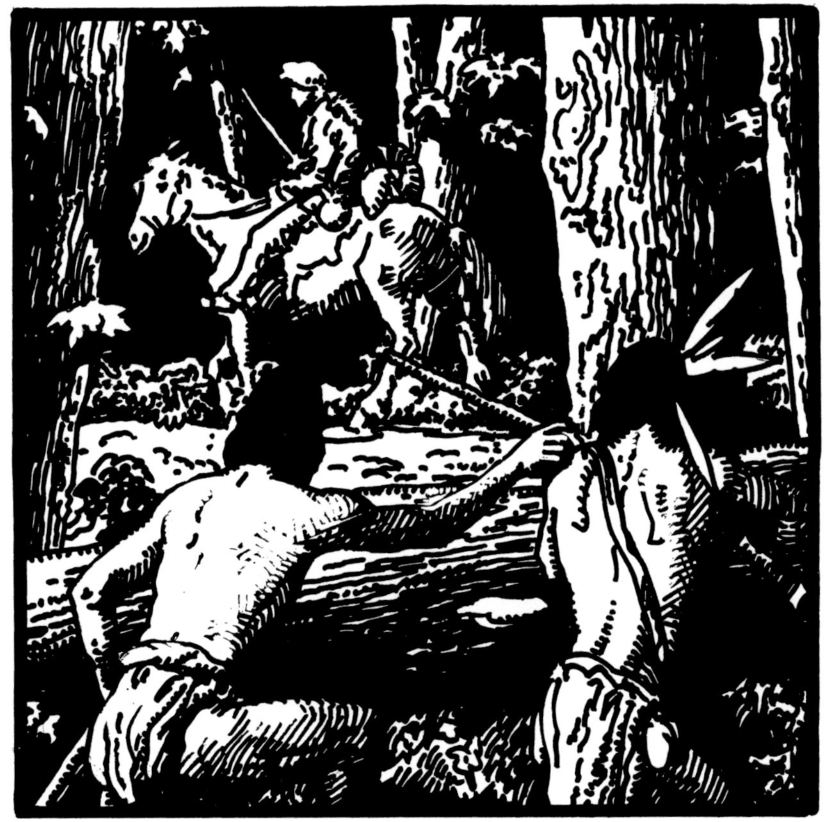

Friend or Foe?

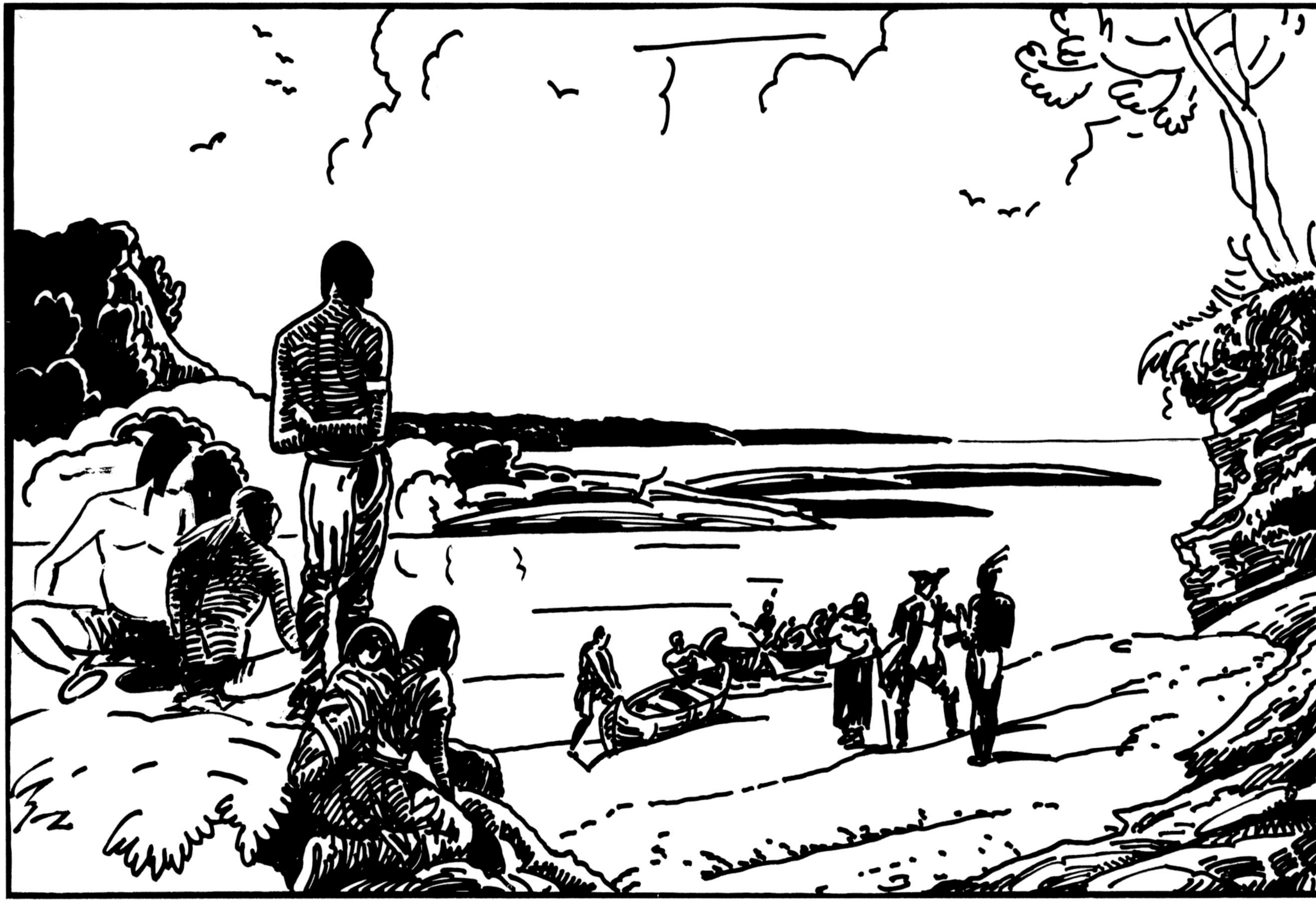

The de Lery Portage; Fort Junandat to Port Clinton

natural camp site that was utilized by Major Robert Rogers, the British colonial adventurer of pre-Revolutionary days.

We are now on the marshy headwaters of the Huron River. The trail leads north over broken and timbered land, crossing the West Branch twice, to Monroeville (Ohio 61) (U.S. 20) where the land is smoother again. It leads from here more to the northwest, down gently sloping land broken by an occasional marsh or sink hole in the limestone subsoil, but where streams are few, until when near the Blue Hole, the Lake Trail is joined, the route passing through North Monroeville and Sandhill.

Rogers is reputed to be the first white visitor to the famous Blue Hole where the lost waters of the hinterland gush forth from the depths. From here the route followed the Lake Trail to "Dunqueindundeh," probably synonymous with the French post of Junandat where Bark Creek enters the Sandusky, although there is doubt as to the exact location of the old post.[6]

The Great Trail is represented on the map published by the Ohio Archæological Society as progressing separately from the Lake Trail by a more southerly route to the mouth of the Maumee, where stood the trading post of Peter Navarre on the east side of the mouth between two marshy streams near Ironville. The route from Junandat was across the heads of the streams falling into the bay, via Lindsey, Elmore and Genoa, and following approximately Ohio 51. The Lake Trail evidently passed north of Junandat via Oak Harbor, Limestone, Willeston and Momeneetown to Navarre's, known today as Harbor View. Crossing the river here, the combined trails led via U.S. 25 to Detroit.[7]

The Great Trail passes through a variety of scenery, and may be said to traverse some of the most attractive country in the state, with the possible exception of the flat district between the Blue Hole and Toledo.

[6] The exact location of Fort Sandusky, or Junandat, is in doubt. Early records place it at a point decidedly unfavorable for building, and it has been variously located at points between Fremont and the actual shores of the lake near Port Clinton. One account states that Fort Junandat was built about 1754 and occupied but a short time as a trading post; another that Fort Sandusky was built by the French about 1750 on the left bank of the Sandusky, near Sandusky City. It was a trading post, and abandoned after 1763.

[7] Pierre Navarre was a French trader who built a cabin and trading post on the east side of the mouth of the Maumee. His activities extended from there to Fort Wayne.

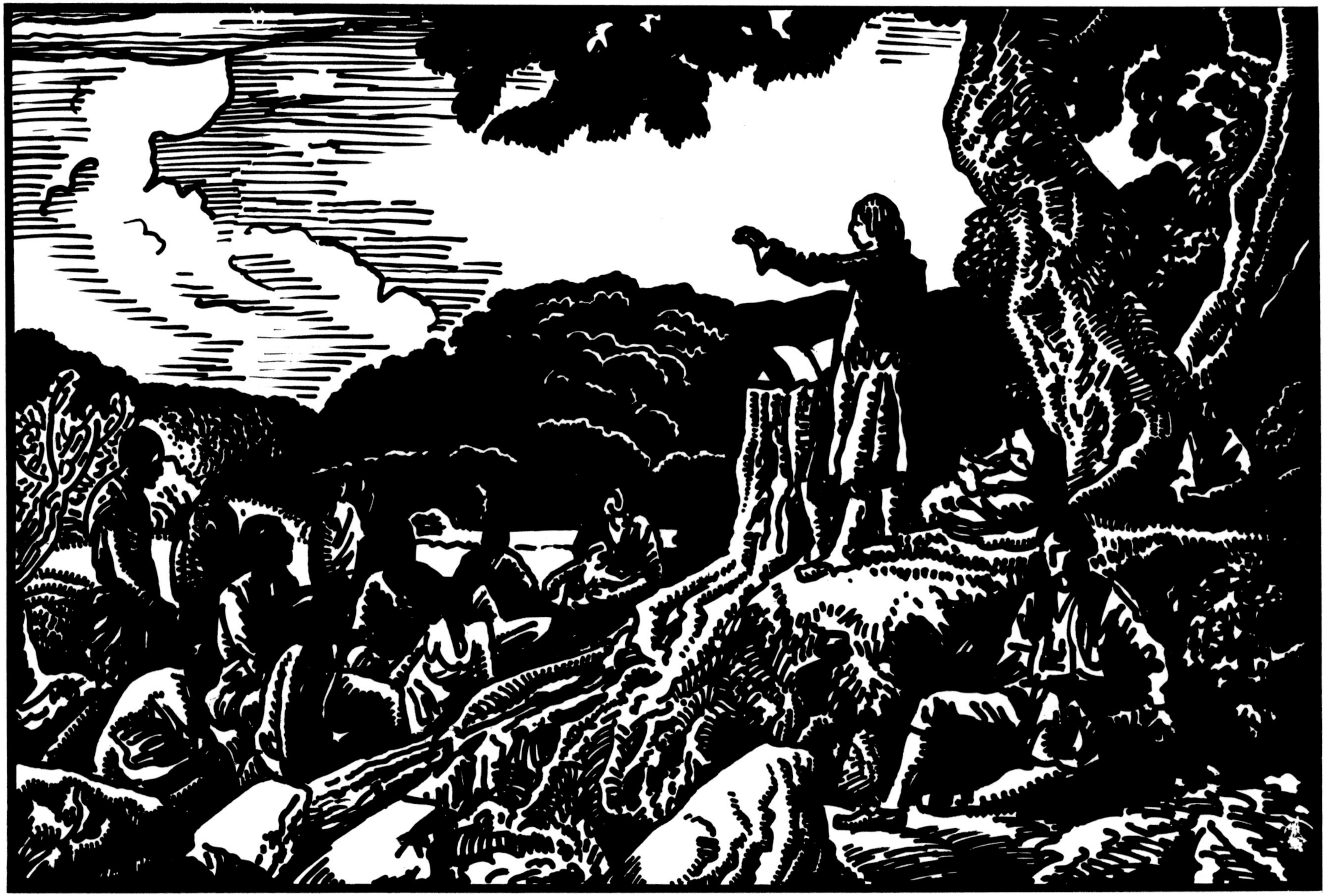

Nicholas Cresswell Visits Heckewelder at Schonbrunn

The Muskingum Trail

Marietta, that first settlement in Ohio, has patriotically preserved the records and relics of her early days, and is situated so picturesquely that that place affords a stimulating starting point for the study of the Muskingum Trail.

Fort Harmar, opposite, was built where this trail descended the western hill of that name to meet the Ohio shore. From the summit of the hill the view up both rivers is superb, and from that height the town seems lost in the splendid trees that have developed, since those early days, to magnificent proportions.

It is said that the lower portion of the Muskingum Trail was little used until white settlement, but it preserves in many places its aboriginal character. It led north and away from the Muskingum at the first bend, and heading Indian Run, meandered north on the hilltops to a point above Lowell, where at the top of the steep road to the river there is a splendid view of the valley immediately below. Bearing west on the hilltops again, as if on the top of the world, it led down abruptly into Waterford.

In Indian days the views from this stretch were possibly few, and the impression must have been one of a well beaten path on the edge of steep ravines, the opposite sides showing like distant green upholstered walls gleaming in the sunlight, or misty blue on the gray days.

At Waterford the trail crossed the crescent bottom land of Wolf Creek, and taking again to the ridges, cut west and south around a great salient of the river and then west again around to Stockport.

On the bluff heights just below Stockport, the trail is said to be distinct opposite the Big Bottom (Ohio 266). On these still densely forested heights the Indians are said to have lurked, watching the blockhouse before the massacre at that place. This is a particularly beautiful reach of the river. To the northeast, Council Rock projects above the valley.[1]

The trail now leads along the modern ridge highway somewhat to the west (Ohio 60) past Malta, and onwards on the hilltops, then down the Fatler Ridge to Philo and Duncan's Falls, where the Mingo Trail reached the river. From the peak of the ridge the trail continued again to follow the big bend below Zanesville, and descending the Moxahala Ridge and crossing the mouth of the stream of that name, led on to cross the Licking at its confluence with the Muskingum in West Zanesville. Then it mounted the long ridge to the north from which a surprising view of the valley is seen eastward from Stringtown and Kelley's Store. The path then descended through sweeping hills to Dresden, on the broad flats, and across beyond Trinway turned eastward on the northern hills (Ohio 16) and mounting between the Mill Fork and the Muskingum, tended north to Roscoe, opposite Coshocton, where it crossed the flats at the confluence with the Walhonding.[2] It then led north past the old town Gosehoking, with its Lichtenau, two miles below on the flats, and following the east ridge of Mill Creek (Ohio 76) turned up Spoon Creek three and a half miles north; there taking the highest ridge to the east, it led over White Eyes' Creek, at the mouth of which, opposite West Lafayette, stood his village; then over Buckhorn Creek it led down to the old Newcomerstown.[3] Here the trail turned to zigzag northeast above Port Washington to Fry's Creek, where it probably touched at Gnadenhutten (U.S. 36) opposite Lock Seventeen, at which point the Moravian Mingo branch met the river.[4] From here it swung north around Mud Valley to descend the ridge back of Goshen where sleeps Zeisberger,[5]

[1] Interesting rock formations are reported on the eastern cliffs of the river near Stockport. A section of the original trail is said to be visible, in its original state, on the ridge by the river immediately south of the town, and across from the Big Bottom State Park.

[2] Coshocton was the scene of repeated attacks by the whites on this cluster of Indian towns. One such was led by Brodhead from Wheeling by way of St. Clairsville. It is reported that Louis Philippe, later King of France, in his bourgeois youth sought adventure in the west. He is said to have taught school in the vicinity, and is reported to have been ejected forcibly from a tavern on a certain occasion. There are in the Coshocton Museum certain plate and china presented by him at a later date to local residents.

[3] The Moravian towns of the Muskingum consisted of two towns below Coshocton and White Eye's Town, one of which was Lichtenau, distant two miles south.

Salem, a short distance below Gnadenhutten, was like Gnadenhutten and also like Schoenbrunn, which was built to remove the Christian Indians from the proximity of the trail of Pipe and his evil influence.

Schoenbrunn, furthest north, was never attacked, but was abandoned before the forced assemblage of the congregations at Gnadenhutten for the exodus to the Sandusky.

[4] The site of the first house in Gnadenhutten is the southwest corner of Main and Cherry Streets.

[5] Zeisberger died at Goshen in 1808, at the age of 87

Heckewelder, the associate of Zeisberger, the Moravian missionary to the Delawares, was born of Teutonic parentage in Bedford, England, in 1743. He came to Bethlehem, Pennsylvania, where he entered the service of the Moravian congregation. His narrative of his experiences casts interesting light on the politics and circumstances of that day.

The following is a brief account of the wanderings of the exiled Moravian Indians: The congregation, including its leaders, was led up the Walhonding and northwest, where they were established at old Wyandot Town on the Sandusky by Captain Pipe, Girty and Elliott. They suffered intensely and the leaders were marched to Detroit, where their sufferings were somewhat relieved by the friendly commandant. They were urged to remain at Sandusky on account of the unsettled condition of the war, but were starved and persecuted by Girty and the Wyandots. To relieve their plight some were permitted to go to Gnadenhutten for a store of unharvested corn. While there, ninety were massacred by Americans under Williamson.

and then continued to New Schoenbrunn across from the Old Town that has now been restored by the State (U. S. 250). Traversing the flats to the northwest the trail now crossed Sugar Creek, where the river runs between New Philadelphia and Dover, and leading through the site of Dover passed through Parral (U. S. 250) and swinging north and east led down to Fort Laurens, south of Bolivar, where it crossed the Great Trail. Just beyond Bolivar in the flats opposite the mouth of the Sandy lay old Beaver Town, in the sharp loop of the Tuscarawas. Above Coshocton, where the Walhonding enters, the river was once known as Muskingum also.

Crossing the Tuscarawas, the trail swung to the northwest, over hills that still are primitive, to Navarre. From this point it led north on the present highway (U. S. 21) along the eastern levels to where Massillon now stands. It then followed closely the eastern bluffs of the narrowing Tuscarawas, crossing the bend at Crystal Spring, and led somewhat westerly

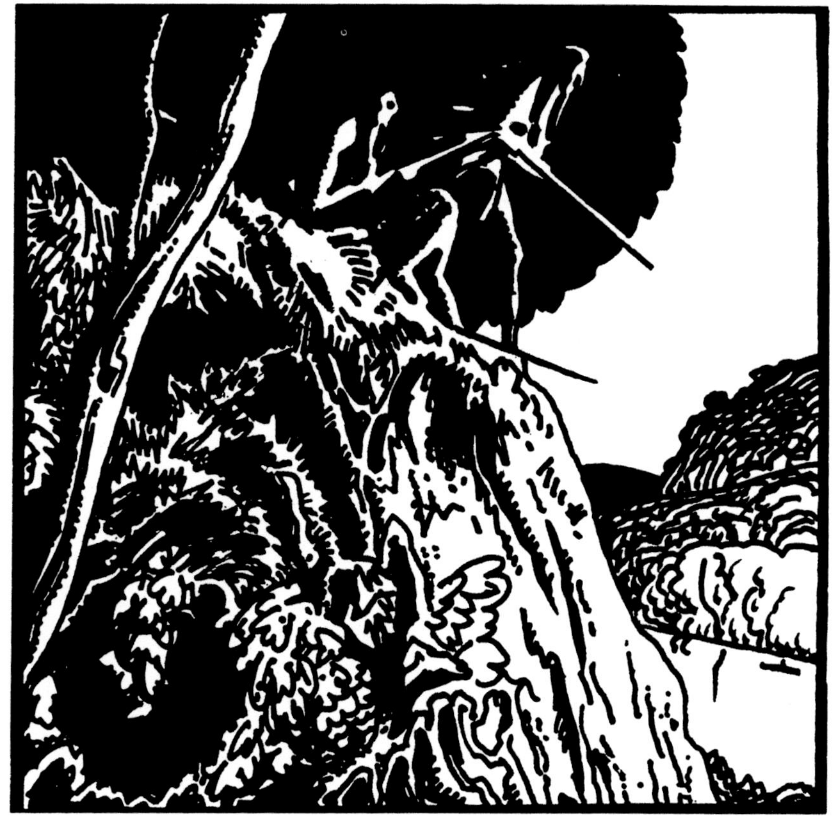

The River Trail

They appealed to Detroit and were conducted to the Huron River north of Detroit, where they settled. The Chippewas resented the occupation of their lands, and they built Pilgerruh on the Cuyahoga, planning later to re-enter the Muskingum Valley.

The Pipe, resenting the actual settlement of the country, urged them to settle at Pettquotting. They did so, but could not tolerate his attempts to alter their convictions. They appealed to Detroit again, and were settled at Fairfield on the River Thames.

The Indians were intending to settle them at Kegeyunk or Fort Wayne, and a few going there were persecuted by the Prophet, brother of Tecumseh.

Zeisberger returned to the Muskingum to investigate the possibilities of a second settlement there. A new attempt was made by groups from Fairfield at Pettquotting, or New Salem, which lay nearby, but was broken up by land sales in 1804. Zeisberger died at Goshen on the Muskingum between Schoenbrunn and Gnadenhutten in 1808, aged eighty-seven. The rest of his helpers withdrew to Bethlehem, Pennsylvania.

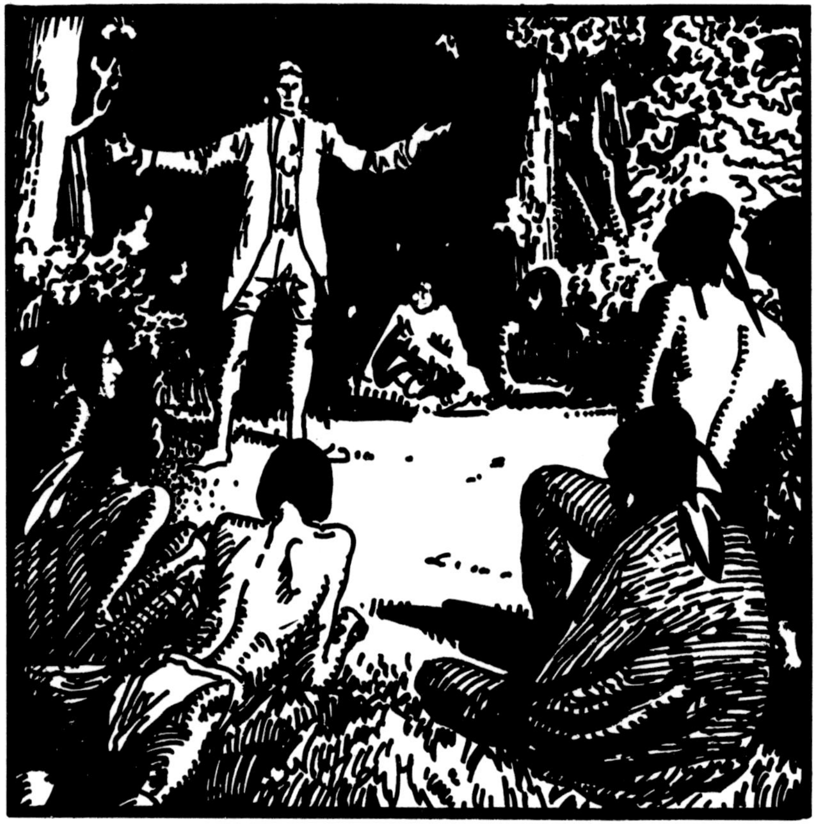

The Missionary

over hummocky land to Nimisila (Ohio 236), and then north to the farther end of Long Pond [Nimisila Res.] where lay Pipe's Town; it continued north by the west shore of Summit Lake and along the ridge west of Akron, and so over West Market Street by the Portage Path to the portage at Cranmer, where it crossed the Watershed Branch of the Mahoning. At Summit Lake it was probably joined by the Cuyahoga War Trail from the southwest, and it may have continued from the portage northeast as part of the Mahoning to the mouth of the Cuyahoga. From certain evidences its main continuation was perhaps past Onondaga George's Lookout,[6] north of the portage, to Botzum on the west bank of the Cuyahoga where the two large mounds are to be seen, and up Pleasant Valley at Ira with its Indian town on the dividing ridge of the little valley, and so up the east side of Furnace Run to the Brecksville Road (U.S. 21).

Adjacent to this district are Bath, Ghent and Richfield, all reported as former Indian villages. After meeting the present Brecksville Road on the Brush estate, the trail evidently followed the present national highway (U.S. 21) through Brecksville and Independence, where it crossed the Mahoning Trail at the Willow Promontory, and, taking the most direct course for the mouth of the Cuyahoga, led up East 71st Street hill (U.S. 21) across the river; taking the bluff to the left at the top, it passed east of the lake in Forest

[6] Onondaga George's Lookout, the high hill northwest of the portage on the Cuyahoga, received its name about 1812, when this place was used as a mustering point for militia from the Western Reserve. For many years the portage had been known as a trading post.

City Park, touching the river at the mouth of Morgan Run; at the Jefferson Street bridge site it passed over the land now occupied by the steel furnaces, and ran below the bluffs of Ontario Street, once known as Vinegar Hill, to the crossing at Union Lane, where it finally reached the Lake Trail and the river mouth.

The old Ohio and Erie Canal lies parallel to this trail all the way from Dresden. It is interesting to imagine the appearance of this trail as it entered what is now Cleveland. The flats of that day were probably densely filled with marsh willows, and the bare, shaly bluffs presently crowned with the skyline of buildings were then draped with green, and presented no dingy and dim outlines through a reek of smoke. The Muskingum Trail passes by an almost continuous river landscape. For this reason it is uniquely beautiful among the scenic routes of the State.

So many Indian villages lay upon this trail that it may be well to review them. Below Zanesville at Duncan's Falls lay Will's Town. Below Coshocton were two Delaware towns, one of them known as Lichtenau, while up the Wakatomika lay the town of that name. White Woman's Town lay not far up the Walhonding. Not far north of Coshocton were Muskingum and Con-cha-ke. Eastward lay White Eyes' and Newcomer's Towns, while below New Philadelphia lay Gnadenhutten, the two Schoenbrunns, Tuscarawas and Three Legs Town. To the north were Old Town and Tapacon Town. At Bolivar were another Tuscarawas and a Beaver Town. At the Akron Lakes were Pipe's Town and others. North and east of Akron were the several Cuyahoga Towns.

Around Bath, Ghent and Richfield were Mingo towns, and around the Willow district were Saguin's Post and Ottawa towns. The trail was evidently a Delaware highway south of the portage, and northward a roving, mixed population followed the Cuyahoga.

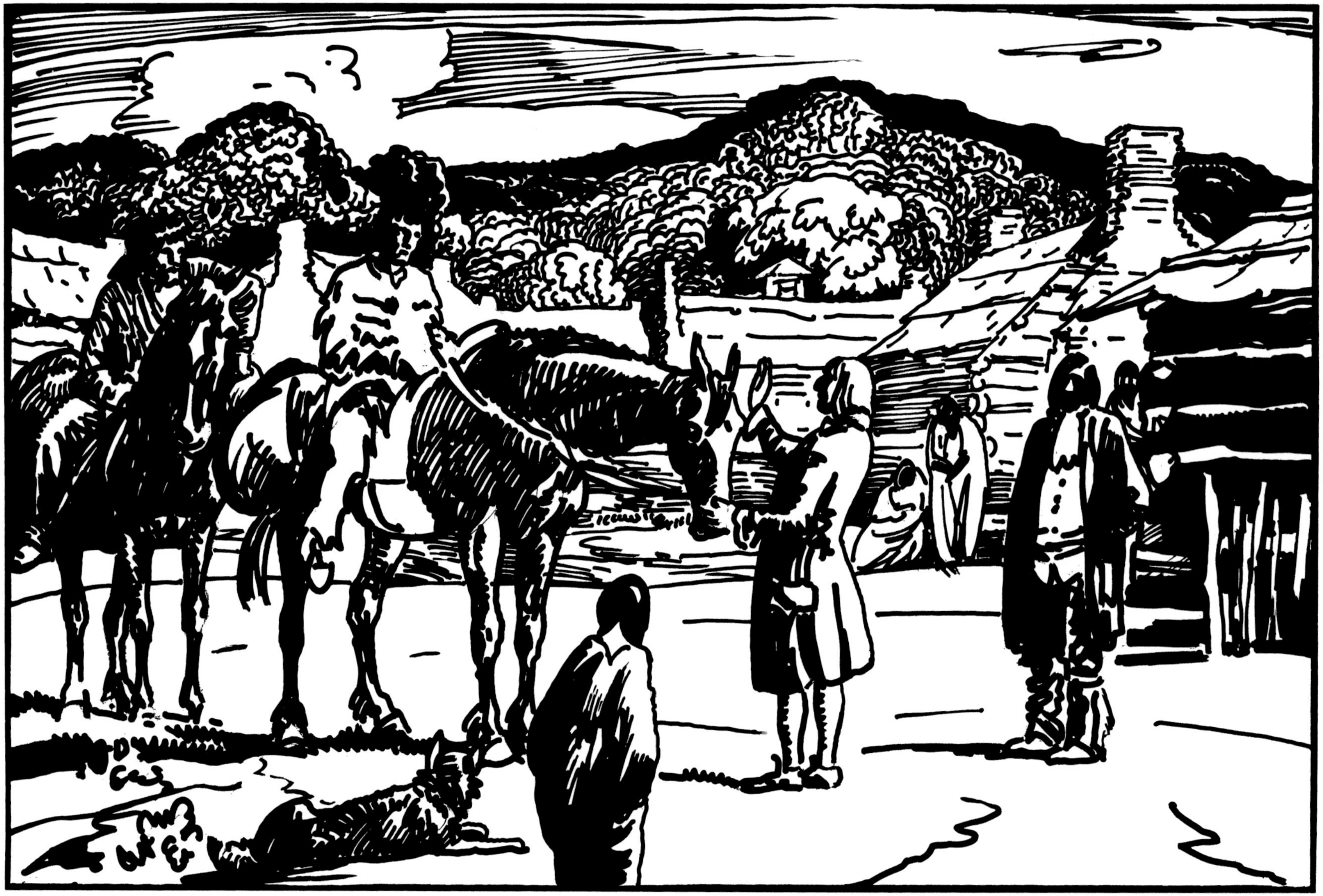

Heckewelder Preaching to the Delaware at Coshocton

The Moravian Trail

Columbiana County contains several narrow entrances through its abrupt hills to the interior of Ohio. The first, the Great Trail, led in at Negley from across the State Line by way of the Beaver and continued across at Lisbon.

One phase of the Moravian Trail was a branch of the Great Trail from that point down southwest to Dungannon, or Painted Post, on the Little Beaver-Sandy Portage.

The mouth of Little Beaver may have afforded another entry; it lies a mile above East Liverpool. Beginning on the hill to the left of the mouth, it led on the ridges northwest through Calcutta, Cannons Mill and West Point, and up the ridges of the West Fork through Gavers on the river to Dungannon.[1]

One account of White Eyes asserts he was shot at Fort Laurens by an American

[1] Captain White Eyes, the Delaware, met his death at the hands of a youth named Carpenter at West Point, Ohio, on Little Beaver Creek. He was shot while drinking at a spring, under the belief that he was stalking the Carpenter cabin. The trial of Carpenter aroused much excitement and dread of an uprising in the region. The spot where he was buried may be seen a short distance southeast of the bridge at West Point.

The records of Jefferson County state that William Carpenter was indicted in the first case of its kind for the murder of Captain White Eyes. The Indian was intoxicated and apparently only intended to frighten the boy. Neighbors, including Bezaleel Wells, one of the founders of Steubenville, raised funds to reconcile the Indians. The shooting took place at West Point, Ohio.

Captain White Eyes was the dissipated son of the great White Eyes, the Delaware.

White Eyes, the Delaware Chief, stood for peace between England and America. He refused to listen to the accusations of McKee, Elliott and the Half King against the Moravian Indians. He was the friend of Heckewelder and Zeisberger.

Thomas White Eyes, an Indian educated at Princeton, is mentioned by Heckewelder as having been murdered at Georgetown, near the Ohio. This is probably the same White Eyes as referred to in the Carpenter episode, and not the first White Eyes of Coshocton. That famous Indian, according to Heckewelder, died of smallpox while with McIntosh at the building of Fort Laurens.

The most direct entry to this region would have been on the ridge back of Wellsville, keeping Little Yellow Creek on the right, past Salineville and west to Carrollton (Ohio 39).

In any event the size of Yellow Creek below Wellsville may have suggested its utility and the valley of the larger river would have led through Irondale to Carrollton as well.

The story of the battle of the Poe brothers with the Indians at the mouth of Yellow Creek, the story of the Greathouse Massacre of Logan's children across the Ohio at that point, and the suggestions made by Nicholas Cresswell in his diary all tend to indicate that this was probably the Ohio end of a route to the Moravian towns on the Muskingum.

From Carrollton in the tumultuous hills of Carroll County, the route led down the Indian Fork of Connotton Creek, and crossing at the confluence, passed over the dividing ridge southwest to Philadelphia Road on the Little Stillwater, thence west down that stream on the north edge of the flats, over the ridge north of Dennison, and southwest over the flats at Uhrichsville (U.S. 36) and so through the narrow gap of the hills westward to Old Tuscarawas. Thus six miles above lay the Schoenbrunn Towns (Ohio 16), and three miles below, Gnadenhutten at the end of the Mingo Trail (Ohio 16) (U.S. 36).

On the ridge beyond Lock Seventeen to the west passed the hillcrest Muskingum Trail, and below along the prairie flats, mentioned in early records as unique in the wilderness of forest where forage was scarce, lay the numerous towns toward the forks of the Muskingum at Coshocton—the lower Moravian towns of the Delawares.

This was the route which in later days was widened as a wilderness road, and by which, from Pennsylvania, came the thrifty Germanic settlers of the Tuscarawas Valley. The trail is still traceable in the hills of Columbiana and Carroll Counties. It is difficult to follow today, as it is almost entirely a hilltop trail.

Returning to Dungannon, or Painted Post, the early pioneers entering Ohio by the old Great Trail seem to have passed southwest of Lisbon to that point and to have descended Willard Run to Millport, at its junction with the Little Beaver Creek, and then to have continued over the ridge of Summitville southwest to Mechanicstown and thence (Ohio 39) to Carrollton; thence westward, possibly crossing the narrow valley several times, to have passed through Dellroy (Ohio 39) and continued along the stream, reaching the confluence with Connotton Creek. The trail then evidently crossed the southwest ridge, following up perhaps Dog Run, and descending into Beaverdam Creek, crossed another narrow ridge and passed down the ravine south of the Tuscarawas County Infirmary; moving west across the present highway (Ohio 8), it arrived at Old Schoenbrunn, four miles above the end of the Yellow Creek Route, which reached the Tuscarawas via the Stillwater at Midvale, a community known in that day as Three Legs Town.

The Moravian Road from Lisbon via Painted Post and Carrollton to Schoenbrunn may have been mainly a later

soldier, either treacherously or accidentally. (*Butterfield,* Washington Irving Correspondence.) This work served to correct "many errors of statement by early writers." Captain White Eyes, slain by Carpenter, is named as the son.

wagon road, which, utilizing part of the Great Trail and the Mingo Trail, established a direct route from Pittsburgh to the upper Tuscarawas towns.

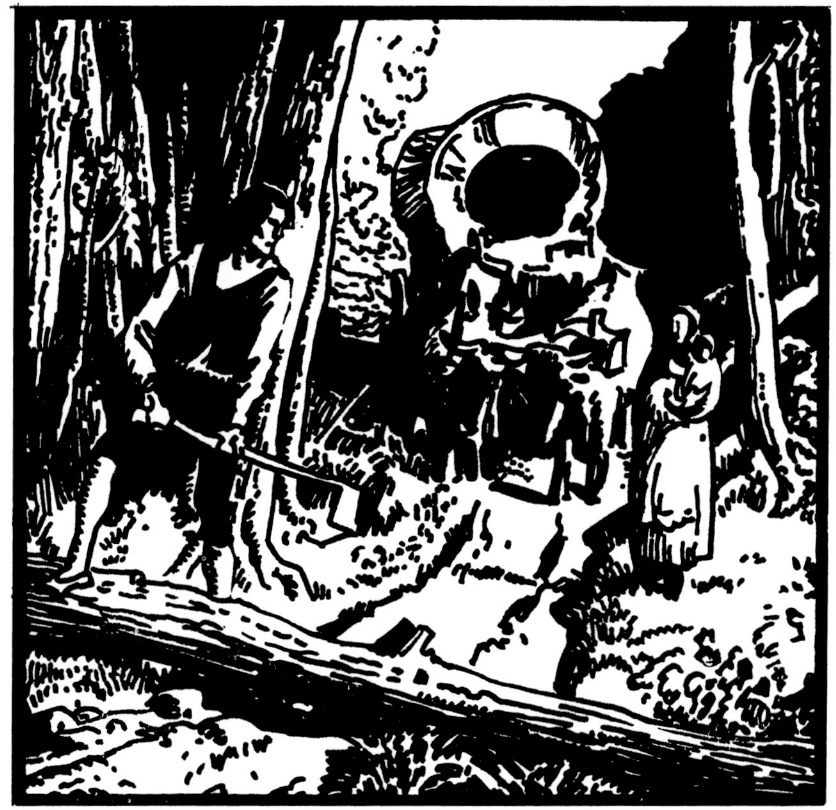

The Pioneer's Progress

The Tuscarawas Trail

Parties having entered Ohio by the Mahoning-Beaver Trail, and visiting the Salt Springs near the site of Niles for the sake of replenishing their salt supply, may have then bent their course toward the Tuscarawas for the purpose of reaching the west rather than to traverse the untenanted lands of the Reserve.

The course of the Alliance branch of the Pennsylvania from Niles follows an easy highland course which may well coincide with a course followed by a good woodsman to the south. The route led generally southwest between the Meander and the upper Mahoning, crossed Mill Creek northeast of Sebring and the diminished Mahoning again at a lake east of Alliance and southwest of Sebring and, ascending a ravine southeast of Mount Union immediately south of the Country Club, approached the swamps at the head of Nimishillen Creek through which passed the Pennsylvania and the Lake Erie, Alliance & Wheeling.

It then pursued a zigzag course over the west ridge of Black Run to the west of Robertsville, and following south on the ridge between the Little Sandy and Armstrong Run, met the Big Sandy about three miles west of Malvern. It then proceeded west, as part of the Great Trail, to Old Tuscarora Town at Bolivar, down the Sandy Valley. This route was over marshy uplands until it met the rising hills just north of the Sandy.

The Salt Springs Trail

The scarcity of salt on the high lands of Ohio led to a high value being set upon springs from which, by boiling the water, the Indian or pioneer could procure this rare commodity. These springs were important also because the fondness of the deer for this water made them favorable spots for hunting.

The Great Salt Lick near Niles was noted in early days, and it is more than likely that some connecting or cross trail led from the junction of the Great Trail with the Moravian trace north to the Mahoning over the high levels.

There is a definite diagonal road direct to Lisbon that was once a cart track to that town, and doubtless a shortening of the original Great Trail to Painted Post. From Lisbon a secondary highway leads through Franklin Square, up the middle fork of Little Beaver, on through Washingtonville; then leaving the modern direct route at that place, the trail probably kept close to the edge of the river, where a lesser road exists, and turning northeast on the line of the Reserve, led to the high land at the headwaters of the Meander Creek, down the east ridge of which, adhering more or less to the line of the Lisbon Branch of the Erie Railroad, it ran to Ohlstown, and crossing the creek, led north to the Spring at the head of a ravine running northward to the Mahoning.

This trail extended from the somewhat mountainous region of Columbiana County to where, east of Salem at Washingtonville, it reached the rolling levels of the southern Reserve. Crossing the height of the plateau one mile west of Canfield, it then descended to the Mahoning. This region was doubtless heavily forested.

The Ashtabula Trail

An attempt by early Frenchmen or their allies to enter Ohio from the lake, with a view to reaching the Ohio River at a western point, may have encouraged an attempt via the Ashtabula River. As this stream, like the Grand River, is turned eastward by the watershed, such an expedition may have crossed the high land along the present line of the Pennsylvania Railroad via Munson Hall to Austinburg, at the bend of the Grand, and continuing up its eastern side, reached Rock Creek, and so, crossing the upper tributaries of the Grand past the high marshes to the east (Ohio 45), have come to the Mahoning at Warren and Niles (Ohio 169). Here the trail met the Mahoning and crossed to the Salt Lick. By following the Tuscarawas Trail it would have led via the Muskingum to points west and south. On the highlands this would have been an extremely difficult route either for canoes or footwork, as it must have been exceedingly swampy and overgrown in part. There is a report of a trail having crossed the Grand River at Mechanicsville west of Austinburg. This may indicate that the trail followed up the west side of the river southward (Ohio 45). Early wagon roads probably used it in part in the settlement of the Reserve.[1] This road would have passed through Austinburg, Mechanicsville, Hartsgrove (U.S. 6), Windsor (U.S. 322), Mesopotamia, Farmington, Southington (U.S. 422) and Leavittsburg (Ohio 5).

[1] The cannon balls used at the battle of Lake Erie were cast opposite Steubenville on the Ohio and were transported by pack mules to the lake, probably via Lisbon and Youngstown.

Trails in the Western Reserve

Since most of the trails entered Ohio from the River, and the north had been since the days of the Eries untenanted, the report of a trail along the Chagrin suggests that in the times of the French traders an entrance to this region may have been found in the Chagrin Valley as well as the Cuyahoga where one French post undoubtedly stood at Tinker's Creek. There is evidence of a continuous road from the Lake Trail southward on the Chagrin, which passes through just such territory as is typical of Indian trails. Much of it was appropriated to estates and the Metropolitan Park, and still retains a natural charm.

Departing from the Lake Trail at the mouth of the Chagrin, the trail, judging by the natural course of the present road as seen by looking at the enlarged contour maps, followed the east or west banks over the low flats below Willoughby, and then the principal north and south street on the west of the river (Ohio 174) ; it crossed Johnnycake Ridge and the lowland of the stream to the southwest, where the golf links lie, and mounted the ridge where, to the east, the landmark of Guildersleeve Ridge and, to the northeast, the blue ridge of Little Mountain, with its native stand of hemlocks and pines, are seen. Thence it dipped into the valley beyond Eagle's Mills and rising over the lower ridges of the hills came to Wilson's Mill. Here it crossed to the east bank and entered Gates Mill, crossing again where the Maple Leaf Inn stood, and passing over the low grounds of the present Polo Field, followed up the west side, either on the ridge or the foot of the ridge, to the narrow gorge southwest of Chagrin Falls (U.S. 422). It crossed at this point, followed

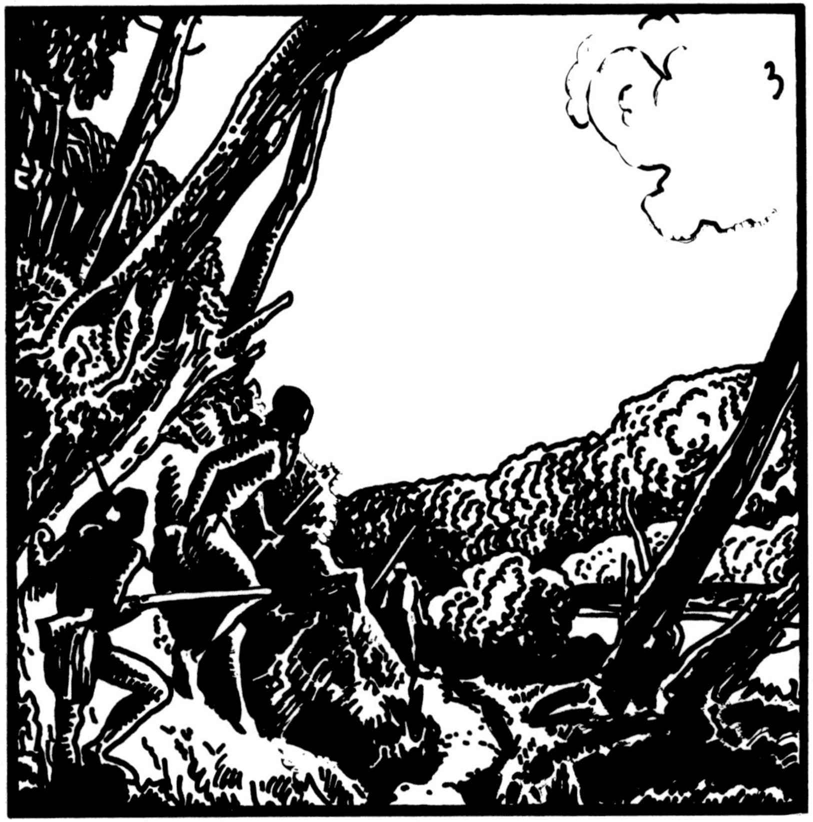

Ambuscade on the Chagrin River

up the Aurora Branch over the McFarland Creek to the Onondaga Town, just southeast of Geauga Lake, and turning southeast on rising ground, came to another Onondaga Town at Aurora.

From here, there must have been a branch trail running west over the marshes at the head of Tinker's Creek to a Seneca Town at Twinsburg (Ohio 82) and continuing west to Macedonia and Northfield, and down to Willow Lake to join the Cuyahoga and Mahoning Trails; also, a branch may have continued down Brandywine Creek to Ponty's Camp, one-half mile north of Boston Mills on the Cuyahoga.

From Aurora Town the Chagrin Trail continued over the pond-studded, rolling land of the watershed, south to Big Son's Seneca Town at Streetsboro (Ohio 43), and so on to the lakes around Kent to join the Mahoning Trail. This it crossed, over more knolls and swamps, south on the line of the Wheeling and Lake Erie Railroad, past Fritch Lake and Congress Lake on the west (Ohio 43), down the Middle Nimishillen, through the rolling hills around Canton, and down the Creek to Sandyville where it joined the Great Trail.

From the junction of streams south of Canton, a branch trail may have followed northwest to Myers Lake, up the general course of the Old Cleveland Terminal and Valley Branch of the B. & O. Railroad, past the pond at Myersville and over the head of the Tuscarawas River, then a mile and a half west of Springfield Lake to the mouth of the Little Cuyahoga at Akron (Ohio 8, 91), then down past the Old Maid's Kitchen to Indian Towns at the Falls, and west past the Old Maid's Kitchen on the north cliffs to Old Cuyahoga Town, the Ottawa Ostionish, in the Indian Cornfields above the Portage (Ohio 5).

Here a short trail may have led northward up the heights to an Ottawa Town at Northampton, and on to the War Trail at Steel's Corners. From Onondaga George's Lookout, the high bluff west of the Portage, a trail may have led up the bluffs on the west, over Yellow Creek, past the Mounds at Botzum, over the dividing ridge across from Hale's Farm at Pleasant Valley beyond Ira, where stood Logan's Town, up the Furnace Run on its east ridge through East Richfield, and via the Brecksville road (U.S. 21) to Willow, where it met the Mahoning Trail, and on possibly to the mouth of the Cuyahoga as part of the Cuyahoga System.

From Kent a trail is likely to have led up the west of the shallow Upper Cuyahoga just east of Twin Lakes (Ohio 43) and following a northeast course have led to Hiram Rapids and so on up to the lakes around Burton, such as Punderson (Ohio 44). Continuing from Hiram Rapids a branch may have led to the head of the Grand River at Parkman (U.S. 422) where lay another lake, and to Nelson Ledges (Ohio 88) and followed the Grand River north on its east bank through Rock Creek to Ashtabula (Ohio 46), or have continued on the north of the river around its bend to the mouth at Painesville (Ohio 45, 86).

The region entered from Lake Erie by the Chagrin Trail or possibly by the Grand River was not tenanted by permanently settled tribes. Judging by the names of reported Indian Villages this region must have been visited by hunting and fishing parties from several directions, and may also have been occupied by renegades from the more organized Iroquois tribes in New York.

It is a high watershed dotted with ponds and affording many pudding-stone shelter ledges. The numerous reports of "Indian Trails" may have some foundation in fact; at least there are many evidences, though unconnected, of Indian occupation. We may assume that the entire state was webbed with subsidiary paths branching from the main system to enter favorable foraging territory.

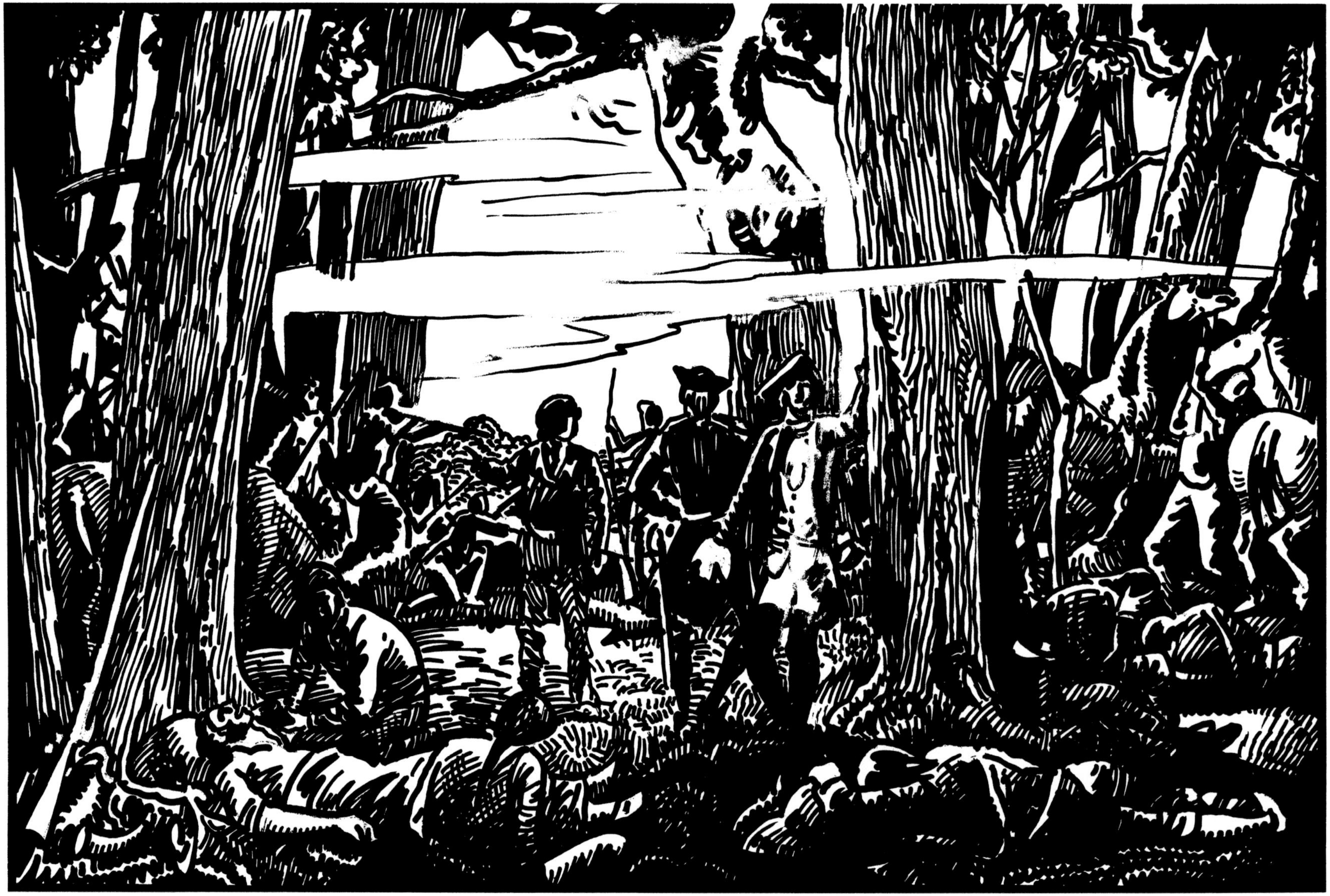

Crawford's Forces Occupy 'Butte Island'

The Mingo Trail

Three miles below Steubenville, where the Ohio flows north and south, lies Mingo Bottom.[1] Across the Ohio is the great gap in the hills of West Virginia, Cross Creek, out of which poured the settlers and borderers who entered the central Muskingum Valley and through which came the brutal murderers of the peaceful Moravian Indians at Gnadenhutten. This point was the beginning of Williamson's Expedition against that town.[2]

Mingo Bottom, now covered with furnaces, was once Indian cornfields and villages. Ohio Cross Creek, just opposite the West Virginia stream, led west across its northern flats into the next important gap, after Yellow Creek, in the hostile green wall of Ohio.

The trail led up the north ridge of the stream to a point about one and a quarter miles below Reeds Mills, where it crossed and struck west up a ridge to Bloomingdale and Hope-

[1] The last battle fought with Indians in southeastern Ohio took place at Indian Cross Creek, or Battle Ground Run. It was known as Buskirk's Battle.

[2] Defenders of Colonel Williamson state that we do not appreciate the conditions then existing, and that the frontiersmen believed that if Christianity did not prevent the English from inciting Indians, they could not, knowing the Indian, trust his Christianity. The Moravians had unsuspectingly purchased garments from a war party which were recognized as those belonging to their victims.

One factor contributing to Crawford's fate at the stake was the existence of the "peeled trees" around his camp at Mingo prior to his march. These trees were peeled in the Indian fashion and inscribed with the war cry "No quarter to an Indian whether man, woman or child." Such inscriptions were habitually copied skillfully by Indians and later translated by willing white men. In this case it was believed that Williamson, the butcher of Gnadenhutten, was involved and his identity confused with that of Crawford.

The monument to the Moravian martyrs at Gnadenhutten stands upon the site of the Indian town, now the modern cemetery. The small mounds mark the graves of the victims whose bones were gathered by the faithful missionaries some time after the massacre. At Goshen, a short distance up the Tuscarawas, is the grave of the leader Zeisberger.

dale (U.S. 22) and then, just north of Cadiz, westerly to the head of the Standingstone Fork of the Little Stillwater.

On this trail was a town called Crow's Town, probably in the vicinity of Cadiz. This is a beautiful country among the coal hills. Today the roads swoop gracefully over rounded hills, and the valleys dip into sharp clefts without many large flats, so that in early days it must have been a sea of green waves.

At a point just above Laceyville it crossed the stream, and taking to the ridge, passed through Deersville westerly to Weaver Run, a branch of the Stillwater. Crossing near the confluence, it followed a northwest ridge to Gnadenhutten, immediately at the foot of this ridge, where the Tuscarawas cuts close to the hills. Old Gnadenhutten lay immediately on the bank of the river where the present cemetery lies.

This trail is a typical hill trail, and the route descends but seldom to low levels. It was, in all probability, possible to scan the surrounding country at all times, and it was the most direct way to the Moravian towns, lying practically east and west. The present absence of improved highways makes it difficult to define without a contour map of the region. It is frequently mentioned as Williamson's Route.

Crawford on his expedition against Sandusky in 1782 started on this route, but dreading the possibility of attack in the southern Muskingum towns, left the trail at the crossing of Cross Creek below Reeds Mills; following the stream instead, he tended more northerly through Jewett (Ohio 9, 151) and down Connotton Creek on the ridge to the south, to a point south of Bowerston on that stream; there he turned southwest down Happy Hollow to Philadelphia Road, and following the Little Stillwater to its mouth through Dennison and Uhrichsville, arrived at Midvale (Ohio 8) (U.S. 250).

Here Crawford seems to have crossed the Tuscarawas at Goshen and following the river northward, close to the western hills, came to New Schoenbrunn, where he found the abandoned cornfields of the scattered Moravian Indians opposite the Old Town.

There was a branch of the Mingo Trail from Cadiz which led southwest to the Muskingum below Zanesville at Duncan Falls. It ran continuously on southerly and westerly ridges, to the forks of the Stillwater at Piedmont (U.S. 22), and so on southwest over the heads of Skull Fork and Salt Fork, and over Leatherwood Creek two miles east of Lore City (Ohio 285). It then followed a ridge westward and southward over Will's Creek, and passing through Hartford Station and Pleasant City, led up Buffalo Fork to Cumberland (Ohio 146).

From Cumberland it ascended Miller Creek, over High Hill (Ohio 284), down the north ridge of Kent Run and into Duncan Falls (Ohio 60).

This branch of the Mingo Trail passes through a tortuous country of V-shaped valleys now scarred with coal mines. It probably was utilized to top the confused territory of the Will's Creek basin, which, though so near the Ohio, would require a very roundabout approach by river, necessitating a journey far to the north at Coshocton and a laborious following of the southeasterly Will's Creek. The present Will's Creek district preserves plenty of suggestion of the period to this day. From Duncan Falls the Mingo may have connected with the Muskingum trail, by crossing the river and ascending the Fatler Ridge west of Philo. At this point the Muskingum pursues its southern trend through an almost gorge-like valley to the Ohio, and the Muskingum Trail may have been little used south of this point since there is little record of Indian occupation between here and the river. At Duncan Falls stood an Indian Village known as Will's Town.[3]

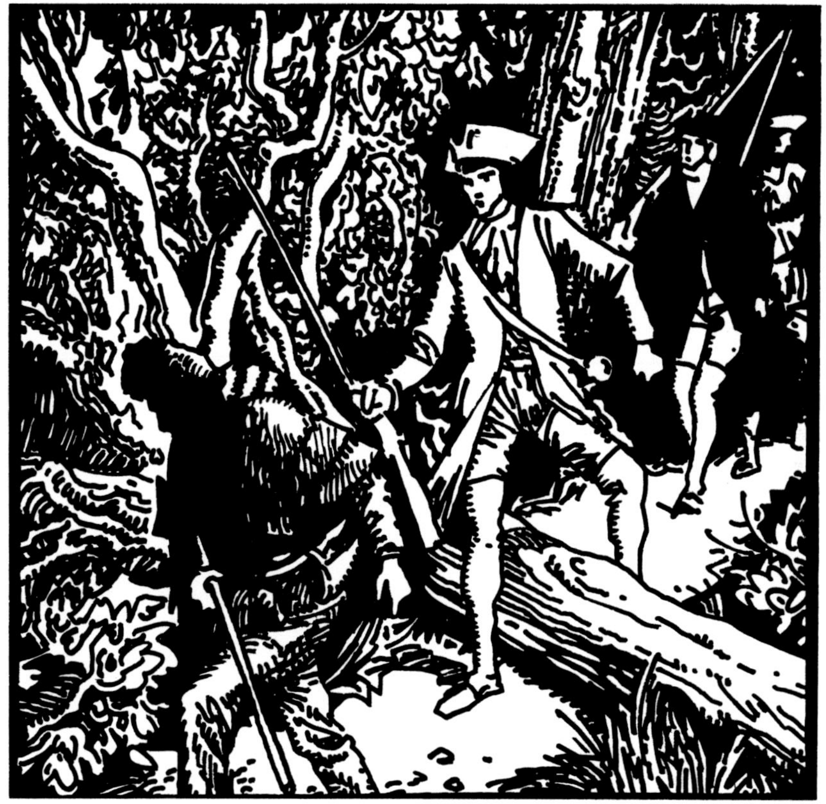

The Trail of Revenge

[3] Duncan Falls takes its name from a white trapper who was ruthless in his punishment of Indians who lifted his traps. He was accustomed to conceal his position by pole-vaulting over the rapids, but his ruse was finally discovered and he was shot in the act.

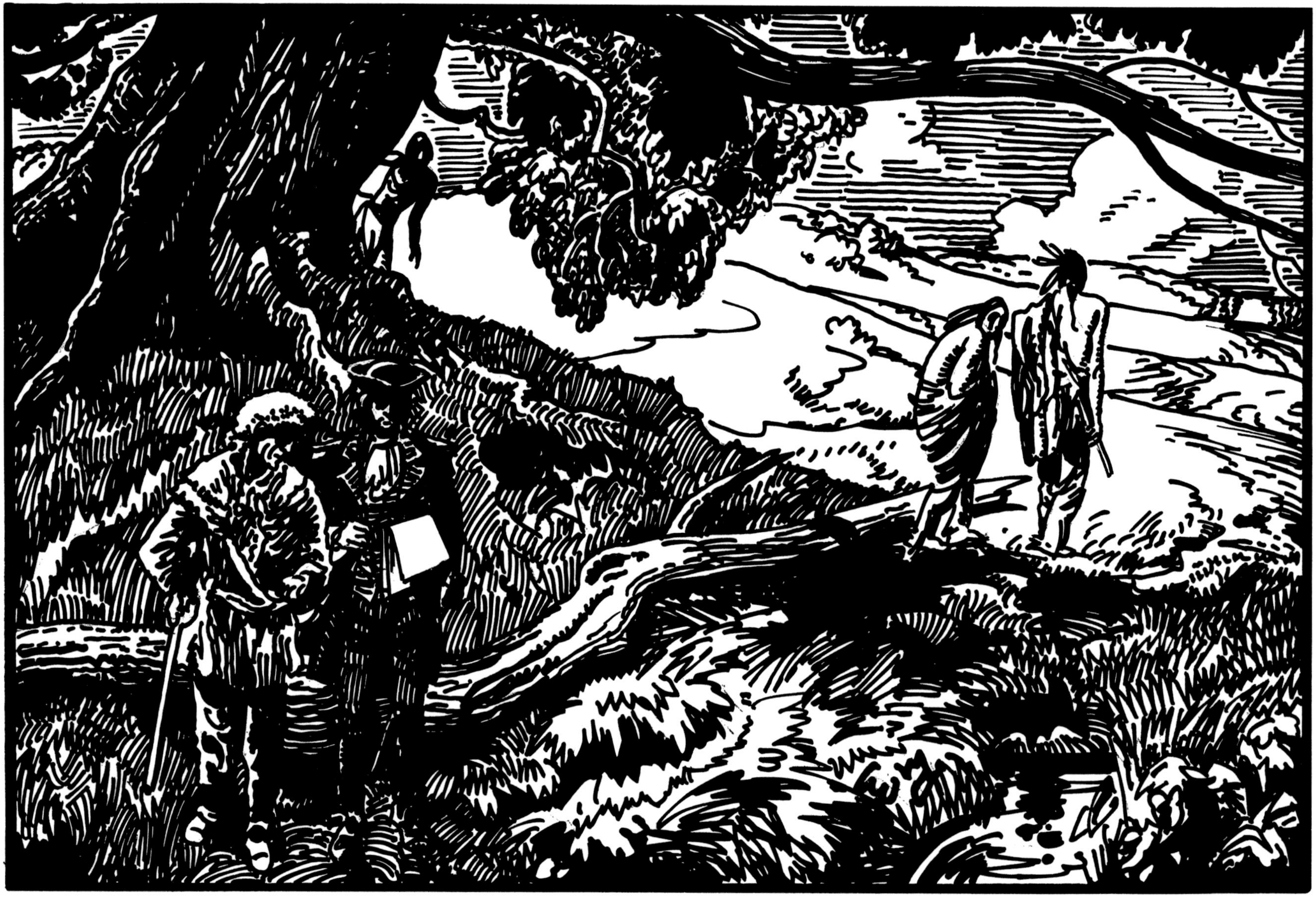

The Ultimatum of Chief Logan

The Scioto Trail or Warriors' Path

The Scioto Trail was the Great Highway of the Shawnee from the neutral hunting ground of Kentucky to the fishing grounds of Sandusky Bay and Lake Erie; his use of it for predatory raids upon the early settlements of Kentucky and the flatboatmen of the Ohio gave it its name.[1]

Crossing from the Kentucky shore, the trail led up along the edge of the high land from present Portsmouth. Across from the town to the west stands Raven Rock, that great river lookout post utilized for years by the jealous red man and by Boone and other venturesome pioneers. The trail lies upon the second bottom of the broad flats (U.S. 23) and leads up past the loops of the Scioto, until the narrower valley through the gap in the Pike County hills causes it to rise from the river and cross the ridge. In this lower course many evidences of the Mound Builder are visible, in some cases the mounds being very impressive. They may in the Indian's day have remained concealed in the uncleared forest, but where not plowed down they appear today in isolated conspicuousness.

The path leads through Wakefield over the hills northeastward, descends into the flats at Waverly to rise again over billowing hilltops, and descends northeasterly to the flats below Chillicothe. This trail is remarkable in that as far as Upper Sandusky it is covered by the modern U.S. 23, and is easily realized.

Chillicothe was one of the many "Homes of the People"

[1] Indian decoy boats, and simulated destitution on the part of Indians and renegade whites ashore, led many an unwary boatman to his death upon the banks of the Ohio. It was difficult to be indifferent to the plight of a fellow traveler in those primitive times.

in Ohio, and its Mound City testifies to its antiquity. From the heights to the south of Chillicothe one sees the triple ridge of Mount Logan, and beyond it Rattlesnake Knob standing above the Pickaway Plains to the north.[2]

Passing directly through the meadows, after crossing the river at the north edge of the present town, the trail touched Mound City in the Camp Sherman area and moved over the rolling prairie, with retreating hills to the right and willowy loops of the river on the left. It passed the famous view of Mount Logan, where the sun rises over the three peaks, a scene which suggested the Seal of Ohio. After crossing Kinnickinnick Creek it entered a region replete with Indian history.[3]

As we reach the Pickaway Plains proper, there are rolling prairies studded with ancient isolated trees growing as they did in Indian days, among them, one mile east of Nash Corners, was the famous Logan Elm, where the great Indian made his tragic and eloquent address to the Royal Governor Dunmore and the victorious Colonel Lewis. This point lay upon the trail circling the plains that bound the bordering Indian Villages.[4]

[2] Daniel Boone, the great borderer of Kentucky, was familiar with the Shawnee country. He was captured on one occasion at old Chillicothe, was more or less adopted by the tribe, and was led on a journey to the salt wells at Jackson. On his return he witnessed preparations to attack Boonesborough, and escaped to warn his old neighbors.

[3] Many natural landmarks still stand in the Pickaway Plains to recall Indian habitation. Among the prehistoric mounds is the Burning Mound of the Shawnees, southeast of Circleville. There are several large elms adjacent to the site of the Logan Elm that are probably almost as old.

[4] The Logan Elm stood in a rolling prairie, a conspicuous and eminently suitable monument to the great Mingo orator.

Beyond Congo Creek, on the southern bank of which stood the Elm, and over Scippo Creek, the trail led past the lookout hill in the center of the Plains known as the Black Mountain; up Scippo Creek a short distance lay Cornstalk's Town and the town of the Grenadier Squaw. To the northeast, and southeast of Circleville, stands the Burning Mound, and off to the left, across the river on the edge of the Plains at Westfall, lay Logan's Town. Maguck, the Shawnee Capital, lay in the vicinity of Circleville, and from it trails branched out to all parts of the State.

The trail continued beyond Circleville and, leading west of north, crossed Walnut Creek six miles beyond; following gently rising ground, it passed northwestward through modern Columbus to a point opposite Olentangy, the Salt Lick Town of the Indian, where it met the trail from the Walhonding.[5]

The trail now led northward, heading many small ravines running into the Olentangy, to Delaware Town, the modern Delaware, and the beginning of the Cuyahoga War Trail

Lewis' Camp in the Pickaway Plains lay on the west side of Congo Creek, two miles above its mouth, in the vicinity of the Logan Elm.

[5] The Mingos were a branch of the Iroquois tribe formerly living at Mingo Bottom near Steubenville and later settled on the Scioto near Columbus. There were three villages. One south of the Ohio Penitentiary, one at the west end of the bridge on the site of the City Work House, and a third near the east end of the Green Lawn Avenue Bridge.

Leatherlips was a chief who was loyal to the American cause in the War of 1812. He was killed twelve miles above Columbus, on the Scioto, for refusing to aid Tecumseh and his brother the Prophet against the United States. Some blame his murder upon Tarhe the Crane, the Wyandot from Upper Sandusky.

Chief among the Delawares in the upper Scioto Valley around Columbus was Buckongehelas, whose name was later known in the vicinity of Bellefontaine and the Auglaize Valley.

to the Cuyahoga Portage.[6] Now, following the west bank of the Olentangy, it diverged at Waldo to the northwest up a shallow valley to arrive at modern Marion. At this point a naturally high, rolling and moderately treeless prairie was reached, burned over by the hunters and teeming with buffalo and prairie hens. The streams ran slowly and bank-full, and the grass was high against the level horizon.

The trail led northwest, crossed the Little Scioto about eight miles from Marion and reached Little Sandusky, on the river of that name, a Wyandot town and the place of portage for the Scioto.[7] Six miles east on the southernmost bend of the Sandusky lies Wyandot, another village of that tribe.

Crossing the Little Sandusky near its mouth, the trail led around a bend of the Sandusky to the northwest and north to the springs where stands modern Upper Sandusky. About three miles southeast of the springs, across from the main trail, lay the town of the Moravian hostages from the Tuscarawas, under the bluff, which town was traversed by Colonel Crawford from Little Sandusky to the Battle Island.

From Upper Sandusky the trail led north to Old Tymochtee, at the confluence with Tymochtee Creek (Ohio 53). Three miles up this stream to the southwest, near the village of Crawford, was apparently another town of Captain Pipe,

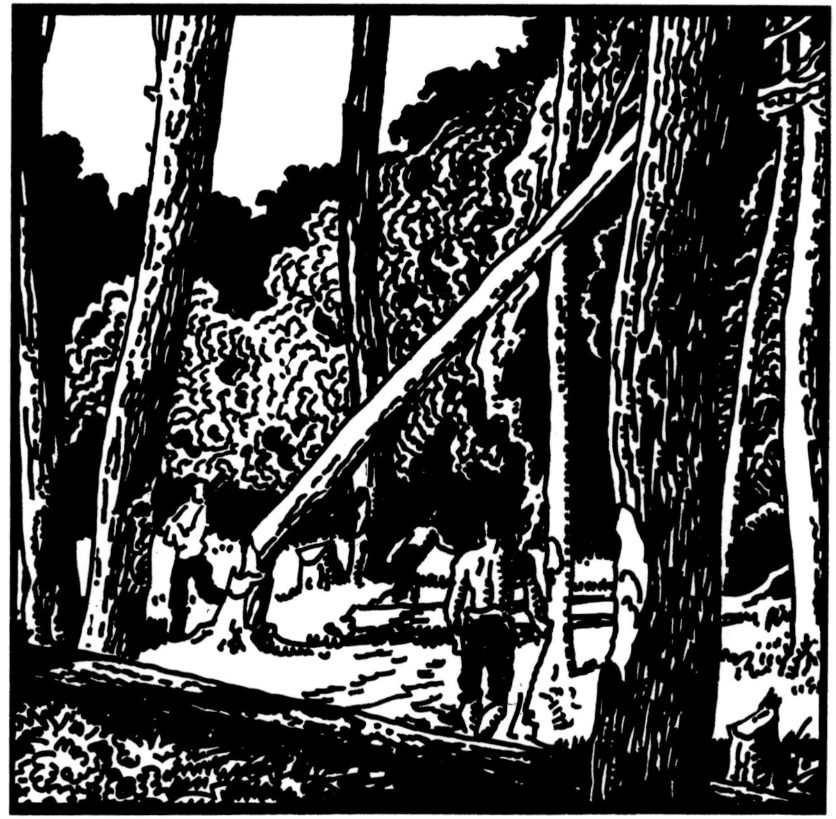

Shattered Silence

[6] The location of the Delawares in Ohio was first on the Muskingum and later upon the Auglaize. They moved finally to the White River in Indiana, a branch of the Wabash.

[7] It is recorded that at a good stage of water, it was possible to ascend the Little Sandusky four or five miles in light canoes, when the portage to the Little Scioto was about four miles.

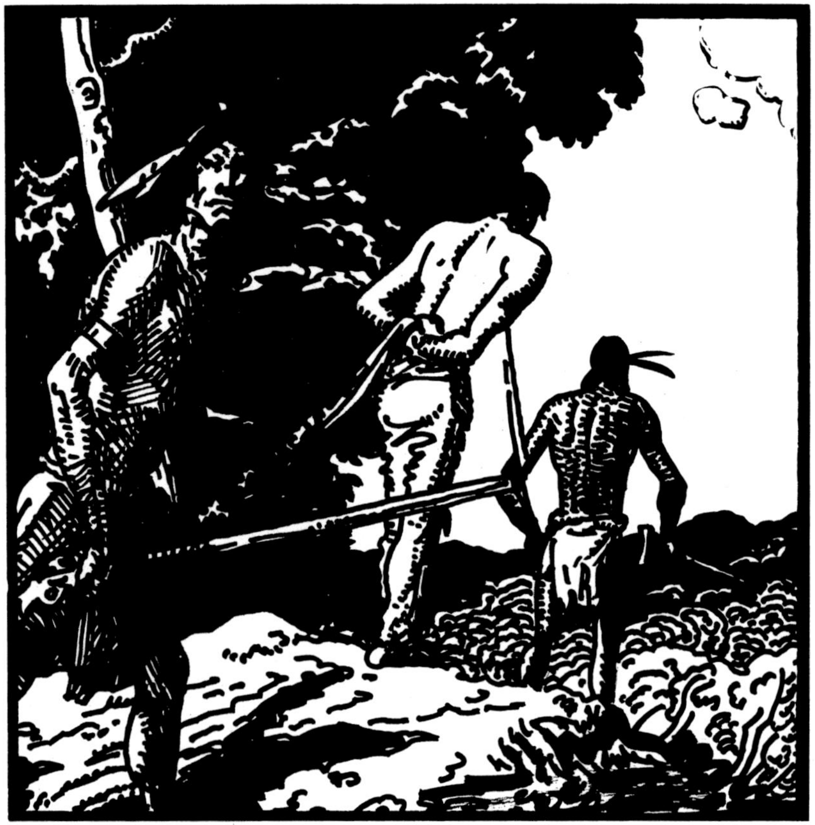

The White Captive

where Crawford met his end. The battle occurred about a mile north of the edge of Upper Sandusky, and is marked by a monument. The few trees remaining on the island are veterans of the old grove, and all around on the flat plain are dense new groves of trees that must look as the famous grove once did. To the east of Upper Sandusky lie the plains, flat as a table, and with black soil from the old vegetation of the prairie.

Leaving Tymochtee the trail continued northeast, and occasionally touching the bends obscured by characteristic dense willows, came to the site of Tiffin. Here it bore due north to Fort Seneca, at a bend of the river (Ohio 53).

At Fort Seneca the trail crossed the river to the east (Ohio 53) and led due north again and then northeast past modern Fremont, of later fame in 1812,[8] and, striking the lower marshes below the rolling prairies, reached the old town of Dunqueindundeh, or the French post of Junandat. This post was situated probably on the east side of the confluence of Bark Creek with the Sandusky, at the head of the marshes of Sandusky Bay, although there is much controversy as to its exact location. Here the Scioto Trail met the Lake Trail to Detroit (Ohio 163, 2).[9]

[8] A half mile southwest of Ballsville is the scene of a skirmish between Captain Ball and hostile Indians, while he was coming to the aid of Fort Stephenson at Fremont in the War of 1812.

There is a legend of a so-called Neutral Nation of Wyandots living at Lower Sandusky. Their villages were a sanctuary for fugitives, but the two towns eventually came to blows and were abandoned.

[9] "The Warriors' Path," or Scioto Trail, may be said to have included the Lake Islands as a route for canoes, voyaging to the mouth of the Detroit River and the north.

The "Warriors' Path" was the most traveled trail of Indian days. It was used many times also by the white man's expeditions, civil and military. It is a level route except for its hilly courses in Pike County and probably knew little of the gloomy woods such as shadowed the Great Trail and others of the eastern woodlands.

The first white man on record to traverse the Scioto Trail was the explorer and surveyor associate of Washington, Christopher Gist, who in 1750 descended the trail from the headwaters of the Licking around Lancaster after a journey through the Muskingum country. His investigations cast much light on this unknown region. Many a captive from Kentucky was led up to a tragic end around the Sandusky Plains, and the Pickaway Plains saw the Scottish troops and Colonial Rangers of Virginia under Dunmore and Lewis. Crawford's forces in the Sandusky Plains were unsuccessful, but the expedition cast light on the unknown northern portions. The French, at an early date, traded on the trail as far as Little Sandusky. The length of the trail was traversed by the American armies in 1812 when Hull's expedition against the British was organized. At that time the strongholds of Upper Sandusky, Fremont, Tiffin, Findlay and Fort Seneca were built, and the Watershed Trail was developed as a route from the east.

Among the Indian towns recorded as lying on the Scioto Trail, beginning at the mouth, were Lower Shawnee Town at Portsmouth, and Wan-du-cha-le's Town at Waverly. At the confluence of Salt Creek and the Scioto was Hurricane Tom's Town and at present Chillicothe was a "Home of the People." Near Circleville was Ma-guck.

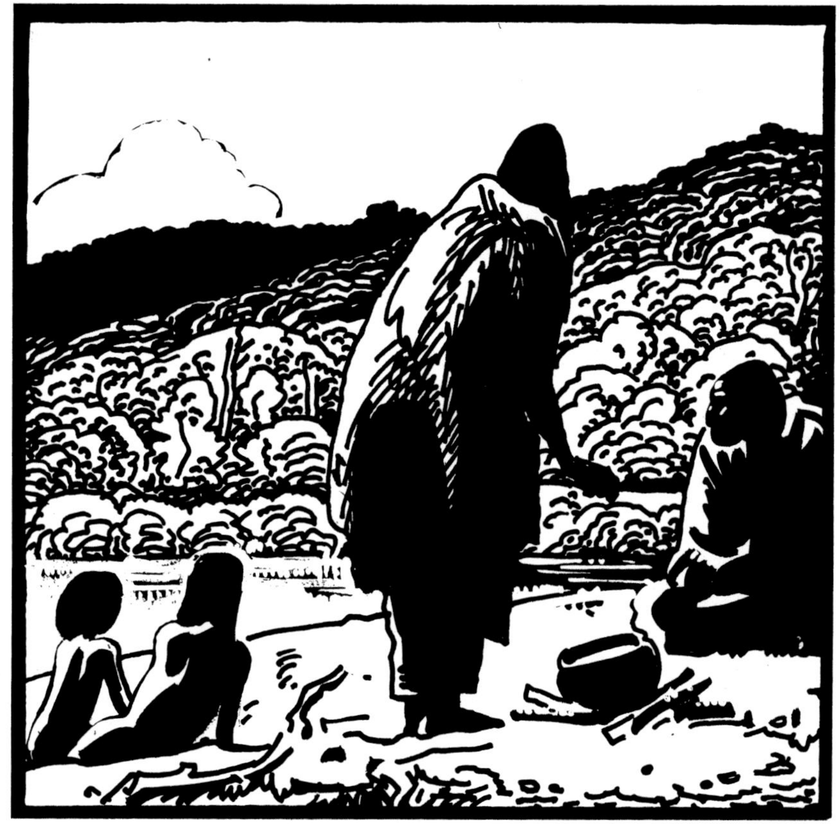

Awaiting the Hunter

Swinging in a half circle to the west between Chillicothe and Ma-guck was a connecting trail tying together several towns to form the western border of the Pickaway Plains. There were: first, another Chillicothe, probably at Slate Mills on the North Fork of Paint Creek (U.S. 50); Wac-ca-chal-la, probably near Andersonville (Ohio 104); Pe-co-wick, possibly Yellowbud (Ohio 104); Piqua Town, at Westfall (Ohio 104); and another Chillicothe, probably Spunkey Town, one mile west of Circleville (Ohio 104, 56).

Five miles south of Circleville and a mile east of the trail (U.S. 23) lay, on the north side of Scippo Creek, Cornstalk's Town and across the stream the Grenadier Squaw's Town. At the head of this stream, half a mile from Leistville, was Dunmore's "Camp Charlotte" (Ohio 56).

Proceeding north on the trail there was a Mingo town at Columbus, and at Olentangy, across the Olentangy from Worthington (U.S. 23), was the Salt Lick Town. Delaware was an Indian town and a Mingo town appears somewhere to the northwest, probably near the Scioto.

We next approach the Wyandot country beyond the plateau in the Sandusky Valley. First came Pipe's Town at Little Sandusky and possibly Wyandot, then the Wyandot Old Town on the east bank southeast of Upper Sandusky, and finally that town itself.

North at Indian Mill was Half King's Town (Ohio 67) and at Old Tymochtee, Old Pipe's Town (Ohio 53).

At the end of the trail was Dunqueindundeh.

The Cuyahoga War Trail

Delaware was evidently a town and mustering place for war parties against the Iroquois of early days. The Cuyahoga War Trail is unique in that it seems to justify its authenticity in many ways. Its long, direct, northeastward trend follows a gentle ridge for many miles, swerving around certain obstructions, and, defying the angular tangents of the surveyed crossroads, strikes directly for the Cuyahoga Portage.

Beginning at modern Delaware, the trail follows first the line of the Big Four Railroad, C. C. C. & St. L., now Penn-Central, over the levels of the once wet and timbered bottoms, but inclines, about two miles southwest of Leonardsburg on the Railroad, towards Alum Creek (U. S. 42). Following up the west bank of Alum Creek, the trail crosses it at South Woodbury, and tending eastward, drops into the Kokosing Valley at Lucerne, and, crossing, arrives at Fredericktown between the river and its north branch (Ohio 95).

From Fredericktown it climbs the ridge to the northeast with Wannegan Valley on the right, and climbing continually into the northern plateau, passes a mile south of Butler (Ohio 95, 97); continuing over the ridges, it reaches Helltown on the Clear Fork of the Mohican one mile southwest of Perrysville, passing through Newville, also a Mohican town (Ohio 39).[1]

[1] Helltown, on the south line of Green Township, on the Clear Fork of the Mohican, was named by a Pennsylvania captive after the German word for "bright." This place was also a residence of the Delaware Captain Pipe, and was a station on the route of captives for Detroit. The old Delaware village of Helltown is on the Clear Creek in Richland County near Newville, on the south side of the stream about four miles from the Ashland County line. It was deserted in 1782 at the time of the Gnadenhutten massacre. The Indians adopted the German word for clear or bright for the name of the town.

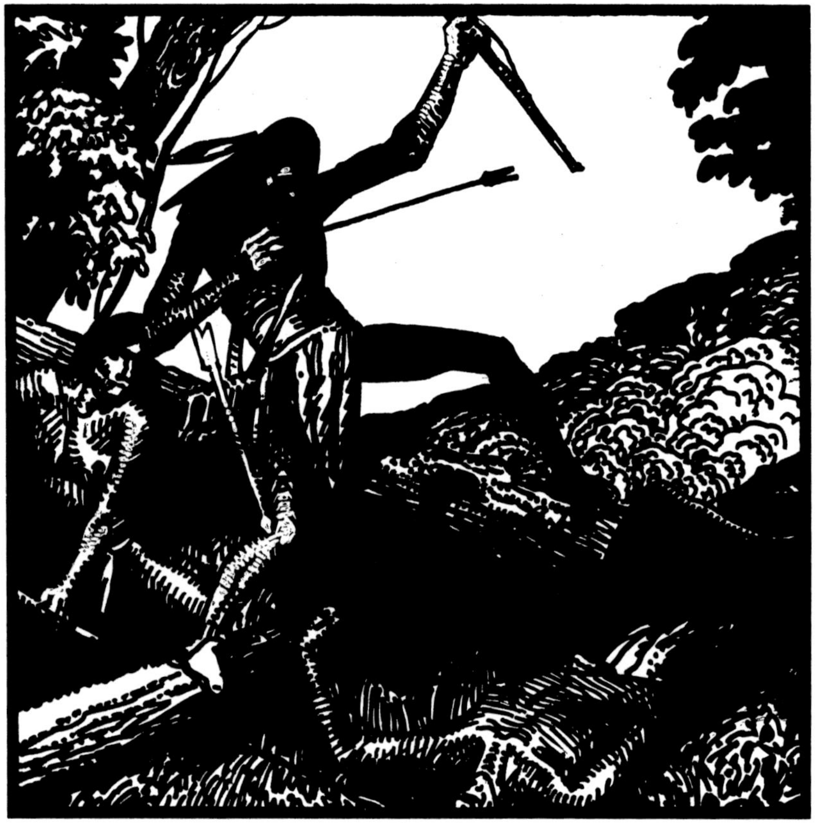

The Last of the Eries

This is a region rich in pioneer and Indian lore and beautiful with its rolling hills, natural and unique stands of white pine, and its hemlock-crowned cliffs. The trail continues over the narrow ridge between Helltown and Perrysville, and passing over the steep hills northeast of Perrysville, crosses Honey Creek one and a half miles from its mouth; then passing over a comparatively rolling high plateau, it arrives at Mohican John's Town, today a little hamlet in the folds of the hills on a small branch of the Lake Fork.[2]

Continuing northeast over a rounded ridge, it passes through Lake Fork, and crossing the wide flats of Muddy Fork, bears to the east on rising ground which becomes high and largely rolling until in the east is seen the deep depression of the Killbuck. Descending the long slope, the trail reaches the confluence of the Killbuck and Apple Creek, where stands the Wooster of today. At the fork of the roads west of town it merges with the trail connecting the Mohican towns to the southwest, around the present Loudonville district and Odell Lake.[3]

Descending to the flats, the trail passes northeast over the level bottom where it crosses the Great Trail tending to the northwest, and following the railroad tracks south and east of town in the narrow valley of Apple Creek, leads across the headwaters of Sugar Creek in the level plateau, and across those of Little Chippewa. The country is rolling, and

[2] Mohican John's Town was occupied by Delawares, Mohicans, Mohawks and Mingos, and by a few Senecas and Wyandots. Captain Pipe ruled the village until 1812.

[3] Killbuck was a Delaware chief, said to have been educated at Princeton, and a great believer in uplift for his people.

judging from present signs, was once heavily wooded (Ohio 5).

This part of the trail is especially interesting in the way it follows the slight direct northeast ridge, the land to left and right showing evidences of former marshy ground. Crossing Chippewa Creek in a wide flat valley and passing a pond at Doylestown Station, the trail swings to the right around Doylestown Hill, and from the modern highway, which passes directly over it, one may see where the old detour re-enters on the further side in the form of a cart track.

The path leads directly on from Doylestown to Barberton, and passing between the modern chemical pond and the town lake on the present highway, bears northeast to the Wadsworth Road, west of Akron, where it joins the Muskingum Trail. Here it becomes the still preserved Portage Path, and descending to the Portage, the old trail leads east through Old Cuyahoga Town to the other villages at the Falls, or here it may have connected with the Mahoning, or Cuyahoga Trails either east or west ridge.

The ancient fort of the prehistoric Eries, lying in the marshes southeast of Montrose, may have figured in Indian history. We are certain that this trail ran between two hostile territories; at least it led into a buffer region between the central Ohio Indians and the Iroquois of New York. The ancient Eries are said to have been exterminated at their fort in the Copley Marshes.[4]

[4] This story may have been founded upon the old French account due to the forlorn appearance of the old Fort Island. There is also a local belief that many hundred Indians lie buried here. Actually the Eries were said to have been the attacking party in their last battle, in which case this would not have been the place. The earthen ramparts are still easily traced around the elevated knoll in the lowland drained by Shocalog Run.

The Walhonding Trail

This vital and direct line of communication between the Delawares of the Scioto and the Muskingum communicated also with the routes leading up the Mohican and the Killbuck to the north, where centered other groups of eastern origin. These secondary routes were also roads by which the Watershed Route could be reached at several points to the east of the Scioto.

It was by part of this trail that the Wyandots, allied with the British at Detroit, conducted the Moravian prisoners to Sandusky.

Departing from Olentangy by the Salt Lick, northwest of Columbus, the trail led across the Olentangy, norteastward, by a diagonal road over Alum Creek to Galena on the Big Walnut (Ohio 3).

The land here is flat with sunken river beds, and early accounts suggest heavy forestation. The path crossed Little Walnut Creek and continued up the Big Walnut a short distance to Perfect Creek, where it crossed the river; tending northeastward it crossed Culver Creek a mile from the Walnut, and followed Culver Creek, tending eastward to Centerburg (U.S. 36, Ohio 3), northeast to Mount Liberty, and up steadily rising hills to the site of present Mount Vernon in the hills of the plateau (U.S. 36, Ohio 3).

The path now traversed the flats south of Mount Vernon, and crossing the river at the foot of the main street, descended the north bank of the Kokosing over the Gambier Campus, apparently to avoid the tangle in the flats to the south, and taking to the ridge reached Howard (U.S. 36), "Coashoskis," at the mouth of Jelloway Creek; thence it followed the present highway (U.S. 36) through Millwood to Zuck or "New Hundy."

Following the widening river with its impressive wooded slopes, it crossed the Mohican a mile above Walhonding, where from the willowy bottoms a long view is visible up that glaciated chute from the plateau.[1]

Below Walhonding, with its rocky southern wall and hemlocks, it appears to have crossed the riffles several times, judging from the modern trail, and after passing the mouth of Mohawk Creek, up the course of which to the south lay the village as today, entered Warsaw (U.S.36).[2]

From Warsaw it led down the center of the meadows and crossed the river just above the confluence with the Killbuck, which here adds to the size of the valley, and following the course of the canal bed, passed by Bouquet's Spring on the steep hillside to the north, just above the mouth of Mill Creek. Here the hills take on a very impressive character, suitable to the united rivers to come.[3]

Tending southward the trail (U.S. 36) now crossed both the Walhonding and the Tuscarawas at Roscoe, and entered Coshocton. At the crossing it met the descending Muskingum Trail (Ohio 76).

[1] In 1758 the English established atrading post above the mouth of the Walhonding.

[2] A short distance south of the Walhonding, near where stood White Woman's Town at Warsaw, is the village of Mohawk, probably once an Indian village; it is pleasantly situated up a tributary of the Walhonding. Just west of Coshocton, on the north bank of the Walhonding and near the mouth of the Killbuck, is a spring called Bouquet's Spring, where he is reputed to have camped for the exchange of hostages by the Indians. This is not far from the site of White Woman's Town, where Mary Harris lived for many years as the wife of an Indian chief. His second wife, the New Comer, killed him out of jealousy for her rival. A monument marks the spot today and the spring has a tablet.

In this vicinity boy scouts of Coshocton have discovered Indian burials, relics of which may been seen in the Coshocton Museum.

[3] Bouquet drew up his 1500 men, including Highland regulars in tartans, Royal Americans, Pennsylvania militia and Virginia backwoodsmen, in full military pomp. The long lines of silent men overawed the Indians. The scene of the exchange of captives was said to have been dramatic in the extreme.

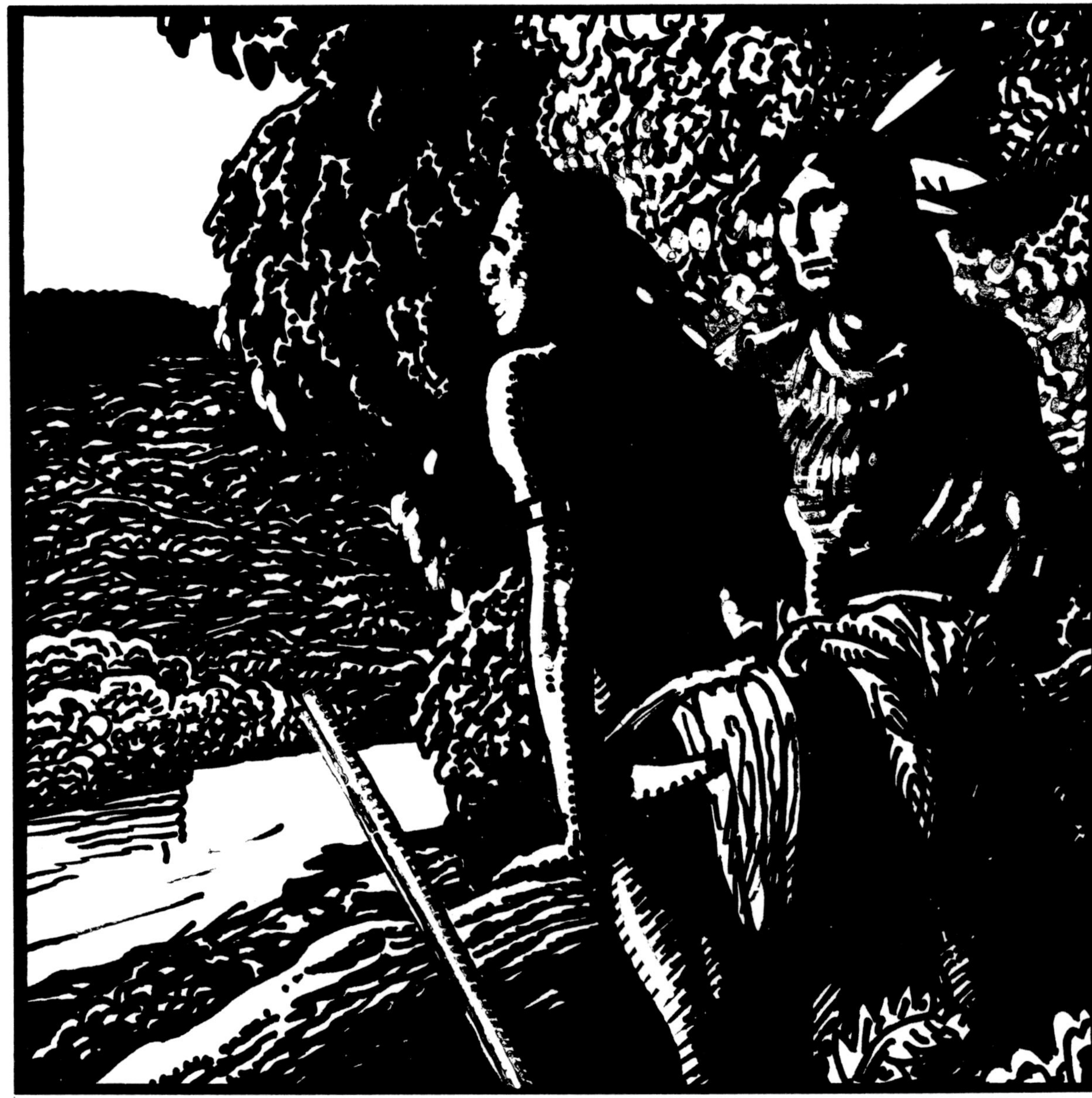

The Lookout

The Killbuck Trail

Retracing to the Killbuck, we shall consider the branch that connected with the Great Trail via that river. At the point where the Walhonding Trail crossed the river to the south side by the canal, it was joined in the flats by the Killbuck Trail. Following this trail up, we find that it had just crossed the Killbuck above the confluence, and following it on the east shore, led north over a ridge to cross again at Helmeck Station (Ohio 754).

It so continued, crossing and recrossing the river, through Killbuck to Millersburg (U.S.62) where Crawford and Rogers had both touched the river in their marches.

The trail continued north on the east side of the now more direct, deep valley, and climbing the ridge at Holmesville (Ohio 76) passed by the flats to the north where the so-called Big Spring, pond or buffalo wallow, lies in the meadows. This may be one of the camp sites mentioned in Crawford's diary. It lies across from a road that follows his course west past Odell Lake to Upper Sandusky.

Continuing northwest (Ohio 76), then north, the trail mounts the moorland heights, where to the west lie the wide Killbuck flats that should have afforded plenty of hunting in the old days. From these heights, up the valley is seen the immense spread of the high plateau back of Wooster, and there is a rapid descent along the heads of many small tributaries to the levels of the State Farm, where the Great Trail is joined before it descends into the Killbuck flats. Across lie the trails from the southwest, converging on the same point at this great trail junction.

The Owl River Trail

Captain Pipe, the chief Wyandot leader during the War of the Revolution, had a town near the modern village of Walhonding, which lies near the mouth of the Mohican River above White Woman's Town. This place he held to keep watch upon the Moravian towns of the Delawares which in the beginning lay at Coshocton and immediately below on the Muskingum.[1]

Pipe's purpose was to influence the Christian Indians against the American cause in the Revolution, to the extent at least that they would not convey any information regarding his activities in the British cause. The Moravian Indians were encouraged by the missionaries to take an absolutely neutral part in the war, on the basis of their faith, but the savages under the leadership of the renegade scouts McKee, Girty, and principally Elliott, imposed upon their known hospitality and their admitted fear of the American borderers.

This purpose led to the making of a definite trail from Pipe's principal town at Old Tymochtee, north of Upper Sandusky, to Lichtenau, the principal Moravian town, two miles below Coshocton. To avoid this influence of the Wyandots and Munseys, the missionaries under Zeisberger and Heckewelder led their flock up the Muskingum to Gnadenhutten and Schoenbrunn.[2]

[1] Captain Pipe was a hostage of Colonel Bouquet at Fort Pitt in 1764.

The dilemma of the Delawares during the Revolution, in regard to their neutral position, caused certain chiefs to move to Fort Pitt, or Pittsburgh, and seek the protection of the Americans. This forced the Pipe to withdraw to Upper Sandusky.

Heckewelder received a letter from Brodhead previous to his campaign against the Delawares, requesting an interview in regard to his position in the war. Brodhead prevented a massacre of the Moravians by his troops in consequence.

Above the Mohican the Walhonding River was known as the Owl River from Owl's Town, located at the site of modern Mount Vernon. The Owl River Trail became then a definite war trail during the Revolution and it was over this trail also that Zeisberger and the Moravian congregation were led to captivity at Wyandot Old Town on the Sandusky, and over which those unfortunates who were brutally massacred at Gnadenhutten later by the American Williamson retraced their way. The trail was known at an early date along the Walhonding and the Owl River, or modern Kokosing, by Croghan and Gist, but its later continuation lay from Mount Vernon northwest, over the edge of the high plateau and down into the Sandusky Plains, where that river cuts a rounded bay into the higher land of the State.

The Owl River Trail left the Walhonding Trail at Mount Vernon and crossed the low land on the west of the Kokosing, passing south of Fredericktown (Ohio 13); then, crossing at Lucerne, it reached the headwaters of the river, and traversing broken land around Chesterville, led northwest to Mount Gilead (Ohio 95) on the heights among the headwaters of Whetstone Creek at the edge of the central plateau. It then descended northwestward and passed over the levels of the Olentangy headwaters, running northeast of Marion to Wyandot on the Sandusky.[3] From Wyandot the trail conceivably continued northwestward but Crawford's account suggests that it led west along the river to the mouth of the Little Sandusky, crossing there and leading through the Old Wyandot Town, to follow through modern Upper Sandusky, known then as the Springs, and nine miles beyond to Old Tymochtee at the mouth of Tymochtee Creek.

This rather unique trail begins as a river trail and becomes a prairie track around the Sandusky Plains. It roughly follows Ohio 95 to Denmark, northwest of Mount Gilead, and then leads across country through Caledonia on U.S. 30S, and through Marion and the village of Tobias to Wyandot (Ohio 231). From the Little Sandusky it becomes, if it followed the longer route, part of the Scioto Trail.

[2] As an indication of the difficulty of travel in Indian days, the exiled Moravians took several days to reach Mount Vernon from Coshocton and eleven days more to reach Upper Sandusky. It was by this march that the Delaware "singing birds" were prevented from communicating with Fort Pitt, according to Captain Pipe.

One of the interesting incidents of the exodus of the Moravians is Heckewelder's account of the hunt by the villagers for a tame buffalo cow, which was grazing with their other cattle at Gnadenhutten. This seems to prove the existence of that animal in eastern Ohio at a comparatively late period.

[3] Between the headwaters of Whetstone Creek and the Sandusky, northeast of Wyandot, stands the monument to the Olentangy Battle. This place lies on the road between Leesville, where Crawford was captured after his retreat, and Wyandot. Here a battle was fought between part of Crawford's forces and the pursuing British and Indians.

The Mohican Trail

This subsidiary trail, branching from the Walhonding, left the main trail just before the crossing of the Mohican at the north of the flats. It led up to those isolated towns in the hills of Ashland County that cluster on its many forks. The lower course of the river is deep and narrow and it is much like the Killbuck in character, but no major roads ascend its steep slopes.

The trail apparently took to the western hilltops and passing around the heads of the short, steep tributary ravines, went through Brinkhaven (U.S. 62) and continued north to the confluence with the Lake Fork, three miles southeast of Loudonville.[1] It followed this shallower valley up over the high flats between Loudonville (Ohio 3) and the three lakes west of Big Prairie (Ohio 3). Continuing up the stream, it struck the branch leading up one and a half miles to Mohican John's Town (Ohio 89) through which passed the Cuyahoga War Trail.[2]

From here it probably divided, one path leading northwest (Ohio 179) (U.S. 30) (Ohio 60) to Ashland, and from there northwest past the Savannah Lakes (U.S. 250) and through the town of that name, continuing down the east bank of the Vermilion River (Ohio 60) through Clarkefield and Wakeman to the lake, crossing above the gorge at Birmingham.

[1] Just north of Loudonville lay a Delaware village in 1808.

[2] Under the charge of Mohican John lived about two hundred Mohicans around Jeromesville and Mohican John's Town. This was the only settlement of Indians in Ashland County in 1812. Jeromesville was named for Jean Baptiste Jerome, a trader who later moved to Huron, Ohio, and fought at the Battle of Fallen Timbers.

Captain Pipe, the Delaware, lived one mile south of Jeromesville and fought at St. Clair's Defeat.

About three or four miles southeast of Ashland it crossed the Great Trail, leading more to the northwest, the meeting place being a high point where streams fall away in all directions and there is no special modern landmark.[3]

Returning again to the fork of the trail at Mohican John's, a trail led north to Jeromesville on the Great Trail and the Jerome Fork (Ohio 89). On this trail, two miles to the south of Jeromesville, on the top of the hill, stood a Pipe's Town opposite the Indian town at Jeromesville.

Northeastward of Mohican John's, the War Trail led nearly parallel to the Great Trail, to converge just west of Wooster. The region of the picturesque forks of the Mohican, with their dark-clad glens and high prairie lakes, was settled by Mohicans. Their several towns were connected by minor trails and traversed by the great trails crossing the Watershed. Down the main branch of the Mohican they were connected with the Muskingum and the Scioto.[4]

The Huron River was the most convenient route to Lake Erie for this region. A trail led southeast from Milan on the ridge and passed southeast of Norwalk to the Vermilion, where it left the Watershed Trail and ascended the west bank to Fitchville (U.S.250). There it crossed the river (Ohio 162); it recrossed at the Big Four Railroad, Penn Central,

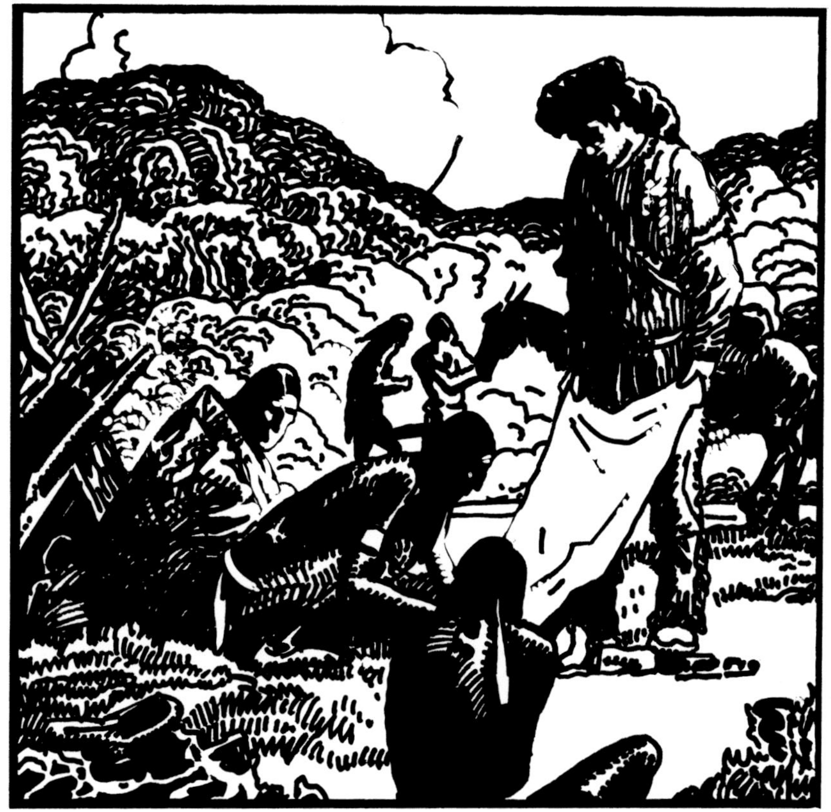

The Indian Trader

[3] Erie and Huron Counties were called the Fire-lands. This region was quitclaimed to reimburse citizens of Connecticut for losses incurred to property during the Revolution.

[4] Two events of importance in the Mohican Valley were the burning of Greentown by militia from Guernsey County and the Copus and Ruffner massacres; the first occurring nine miles from Mansfield on the Black Fork and the second one mile west of Mifflin. These families were early German settlers of the region; the Copus affair involved the death of several of the militia serving in their defense.

and continuing southeastward, arrived at Savannah (U.S. 250) and went on to Ashland. It then crossed the Great Trail, three miles southeast at Ohio 60, and continued over the broken hilly country; it crossed the head of Quaker Springs Run about a mile and a half west of Pipe's Town, situated on the heights above the Jerome Fork and two miles south of Jeromesville, another Indian town. Continuing southeast, it led down a run to Mohican John's Town (Ohio 89).

Among other towns noted in Indian days around Mohicanville was Helltown, over the ridge southwest of Perrysville on the War Trail, and about ten miles southwest of Mohicanville. This town was on the Clear Fork or the first of the Forks. Three miles north of Perrysville, on the Black or Middle Fork, in a northeast angle of the wide flats, was Greentown, also about ten miles from Mohicanville. This town evidently stood on an elevation in the bend of the river flats on the road from Loudonville to Mansfield (Ohio 39).[5]

[5] Twelve miles southeast of Mansfield in the beautiful Mohican Valley is the site of Greentown, the Mohican village. At a bend of the river is an isolated knoll in the flats, now occupied by farm buildings, which is the likeliest location for the old town.

Greentown was named for Thomas Green, a Tory, who joined the Delawares during the Revolution.

The Huron Trail

According to the tales of white prisoners and hostages of the Wyandots, who seem to have had a habit of adopting white people occasionally and taking them on their various enterprises, these Indians seem to have wandered much over the valleys of the short rivers emptying into Lake Erie, for the purpose of hunting, fishing and sugar-making. The story of James Smith is particularly interesting in this regard. He mentions camps at Black River and the Cuyahoga. The existence of a trail from Upper Sandusky to the northeast seems to be proved by these accounts.[1]

The trail led somewhat northeast from the springs at Upper Sandusky (U.S. 30N) about as far as Osceola where it ran up the shallow valley of Broken Sword Creek on the north side to near New Washington. This would have led it almost directly to Plymouth (Ohio 61) where the Great Trail bent northward toward the Blue Hole.

It was on the early part of this course that Crawford approached Leesville after his battle at Sandusky and before his capture. It was possibly from some relic of this expedition that Broken Sword Creek was named.

At Plymouth the trail would have touched the head of the west branch of the Huron, and continuing directly northeastward, would reach that point three miles northwest of Fitch-

[1] James Smith, a captive adopted by Indians, describes a journey up the Walhonding and Mohican and then up the Black Fork to the "carrying place," where they struck the Canesadooharie or Black River, and descended to the lake and a Wyandot village (Lorain). He also crossed the Cuyahoga portage and from the Sandusky to the Big Darby.

The Wyandots were a branch of the Hurons driven by the Iroquois to settle about the straits of Mackinac. They later occupied the country now included in Wyandot, Marion and Crawford Counties, where their principal villages lay.

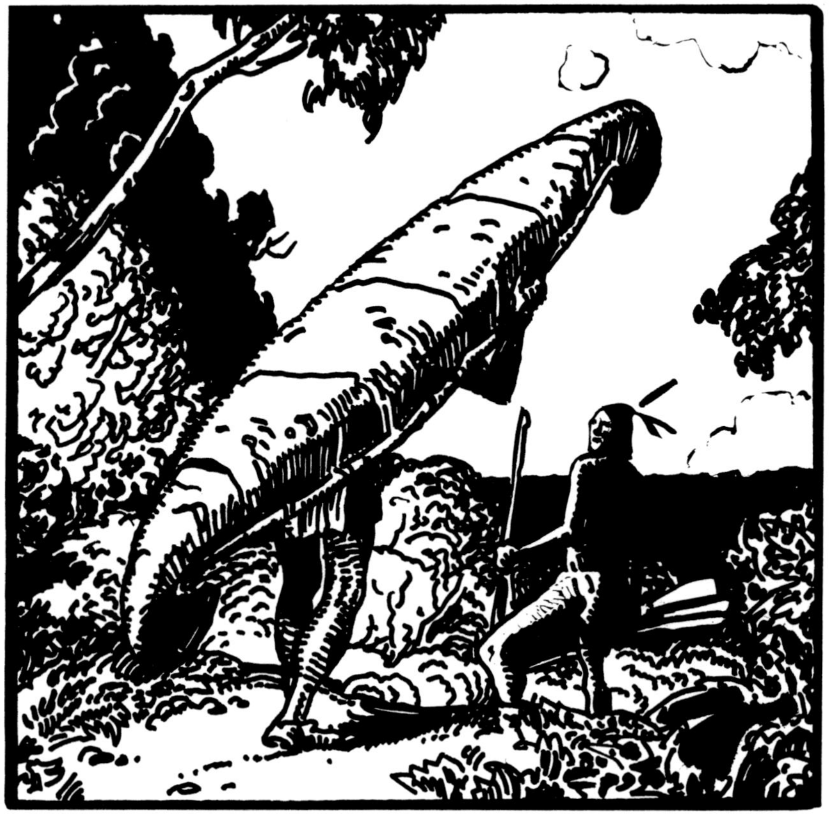

The Huron Portage

ville (U.S. 250) where the Watershed Trail bent north towards Norwalk. This is at the head of Indian Creek, a tributary of the Vermilion River, which enters five miles below Fitchville.

The trail would here meet the trail from the Mohican town in Ashland County. Continuing eastward as part of the Watershed Route, connections were logically established with the headwaters of the West Fork of Black River, near Rochester Station on the Big Four Railroad, and with the main stream five miles southeast of Wellington; then beyond Medina with the west branch of the Rocky River. At Medina, via Weymouth (Ohio 3), the Upper Cuyahoga would have been accessible beyond Richfield.

The Coshocton Trail

Ebenezer Zane blazed his famous Trace across Ohio from Wheeling to Maysville, Kentucky. This famous road, now partly the National Road (U.S. 40) from Zanesville, was laid over portions of an old trail from the Shawnee capital at Circleville to the Delaware center at Coshocton. Zane's Trace led off to the south up the Paint Creek Valley, but the section from Circleville to Lancaster is definitely the old trail.[1]

From Circleville the trail (U.S. 22) led across the flats and climbed the long grade northeast to Amanda, which was an Indian town and which lies about six miles south of Royalton, another Indian settlement. From the heights of Amanda a panorama spreads out, backed by the misty hills around Mount Logan to the south, and nearer are the flats of the Pickaway Plains. Northeast the isolated red tors, crowned with green, appear around Lancaster, the trail rising and falling in long waves.[2] The trail entered Lancaster at the southwest end and converged with the Standing Stone Trail in the railroad flats at that place.

Passing through the town, the trail left the trace (U.S. 22) and continued northeastward on the road to Pleasantville and Thornville, crossing high rolling ridges, and near Pleas-

[1] Christopher Gist, agent of an English and Virginia Land Company, passed over the trail from Fort Pitt to the Indian Towns on the Miami on January 17th, 1751. He visited the great swamp in Licking County known as "Pigeon Roost" or Bloody Run Swamp, five miles northwest of Buckeye Lake or Licking Reservoir and one-half mile south of the National Road.

[2] The site of French Margaret's Town is in doubt, but it was probably in the vicinity of Lancaster. As the name implies, it was probably named from the Canadian wife of some Indian leader.

There was an Indian village on the upper Racoon branch of the Licking near Johnstown.

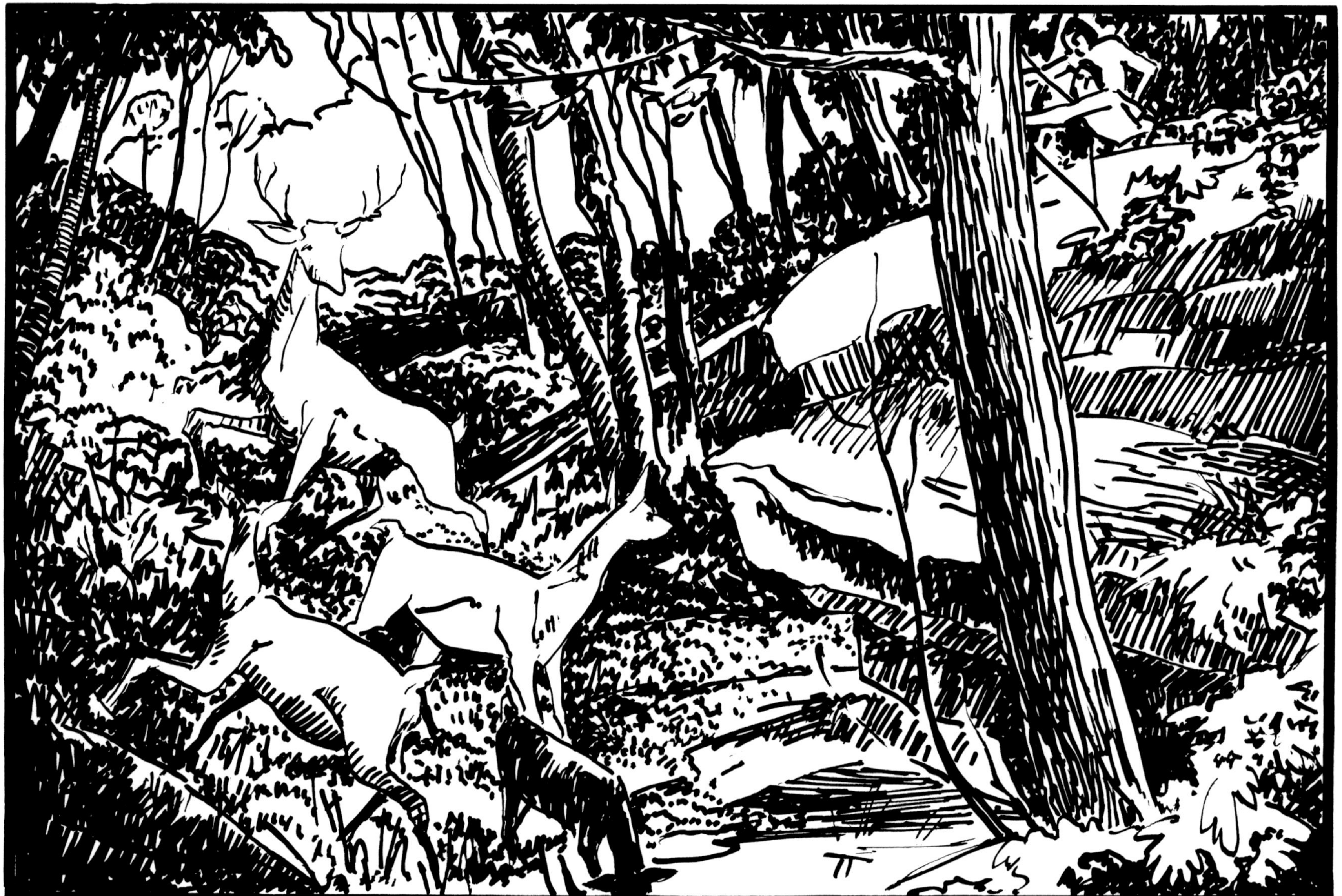

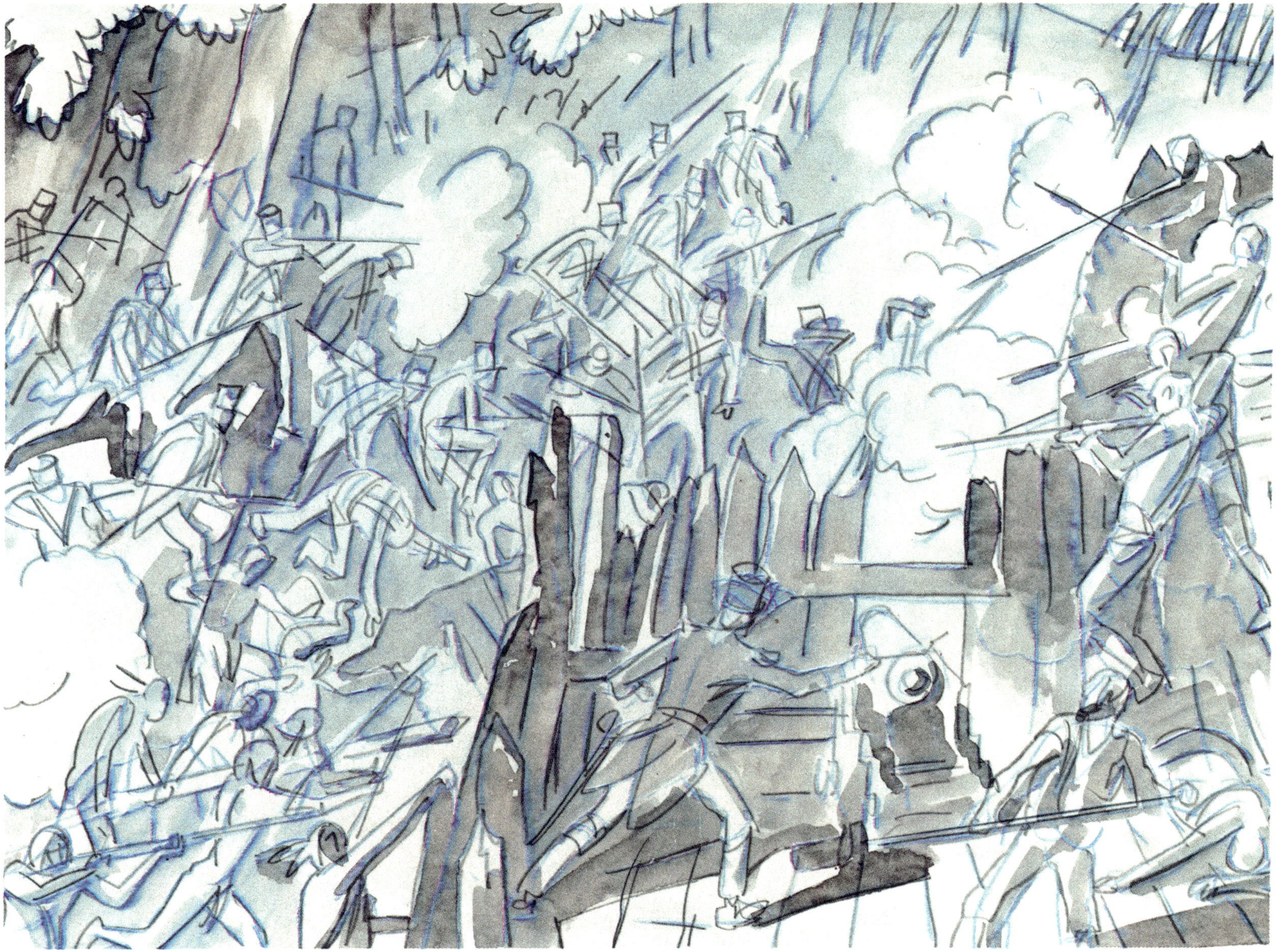

Col. George Groghan

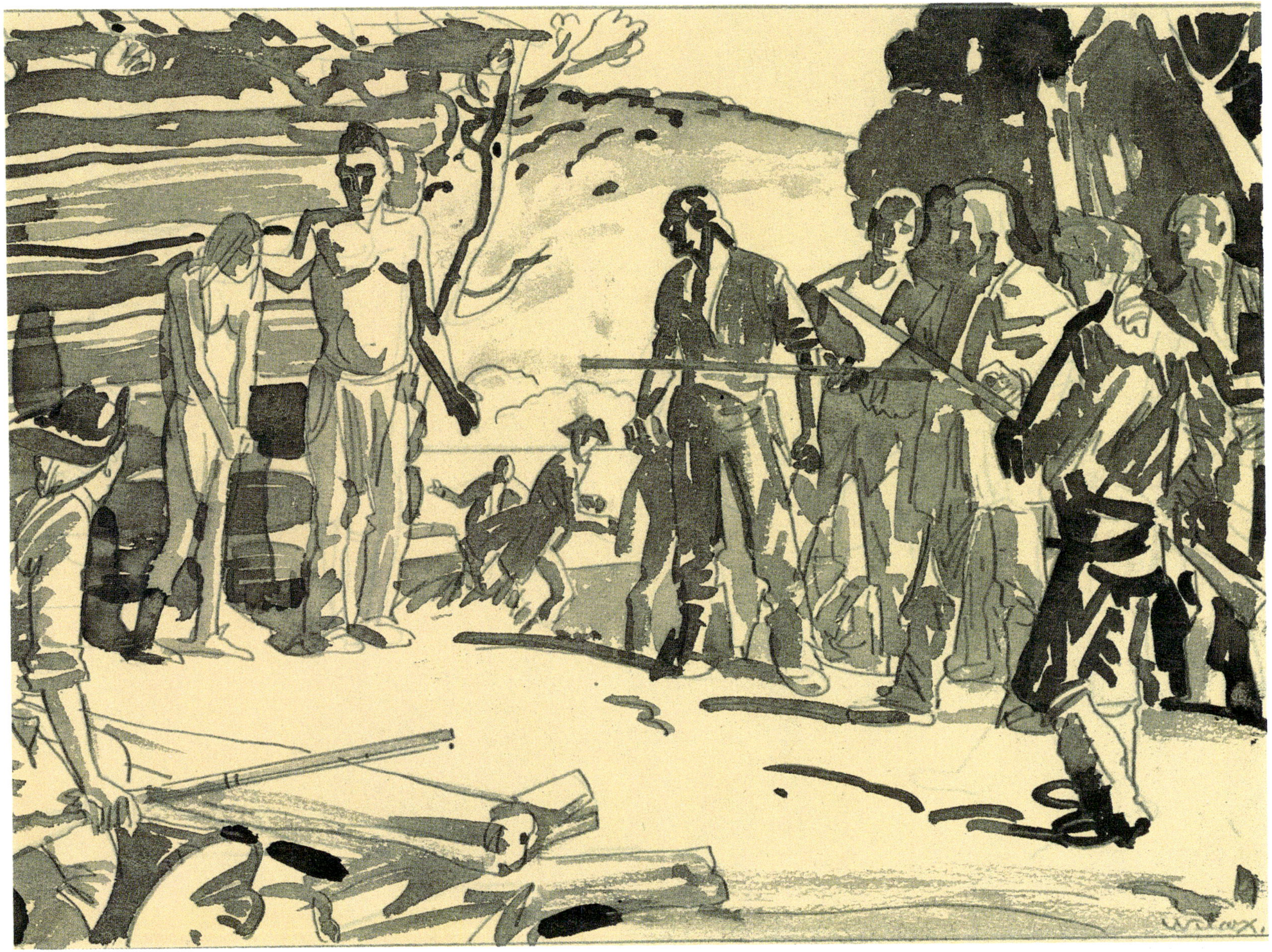

Murder of Cornstalk at Point Pleasant

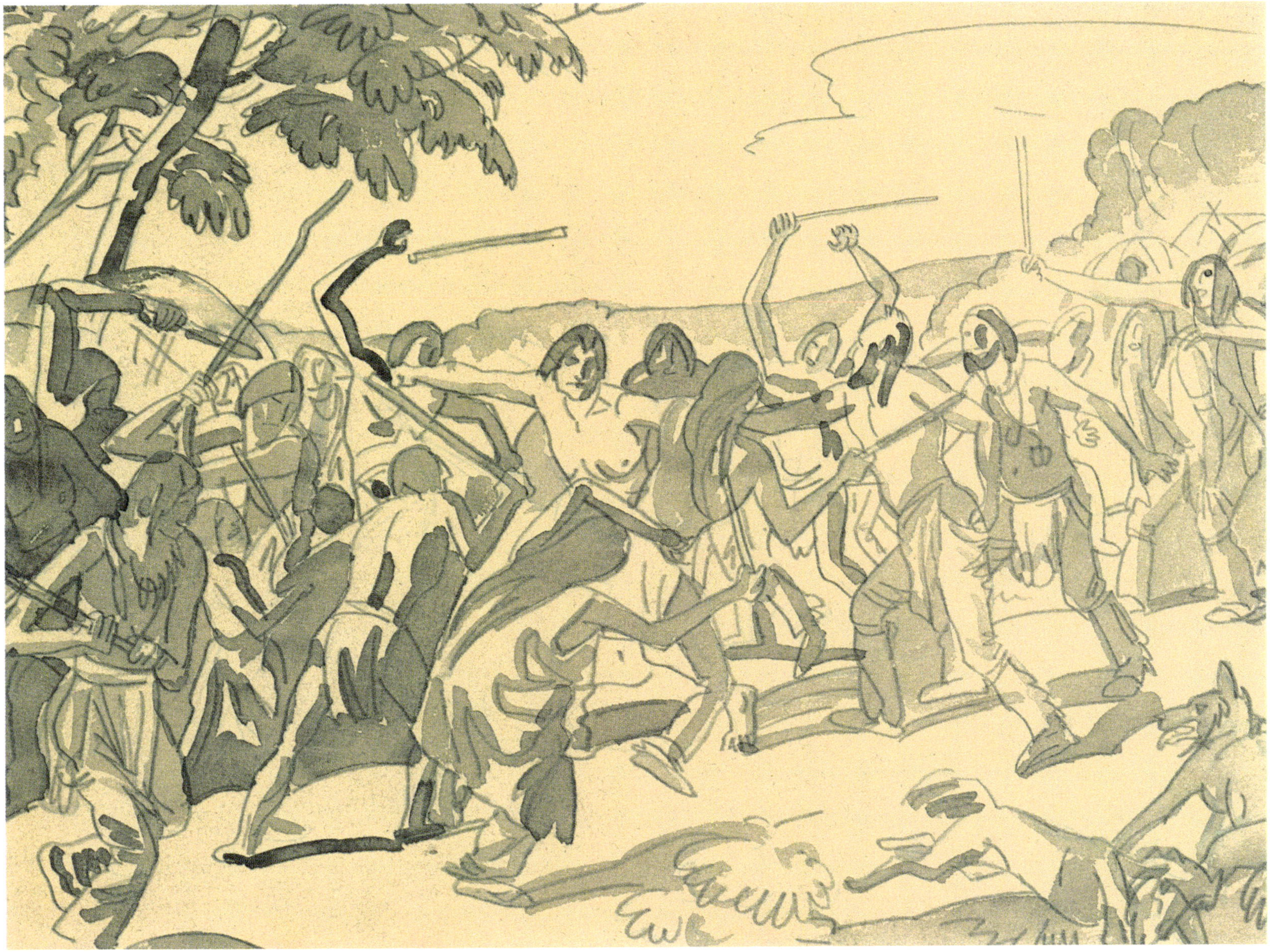

Simon Kenton

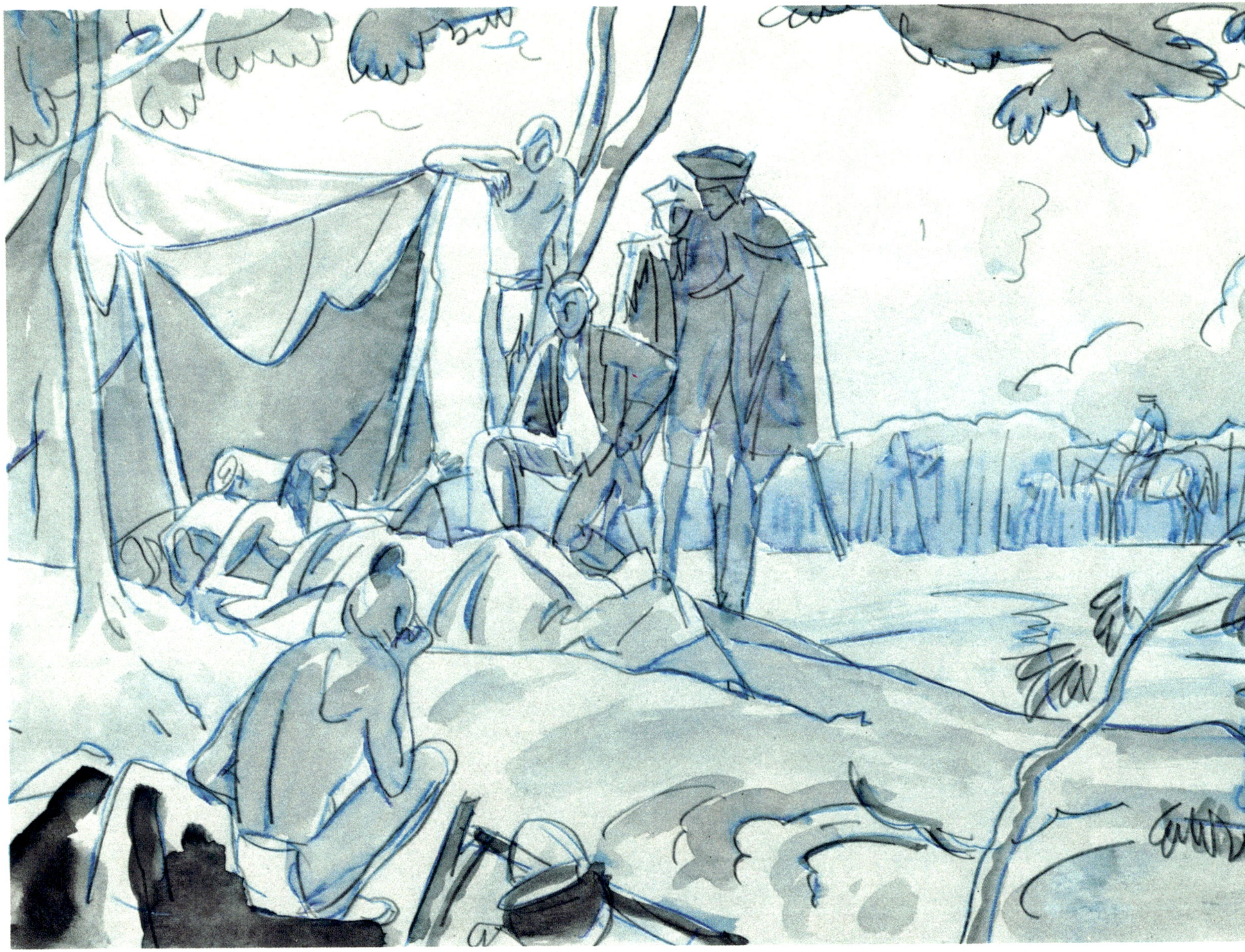

Spemica Lawba (High Horn) at Defiance

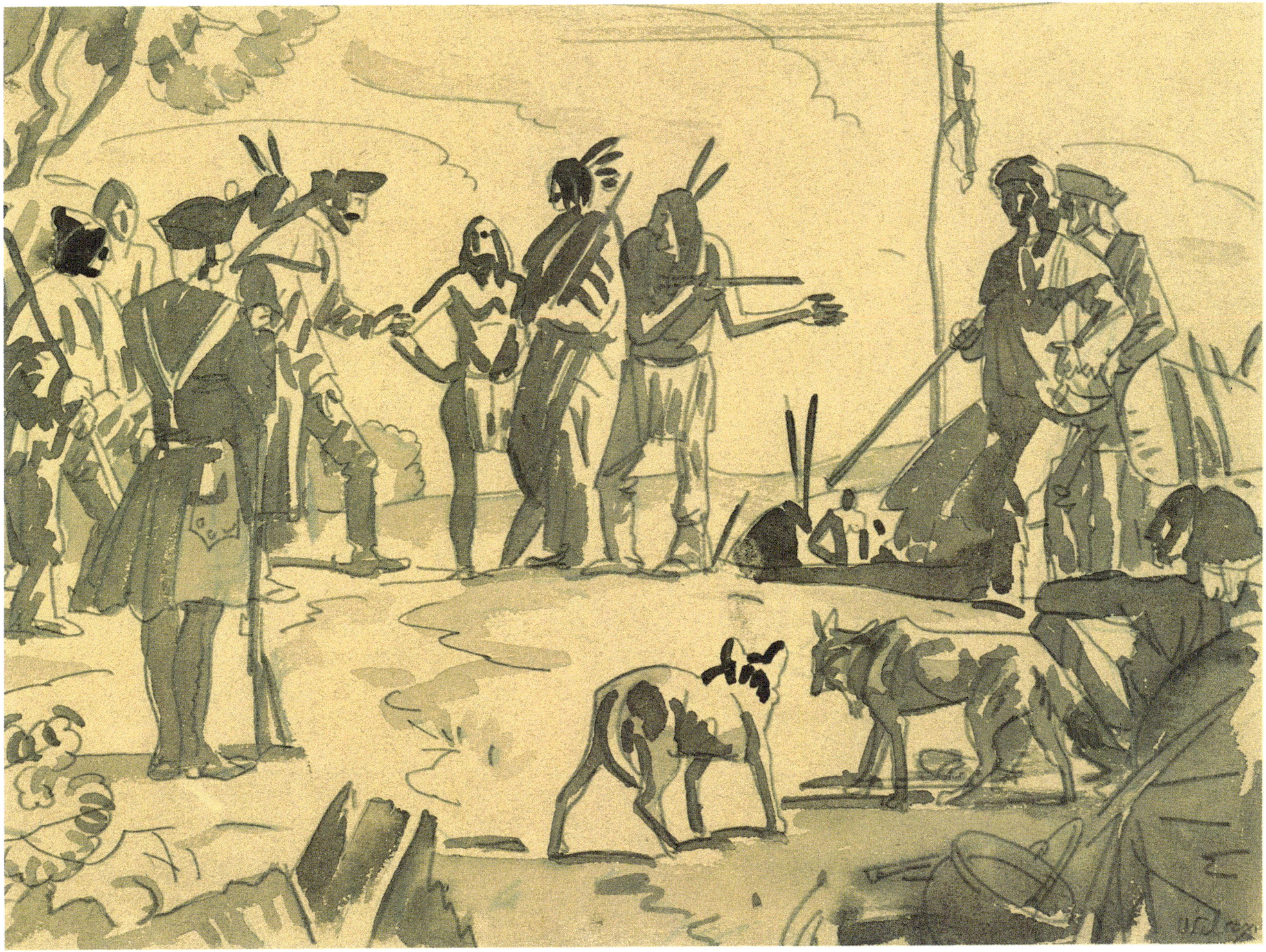

Old Britain Declares for the British at Pickawillany

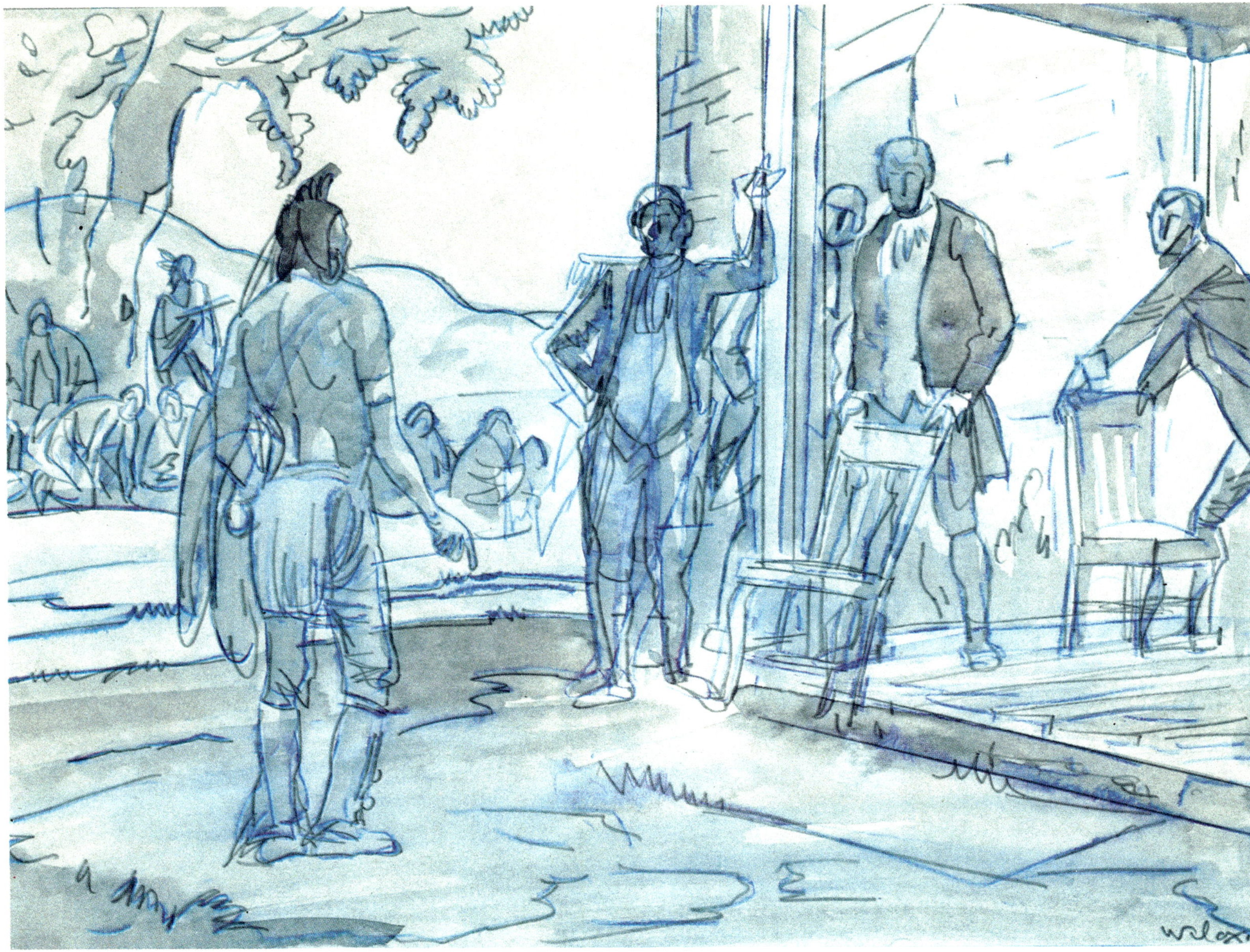

Little Turtle Refused a Chair at Conference

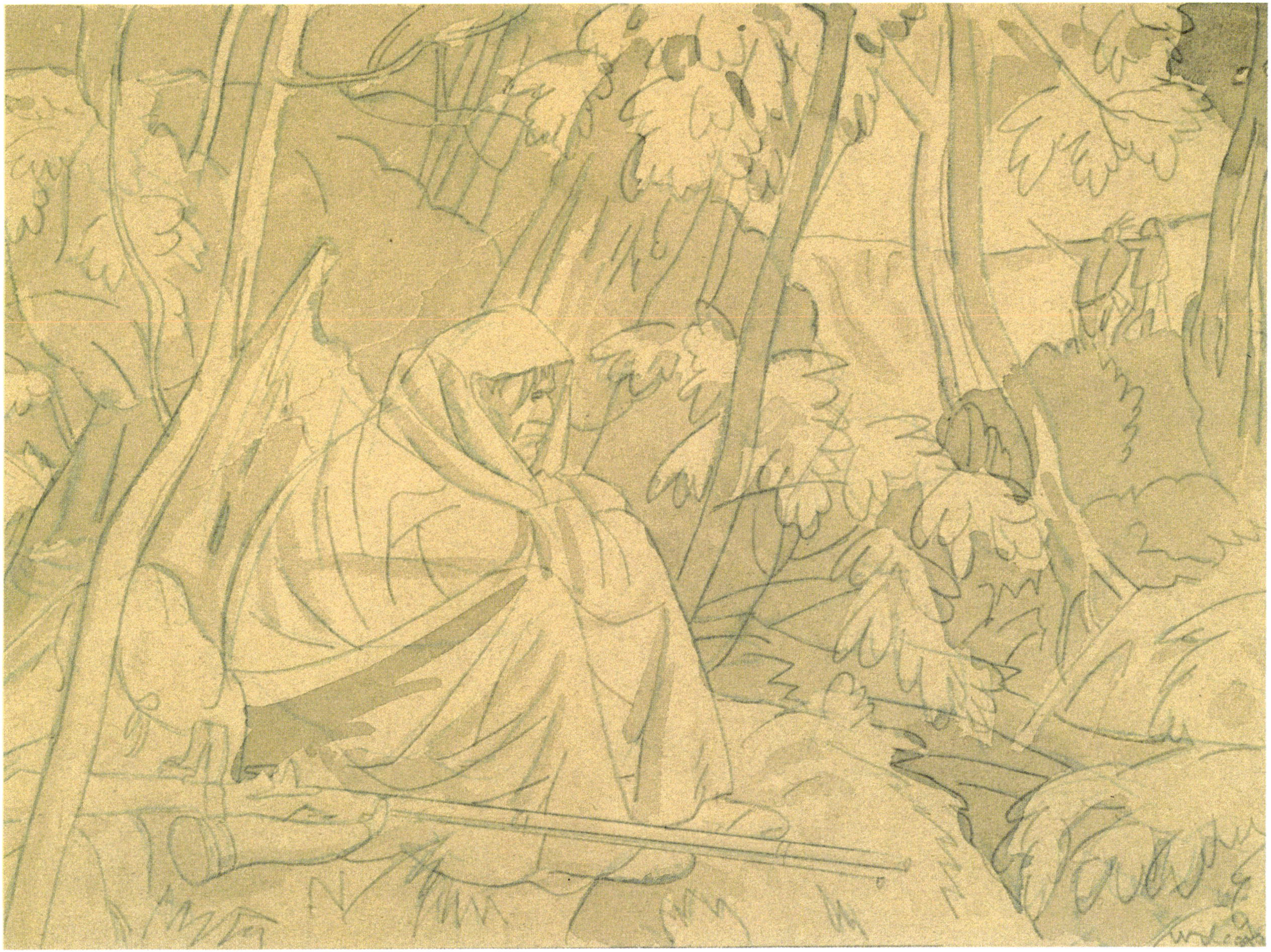

Josiah Hunt Employs Camouflage During Wayne's Campaign

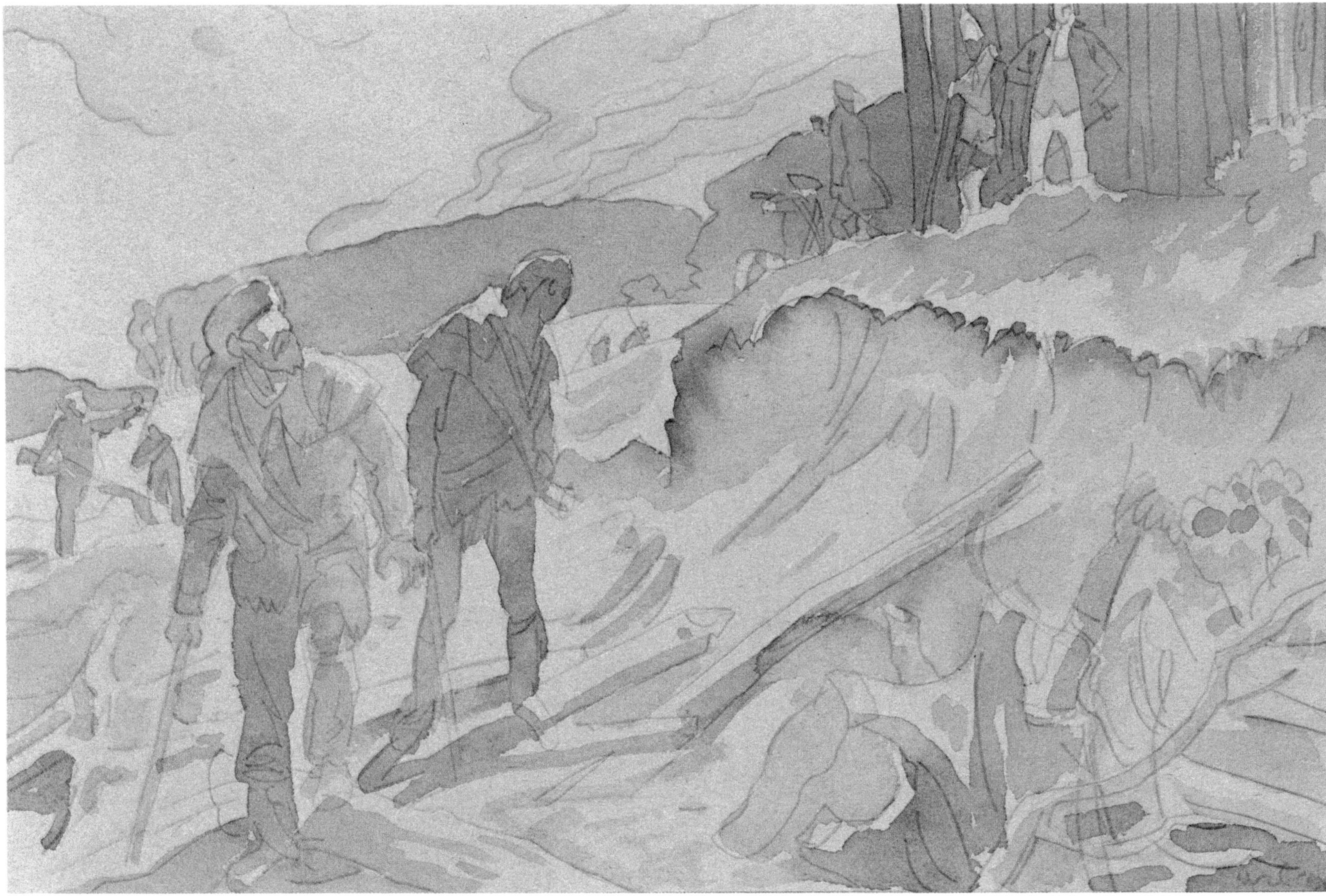

Simon Girty Refused the Protection of Fort Miami After Fallen Timbers

antville descended into the elevated basin of Buckeye Lake. It led to the broken hilly region to the east of the lake at Thornville, and at Thornville Station, at the head of the lake (Ohio 204, 13), turned east up the Jonathan Creek (Ohio 204) and crossed the flat at the forks. It soon turned northeast on the ridges to the north, and crossed the National Road a mile east of Gratiot (U.S. 40).

This is the high portion of the road where it passes over the rolling base of Flint Ridge. It is about two miles east of Brownsville, where on the heights above are the Flint Quarries.[3] Leading up the east side of Kent Run, the trail crossed the ridge and descended to Nashport Station (Ohio 146) where it crossed the Licking. West four miles at Toboso are the Black Hand Narrows, which with the aboriginal signs there and its unique and sombre beauty, should be visited by any trail finder. Apparently the Ridge and the region about were well threaded by lesser trails.[4]

[3] There is an Indian fable that the tribes, gathering to get material for arrowheads at Flint Ridge, were so inclined to war that the Great Spirit ordained it neutral ground. The local residents assert that no war points are found, and that the Indians agreed to abide by the tradition.

[4] The narrows of the Licking River east of Flint Ridge lie between sharp fifty-foot cliffs, thickly overgrown with forest and vines. It is a startling and unexpected sight and is very beautiful. The rocks near the water's edge were formerly covered by Indian Petroglyphs, which were destroyed by the cutting of the Licking Canal.

It is now a state reservation, which will tend to preserve its aboriginal character. The presence of many flint chips upon the edges and on the isolated crags of the midstream suggest its use as a camp site by aboriginal visitors to Flint Ridge nearby.

The name "Black Hand" was given by an Indian carving, now destroyed, and an Indian legend centered about its making.

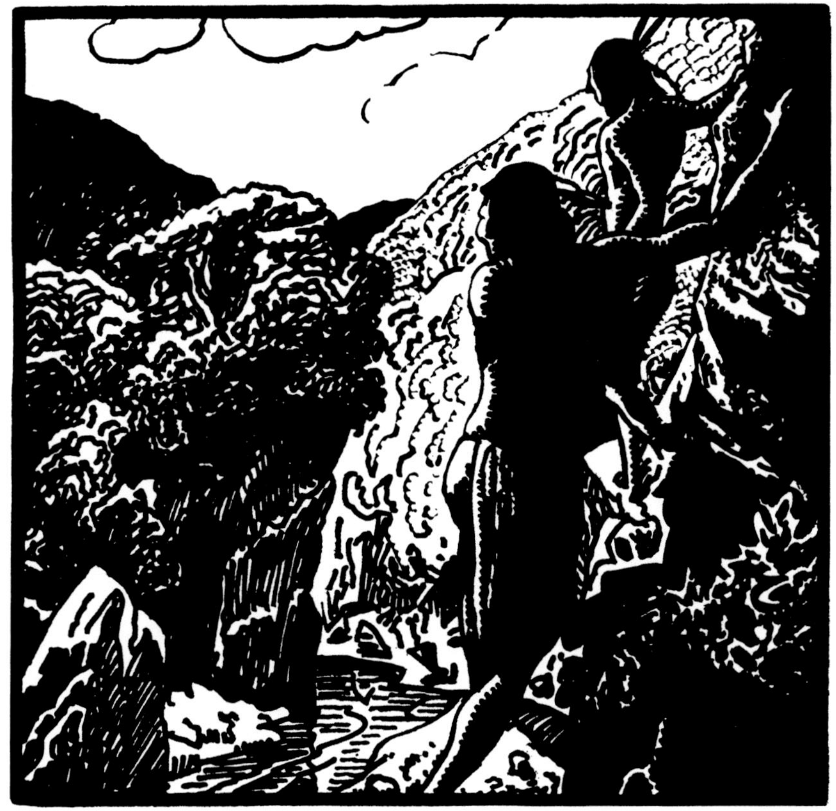

The Black Hand Gorge

At Nashport the trail led north over the flat between two ridges that extend along the abandoned canal to the confluence of Black Run and the Wakatomica at Frazeysburg (Ohio 16). The rivers here surround the highlands, a peculiar triangular mass of hills, which stands on the flats of the Licking, Wakatomica and Muskingum. On the northeast corner is Dresden, the Old Wakatomica (Ohio 60).

Mounting the Graham Ridge to the north the trail converged with the Muskingum Trail from back of Wakatomica, which apparently led from Trinway in the flats (Ohio 60) at the confluence and west up the Irish Ridge. This Ridge converges with the Graham Ridge at right angles on the north of Frazeysburg.

This trail is one of those which, although fairly short, contains unique landscape and much of interest for the student of history.

The Standing Stone Trail

Lancaster, on the high plateau northeast of the Shawnee Confederacy in the Pickaway Plains, and known as Standing Stone, was the junction of a trail from Circleville to Coshocton on the Muskingum and of a trail from the Lower Shawnee Town, now Portsmouth. It stands under a high red sandstone cliff, which gave it its name; to the southwest lie other outriders of the hills, and southward in Hocking County are peculiar flat-topped hills with one abrupt and one sloping side.

From the mouth of the Scioto the trail led northeast up the north side of the Ohio, on the back street of Portsmouth, and coming to the narrow way at Sciotoville, turned up the west bank of the Little Scioto and led north over the ridges to a point near Jackson, where it crossed at the junction of Buckeye and Little Salt Creek, and passing along the west ridge of the Little Salt, crossed it and the Kanawha Trail northwest of Jackson. It crossed the Pigeon Fork of Salt Creek, probably at Byer, and led north in a zigzag hilltop course for many miles, across Salt Creek and Pine Creek to the famous Rock House. The region is exceedingly unique for Ohio; the deep ravines preserve giant hemlocks, and the flat, narrow valley bottoms give an effect of height to the hills. The Rock House, as well as many other caves and cliffs are, and were to the Indian, mysterious and beautiful retreats. It is difficult to describe the trail through this region as it does not lie upon well traveled highways. The entrance today is from east and west.

From the Rock House the trail led down, by the present entrance of Hocking Hills State Park, to Mound Crossing on the road from South Bloomingville to Logan, and so north-

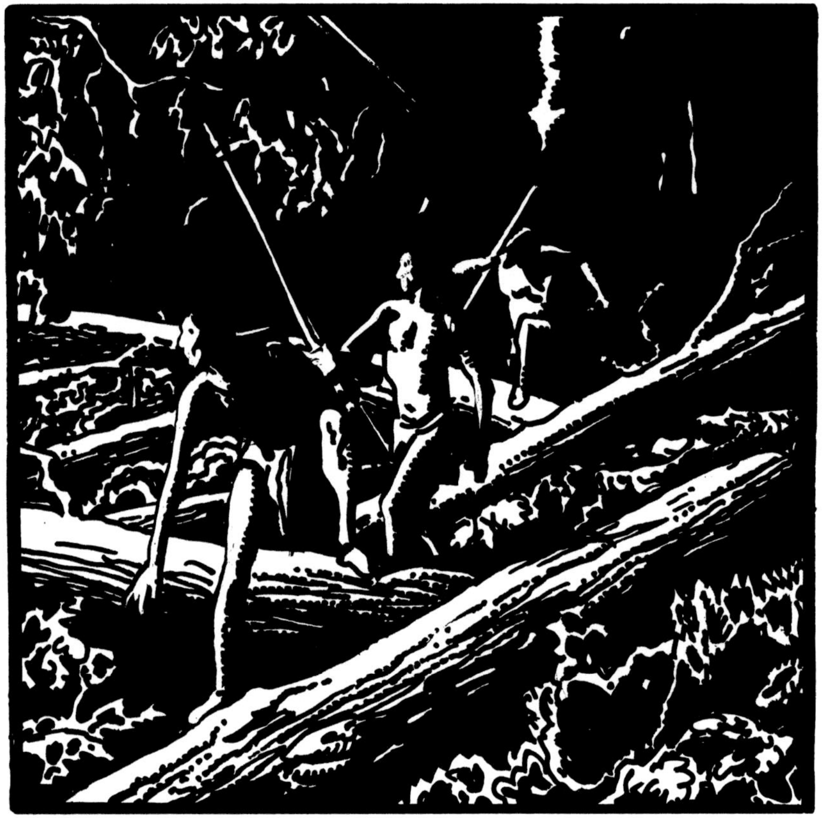

The Trail Makers

ward seven miles to the crossing of the Belpre Trail west of Rockbridge. It followed a northerly ridge to where the State Industrial School stands, and passing east of Jacob's Ladder and Christmas Rocks, led down the tracks of the electric line to Lancaster, where at the southwest end of town it joined the trail to Coshocton from Circleville.

This trail traverses no well improved highways, but crosses a few, more or less at right angles. It is completely a hilly ridge trail and is difficult to trace, although it probably preserves, for that reason, many indications of its original condition. The territory is wild, romantic and inaccessible.

The number of state parks around caves and gorges testifies to its general interest.

The principal highways crossing the trail are Ohio 124, through Jackson, from Piketon to Gallipolis; U.S. 35 from Chillicothe to Jackson; U.S. 50 from Chillicothe to McArthur; Ohio 56 from Circleville to Athens, which passes nearest to the points of interest in this wild region; and Ohio 180 from Laurelville to Logan.

The trail certainly passed near Jackson, since it is known that the Salt Springs were frequently visited by the Indians. This is one part of the state where the modern roads seem to give no hint of the red man's trails.

The Ohio Trail

A trail on the high ridges of the Ohio River hills extended from the Kanauga flats, opposite the Kanawha, to the flats of Belpre, opposite the Little Kanawha at Parkersburg. A branch of this trail led south to the bottoms of the Great Bend in the salient of Meigs County.

Beginning as part of a trail leading from Belpré to Circleville, the Ohio Trail began on the high northern ridge from which Blennerhassett Island is seen far down in the river below.[1] It led west (U.S. 50S), and turning south with the river, crossed the Hocking at Coolville, which lies just above the deep, rocky and picturesque gorge of the Hocking River. It then crossed over the ridges to Tuppers Plains, at a flat place on the hills, and then ran southwest to Chester (Ohio 7). Here it crossed the Shade River, and leaving the present highway, crossed west over more ridges. At Chester the branch to the Great Bend seems to have led easterly and south over the hilltops on the west of the Shade, and reaching the height of land, to have descended Old Town Creek in a southeasterly direction to the bottoms of the Bend, where, judging from the name of the stream, an Indian town doubtless stood.

Returning to Chester, the Ohio Trail continued west and then south around the bend at Pomeroy, but kept well back on the highest ridges. It led through Rutland (Ohio 124), and crossing the modern highway, passed over Leading

[1] Not far from Belpré, and below Marietta, lies in the middle of the Ohio the beautiful island formerly belonging to Harman Blennerhassett, the romantic and impractical Irishman who was drawn into Aaron Burr's famous conspiracy against the United States.

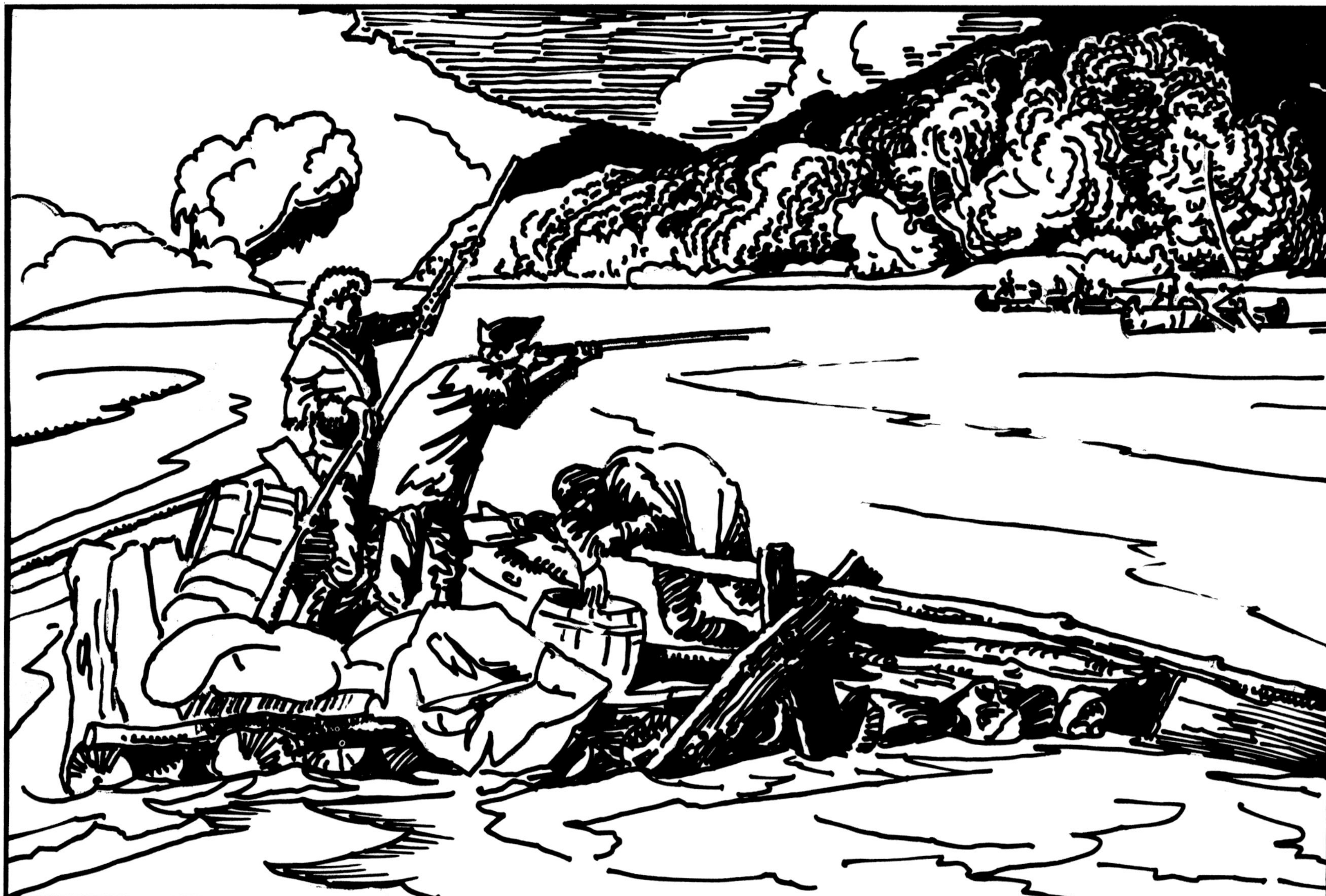

Perils of the Ohio from the Indian Shore

Creek, south down Jessie and Kyger Creeks to the Flats of the Ohio at Cheshire. Here it followed the present highway (Ohio 7) under the cliffs and the narrow flat at Addison to Kanauga.

It is conceivable that this trail was in a sense a war trail for intercepting on the Ohio, between the Great and Little Kanawha, travellers who had descended those streams. The path may have continued from the heights at Kyger, above Chester, southward on those heights, and, crossing Campaign Creek, have descended little Chickamauga to the Kanawha Trail behind Gallipolis.

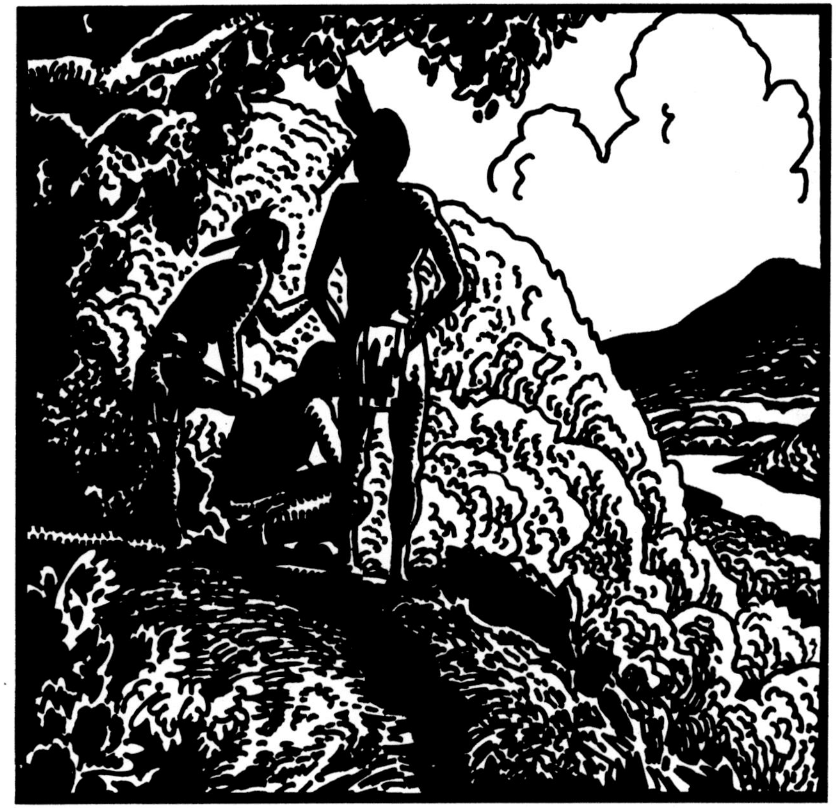

La Belle Riviere

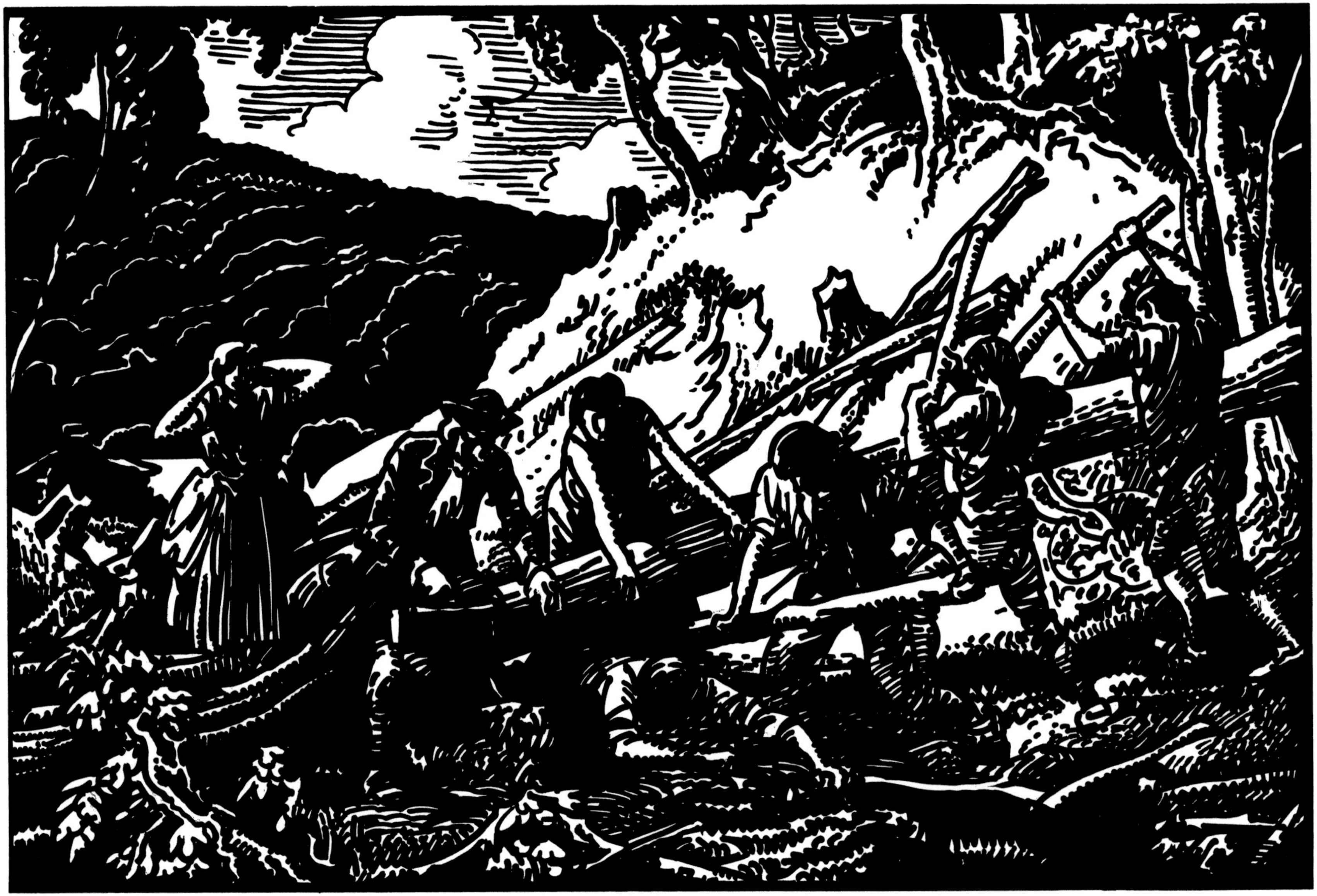

Unhappy Incident Among the French Engineers at Gallipolis

The Belpré Trail

The Little Kanawha was early used as an approach to the Ohio from West Virginia. The route from here to the Shawnee towns lay almost due west. The trail may have been used by the first traders, and it certainly was a direct trail for Shawnee raids.

It left the Ohio Ridge Trail at the head of the Little Hocking and struck northwestward through Vincent and Chesterhill, where, crossing the present ridge highway (Ohio 76), it led northwest on the ridge between Wolf Creek and Federal Creek, and turning west over the east branch of Sunday Creek, passed up Wild Cat Hollow and over Irish Ridge to Corning (Ohio 13). Here it led west (Ohio 155) through Hemlock and Shawnee to Monday Creek. It then led west on the high ridge between Rush Creek and the Hocking, passing probably four miles north of Logan to Rockbridge on the Hocking (U.S. 33).

Continuing westward, it passed through Revenge and Drinkle, where it began to descend the long slopes of the hilly Hocking region and led due west to Circleville over the prairies.[1] This route runs today through a mining region as far as the Hocking. The valleys are V-shaped and the hilltops are seldom flat. It passes north of the more spectacular scenic territory of Hocking County, but crosses the trail from Portsmouth to Lancaster at Clear Creek, about five miles west of Rockbridge. The latter trail traverses this region.

[1] One account places Dunmore's camp in the Pickaway Plains on the Black Mount in the center of the plains near Westfall and a mile from Squaw Town. Camp Charlotte lies much to the east and about one mile southeast of a prominent prehistoric mound. It is marked by a tablet. This spot is about a mile northwest of the village of Leistville, on Scippo Creek, near a crossroads.

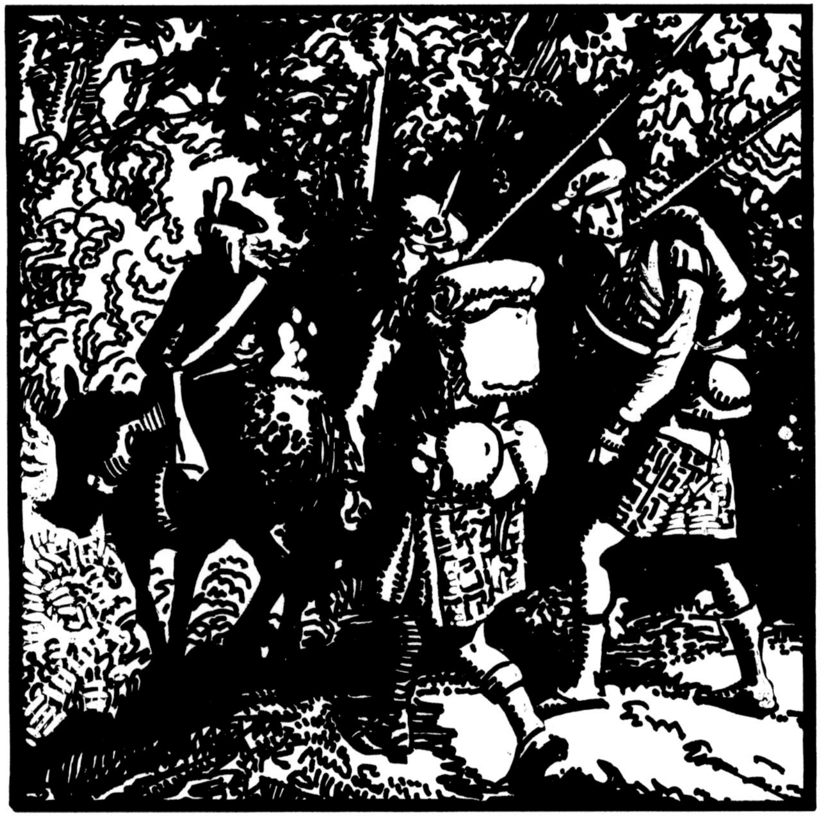

The Forest Invaded

Four miles north of the trail is Amanda, on the slopes of the Scioto basin, a Shawnee town southwest of Lancaster (U.S. 22).

The Kanawha Trail

The battle of Point Pleasant at the mouth of the Kanawha was the first great pitched battle that can be considered a white victory. When Lewis, at last, at the end of the day, saw his adversaries cross the Ohio, it may be assumed that they descended the far side of the flats and entered this trail on their retreat, and that he pursued them to the Pickaway Plains over this route. His dilatory and reputedly treacherous co-leader, Dunmore, had failed to join him at the confluence, but had ascended the Hocking, approaching the plains from the east. In any event the battle is locally construed as the first battle of the Revolution, and it is known that the otherwise successful campaign did not achieve a diplomatic understanding with either England or the Indians.[1]

The trail led from the Indian town of Kanauga, opposite the mouth of the Kanawha, across the flats to Gallipolis (Ohio 7) and climbed the east ridge of Chickamauga Creek to the Mills (U.S. 35);[2] leading west from that point on Buck Ridge it descended to Adamsville on Raccoon Creek, crossed through Rio Grande (U.S. 35) on the next hilltop, followed

[1] In the courthouse yard at Point Pleasant, West Virginia, opposite Kanauga, Ohio, stands the simple monument to the great Shawnee leader, Cornstalk, who was murdered there while on a peaceful mission after the Dunmore Treaty.

[2] The City of Gallipolis was founded under the French Grant. This land promotion scheme was advertised in Paris and brought many inexperienced and helpless Frenchmen to Ohio, by what would now be considered underhanded methods. They survived many hardships in building the community.

Mad Ann Bailey was born in Liverpool, England, and was married first to John Trotter, who was killed at the Battle of Point Pleasant. She became somewhat crazed from grief and vowed vengeance against the Indians. She became a messenger and spy between Point Pleasant and Covington.

Later she married John Bailey and lived at Charleston, West Virginia, until his death, when she became a hermit near Gallipolis.

There formerly plied at Point Pleasant a ferry boat bearing her name and picture upon the paddle boxes.

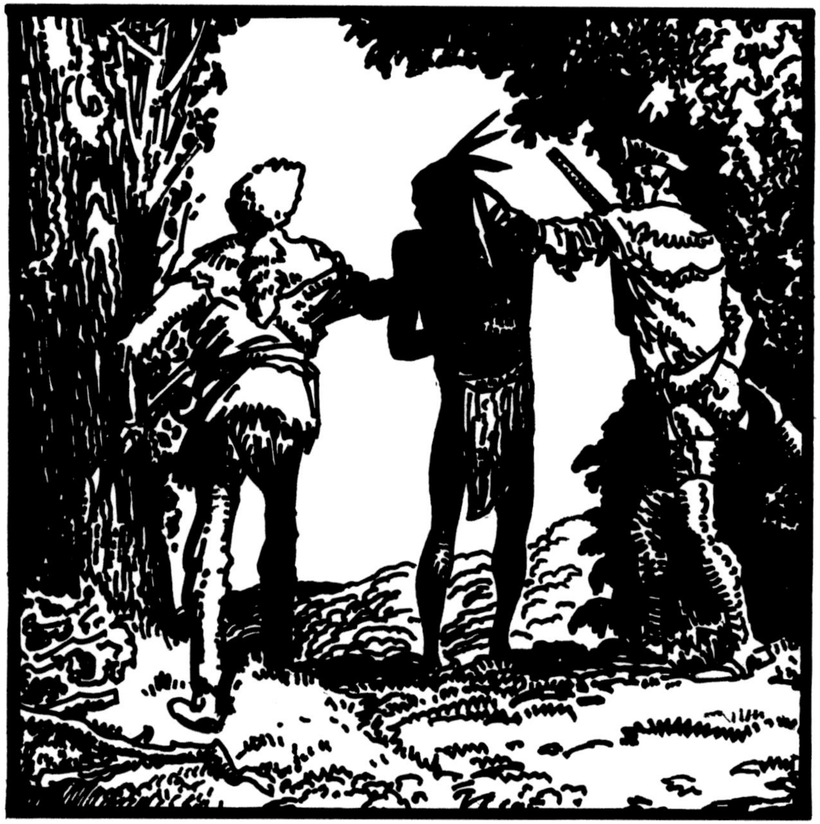

The Red Captive

the ridge, descended over Indian Creek, and followed up that creek to Centerville; continuing northwest through Rempel on Symmes Creek, over country very hilly and broken, it descended Little Salt Creek to Jackson, on the flats at the confluence of several streams. Following Salt Creek on the ridges to the eastward, it descended Little Salt Creek (U.S. 35) to broken land, which, extending northeastward from the Scioto flats at the confluence with the Scioto, forms the basin of Big Salt Creek. This the trail crossed, and (U.S. 35) passing east of Richmond Dale, up Walnut and then Little Walnut Creek on a northerly course, it led between the impressive eastern and western series of knobs that are so characteristic of this region, to the head of Little Walnut Creek, where it reached the flat land beyond these upheavals. It crossed the head waters of Kinnickinnick Creek, and passing northwestward through Kingston, followed down the north bank of Congo Creek past the famous Logan Elm. Crossing Scippo Creek at Cornstalk's and Grenadier Squaw's Town, it led due north to Maguck at Circleville.

Cutting as this trail does the western section of Vinton County, an impressive view of the Chillicothe Knobs is obtained as the descent of Little Salt Creek is made, and as Little Walnut Creek passes between them. The trail passes first through a mountainous region which, changing to broken foothills, ends in the Pickaway Plains.

This route was a direct war trail from the Shawnee stronghold to the earlier frontiers of the Allegheny and the Virginia country.

The Shawnee-Miami Trail

There was a direct trail connection between the Shawnee towns of the Pickaway Plains and the old Indian agency of Pickawillany. This seems likely in view of the length of time that that station, and also Loramie, were in French hands. When these places became English posts at the end of the French and Indian War, they were the centers of turbulence which prompted the Shawnees to match their strength against the settlers who filtered into the region of the Ohio and those agents and traders who penetrated the state by the eastern river gates.

Beginning at Maguck or Circleville, the trail led northwest through Spunky Town (Ohio 56), Mount Sterling and London on one of those state roads that seem older than the present age. It traversed a flat or gently rolling landscape until, beyond London, it became more broken as the headwaters of the Mad River were reached, and descended into the flats to join the trail to Pickawillany from the Lower Scioto Town.

From London it continued northwest through Catawba, and crossing the East Fork of Little Darby Creek, led over the dividing ridge about five miles south of Urbana (Ohio 54) to strike the mouth of Nettle Creek, where it crossed the Maccochee Trail and joined the Pickawillany Trail.

This trail crossed the Scioto basin northwesterly from its center and the long north and south ridge between Bellefontaine and Hillsboro, after which it made an abrupt descent into the Miami. Its course lay between the headwaters of Great Paint Creek on the south and of Darby Creek on the north, and it is a typically direct watershed route.

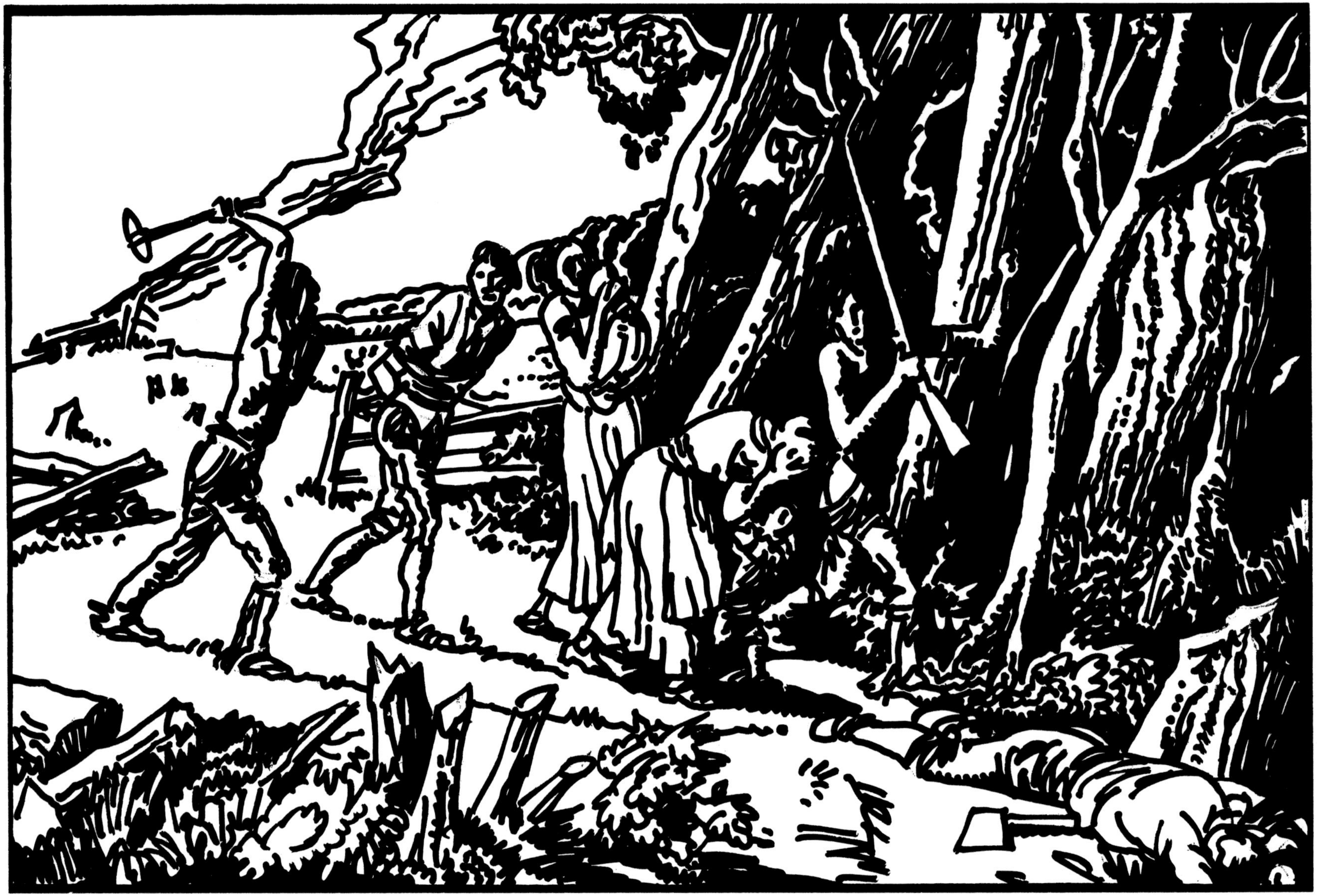

Shawnees Attack a Frontier Settlement

The Pickawillany Trail

The mouth of the Scioto is a spectacular doorway into Ohio from the river. High Raven Rock stands to the west, and back of Portsmouth the hills rise like an impervious wall, but up the Scioto there is a view of wide interior meadows and bottom lands. Raven Rock, that famous old lookout post, still guards to the northwest a primitive, little-settled region where the wild game is protected over many square miles and the forest army has been recruited for its reforestation. In this direction the hills between Paint Creek and the Ohio are loftier. To the west lie Fort Hill, Serpent Mound and the other reminders of the use of this fastness by the aborigines as a refuge from their enemies. It is a fruitful field today for a study of their life history.

Piqua, far to the northwest, lay over the great north and south watershed which extends from Hillsboro up to Bellefontaine, and the Pickawillany Trail crosses this divide. It is essentially an Indian thoroughfare, since most of the white man's expeditions led up the Miami, or up the Mad River, which leads into the divide from the southwest.

The trail, commencing in the flats of Carey Run, mounted the southwest slope of the rocky hill, and leading northwestward, crossed the high choppy hills to Scioto Brush Creek at Henley (Ohio 73) and followed the great northerly ridge of Mount Joy west and north to Duke. The path follows in this region no major highways, but traverses still primitive hilltops.

From Duke the trail meandered over Laurel Ridge, over Chenoweth Fork of the Sunfish Creek at Arkoe; then up Long Run and down another run to Sunfish Creek a mile below

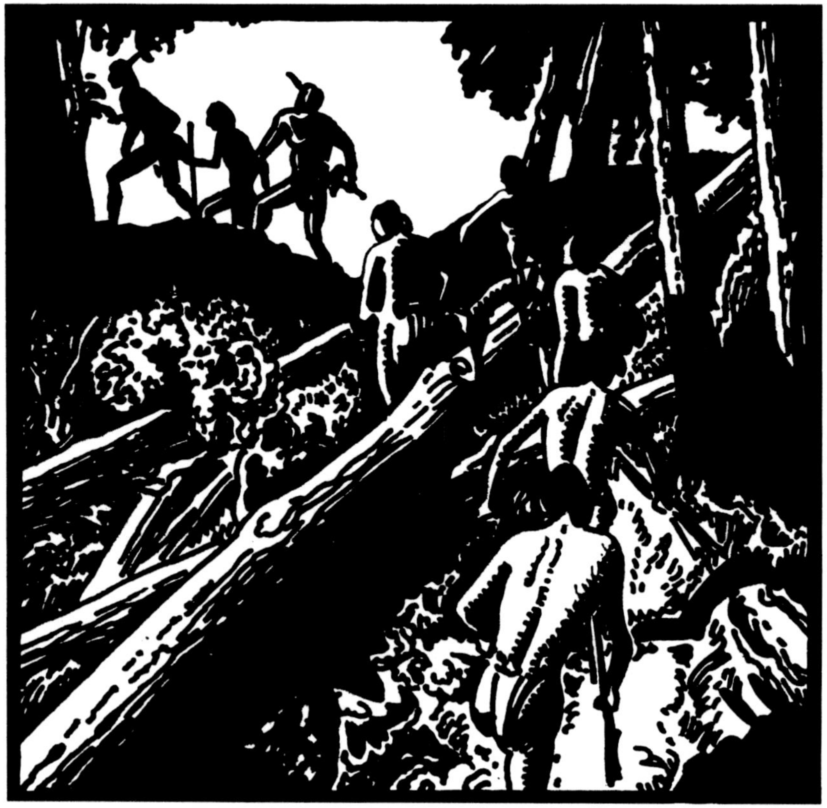

The War Party

Latham, where it crossed an improved highway to Sinking Springs westward (Ohio 124, 41). In the region of Sinking Springs are Fort Hill and other spots of definite interest. From Fort Hill, with its aboriginal traces, a splendid idea of the region can be gained.

Continuing from the highway, the trail led up the north bank to the town of Latham; it led northwest up another run and over high ridges to Fairview Ridge, which tends southwest and northeast. This it crossed and descended in the course of half a mile to Beech Flats, surrounded by small peaks such as Round Top and Shepherd's Mountain. This is a spectacular region with its round tops crested with woods and its once-tilled slopes reverting to the primitive. In Indian days it must have held still more of its misty blueness. Looking west across the flats, one sees Fort Hill six miles to the southwest.

On rising ground the trail passed between Iron's Mountain and Core Hill into the flats of Cynthiana (Ohio 41), thence northward across the highway, through more hills or knobs, until it reached Barrett's Mills on the Rocky Fork of Paint Creek; crossing the stream and leaving the knob country, it lifted to the rolling plateau northwest through Rainsboro (U.S. 50), then over several tributaries of the Rattlesnake, and up the south ridge of Bridgewater Creek to Highland, following the highway from Rainsboro (Ohio 28 to 72).

From Highland the path led northwest over the rolling plateau broken by brooks for many miles to Port William above the Mad River Basin, not far from the modern highway (U.S. 68). The country now presents a surface cut by

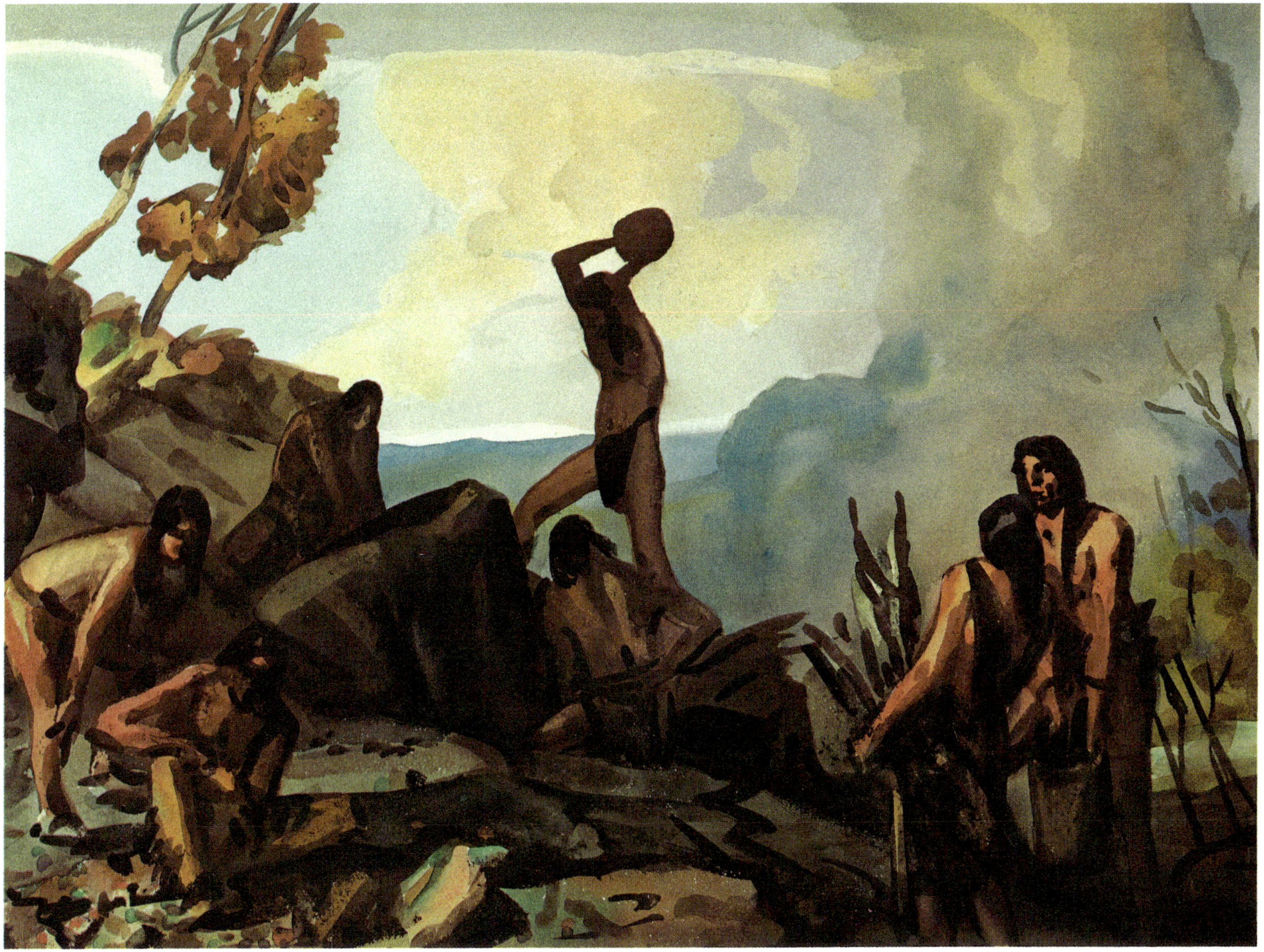

Prehistoric Flint Quarry, Newark

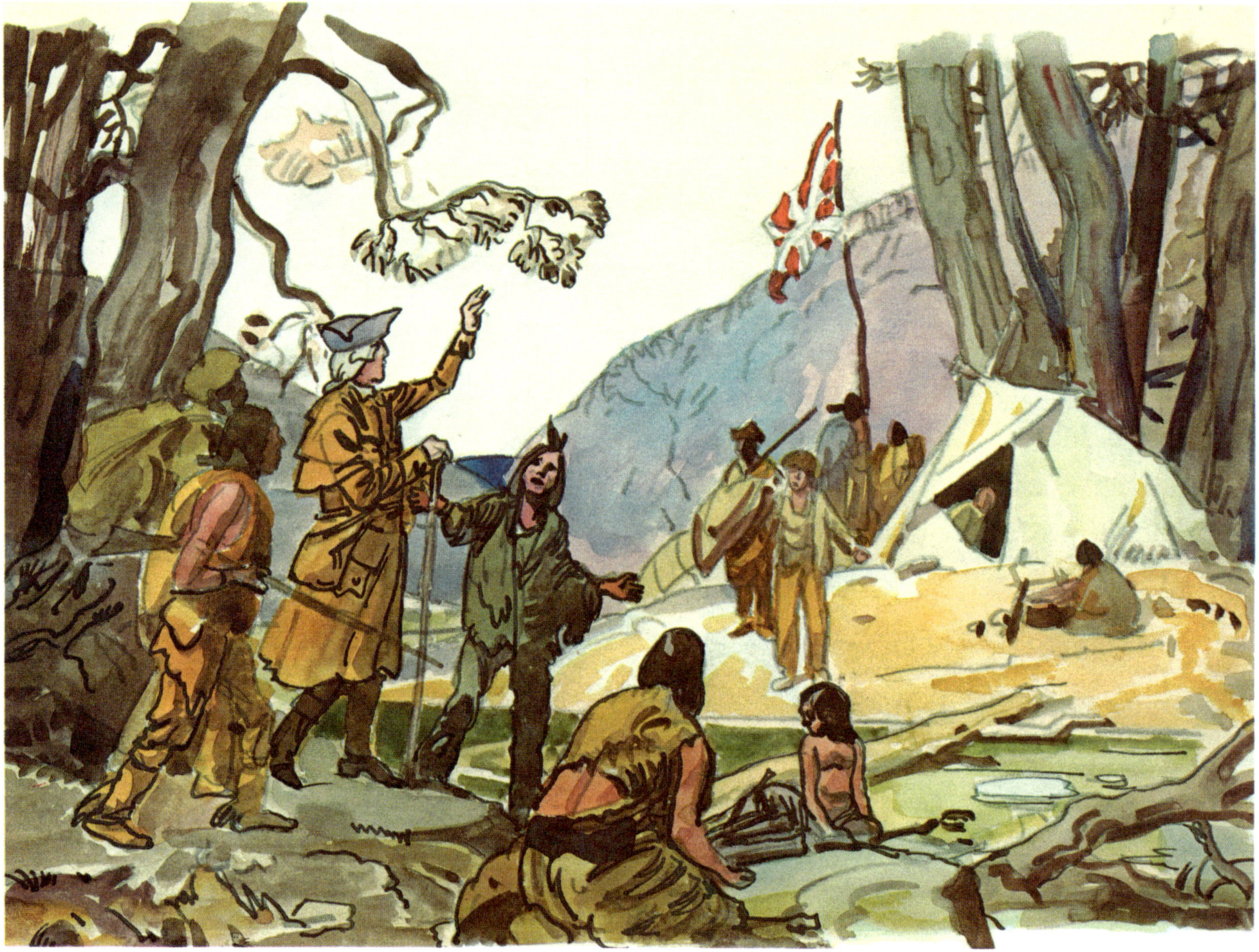

George Croghan and Christopher Gist on the Walhonding

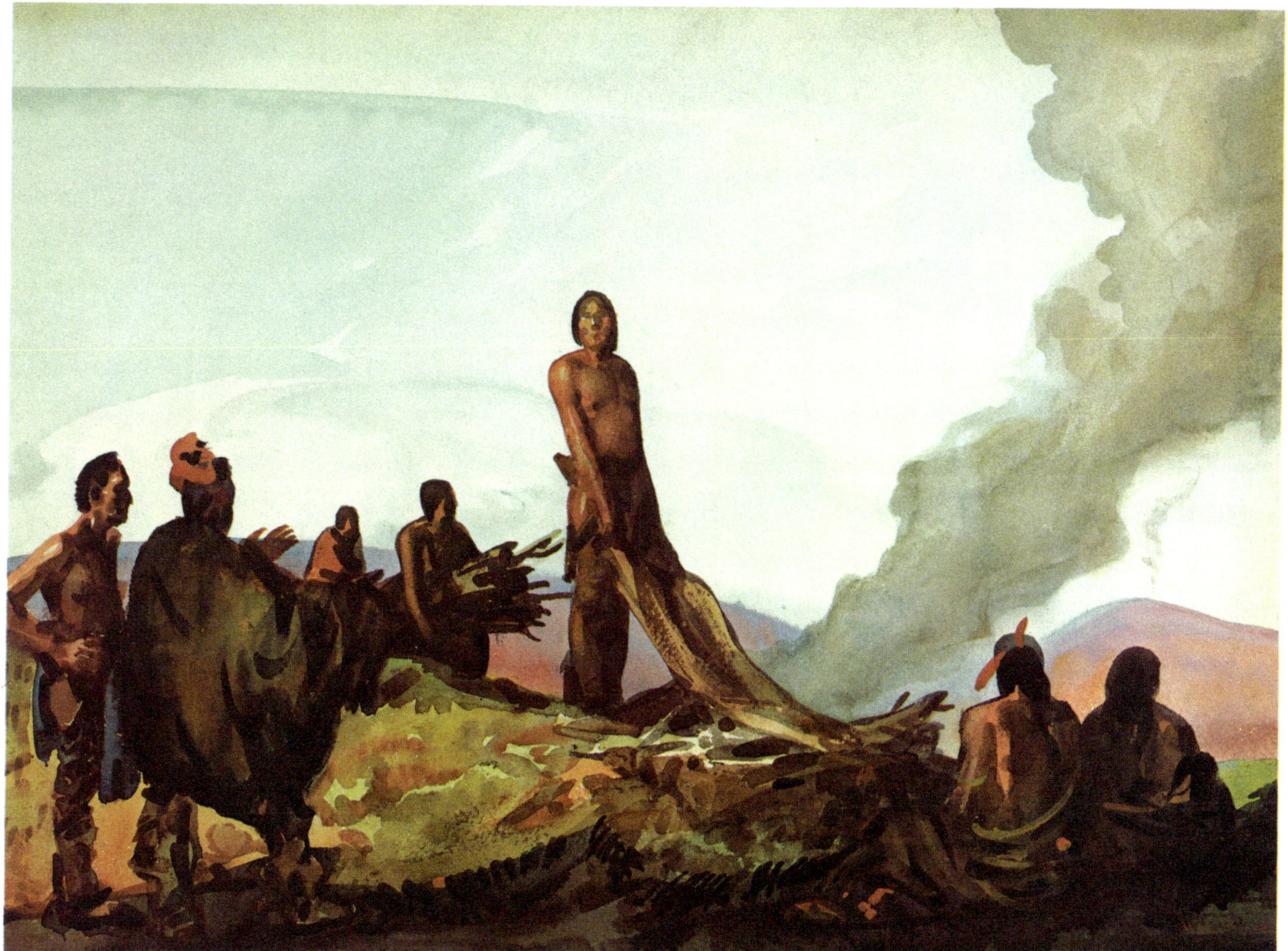

The Smoke Signal

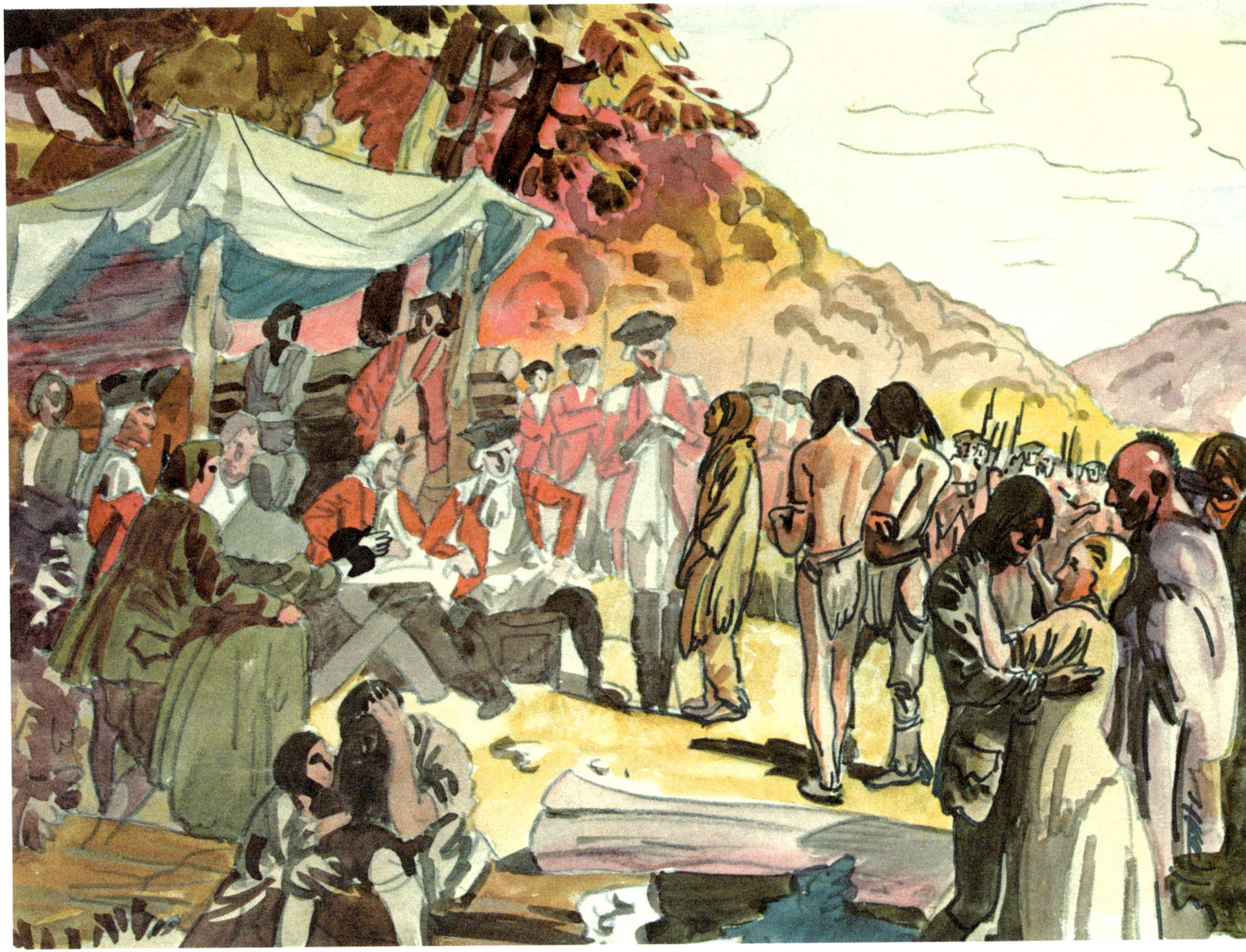

Col. Bouquet's Exchange of Prisoners at Coshocton

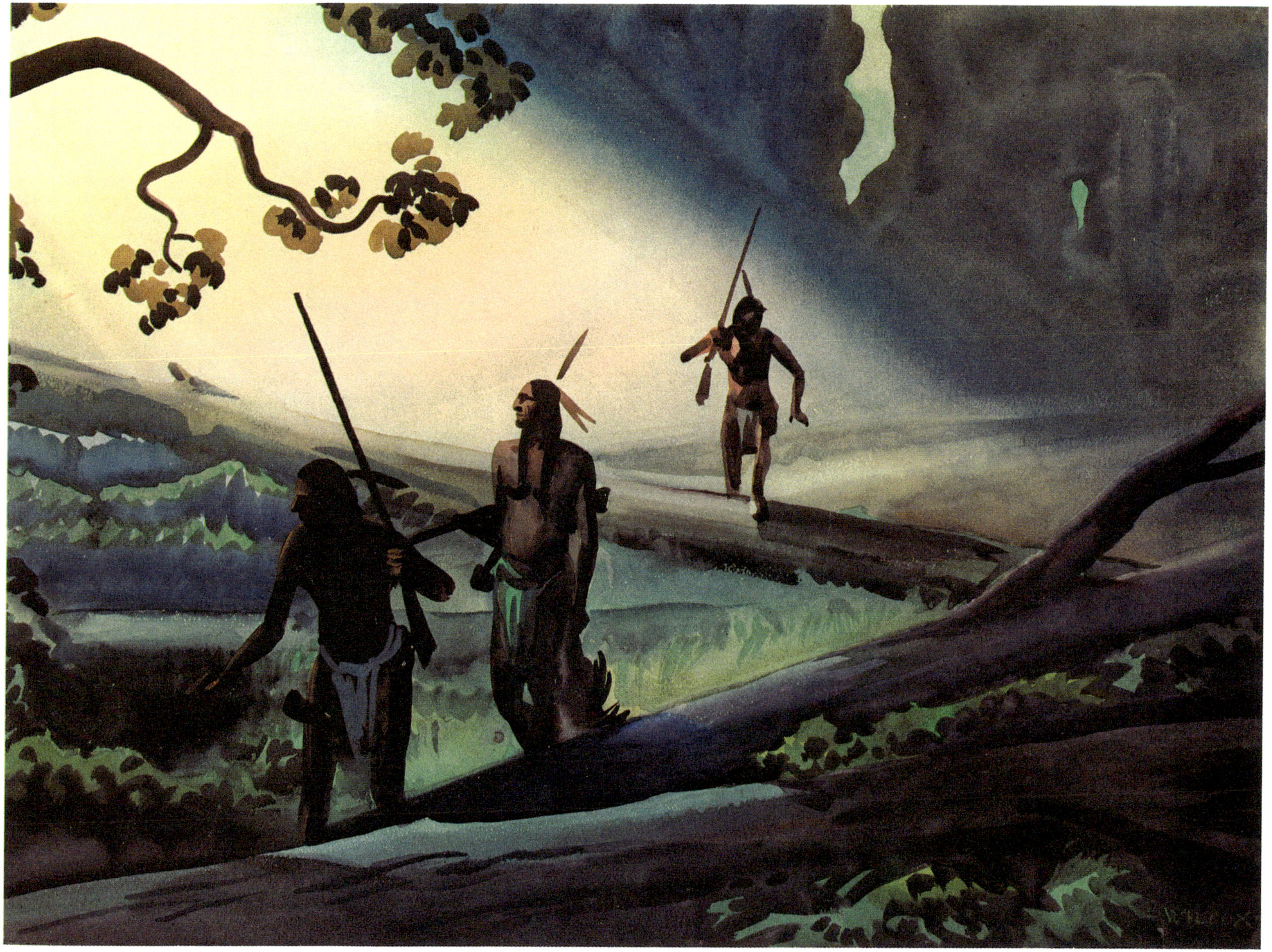

The Standing Stone Trail

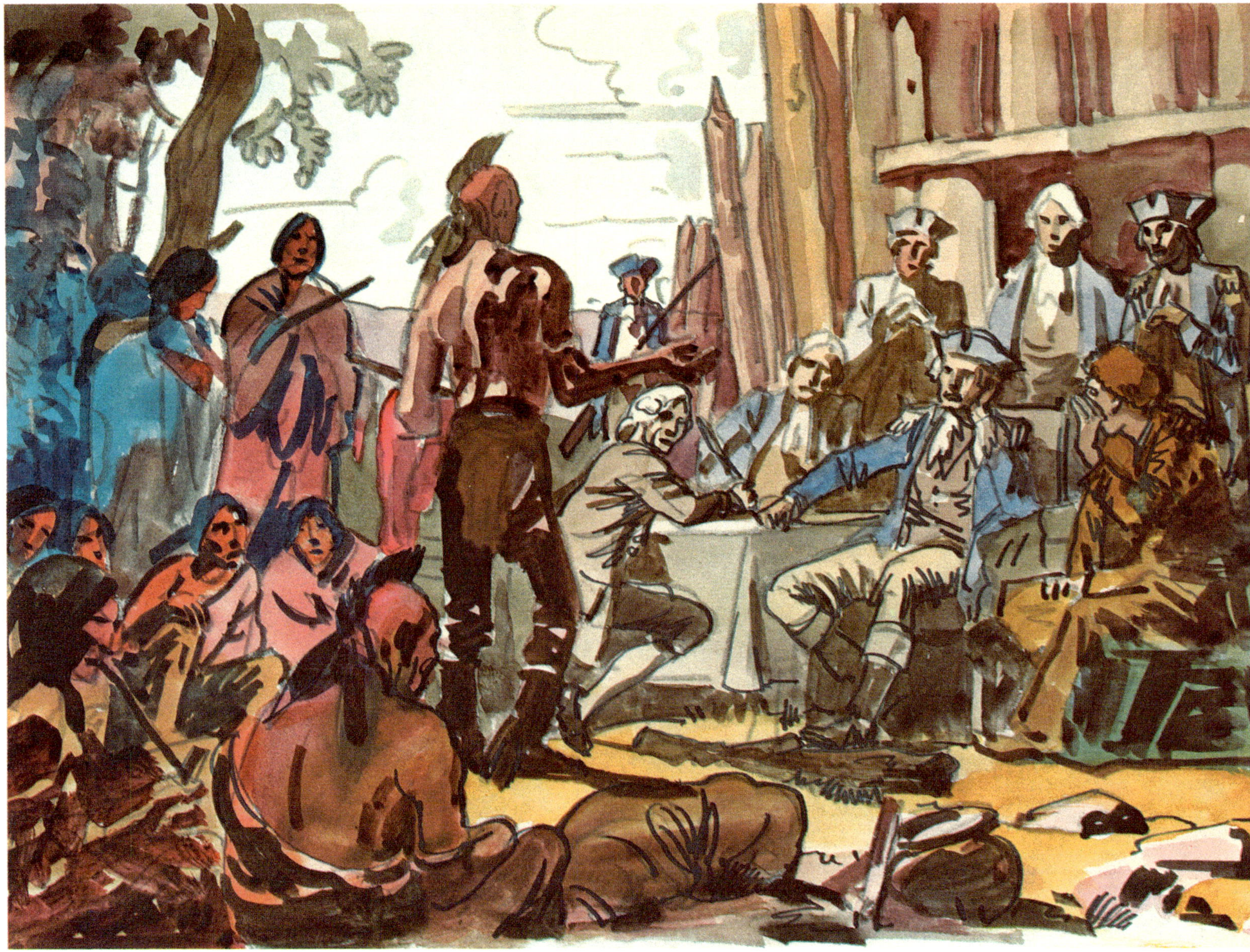

The Treaty of Greenville

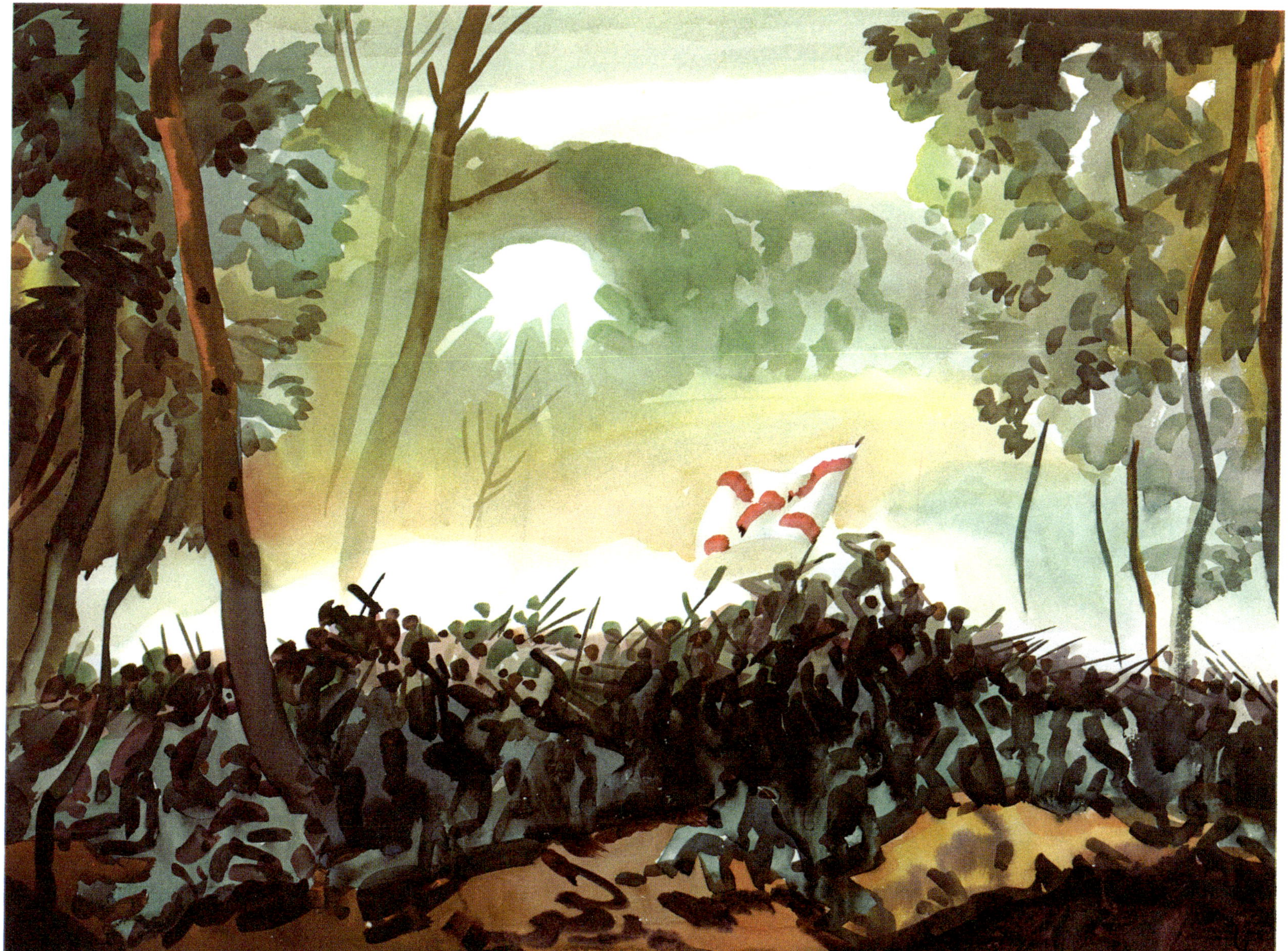

The Battle of the Wilderness

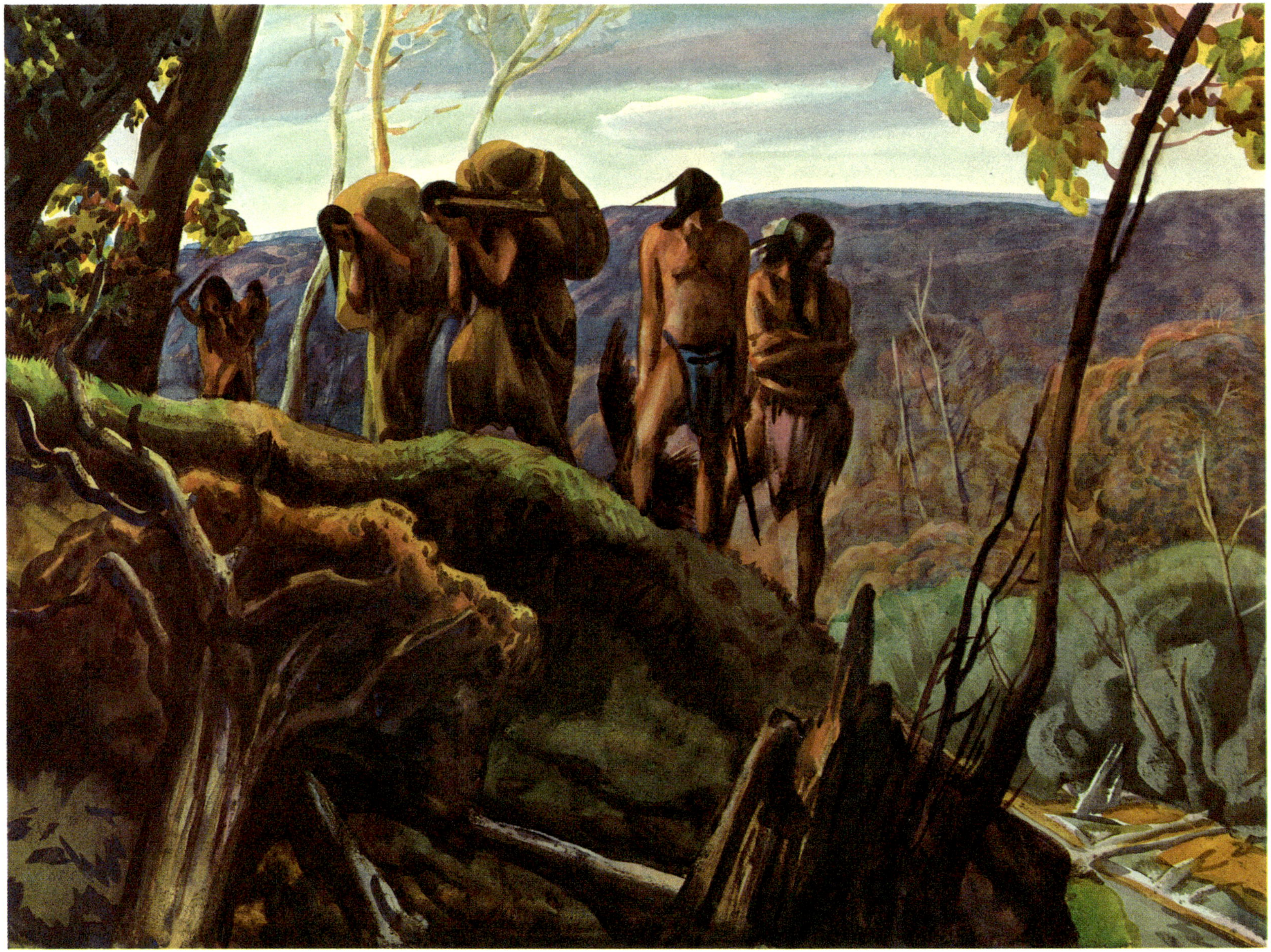

Dispossessed

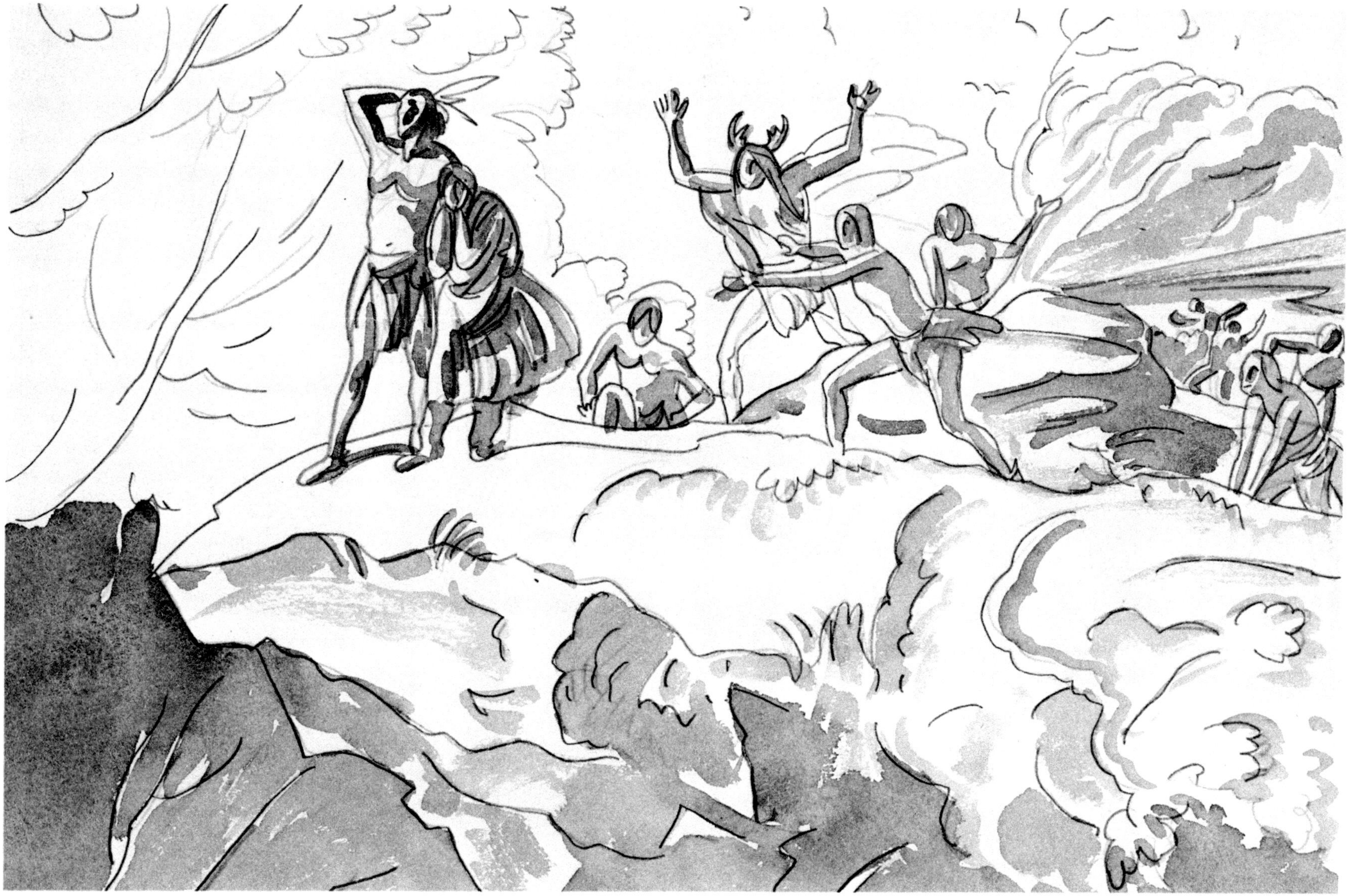

Legendary Sacrifices at the Serpent Mound

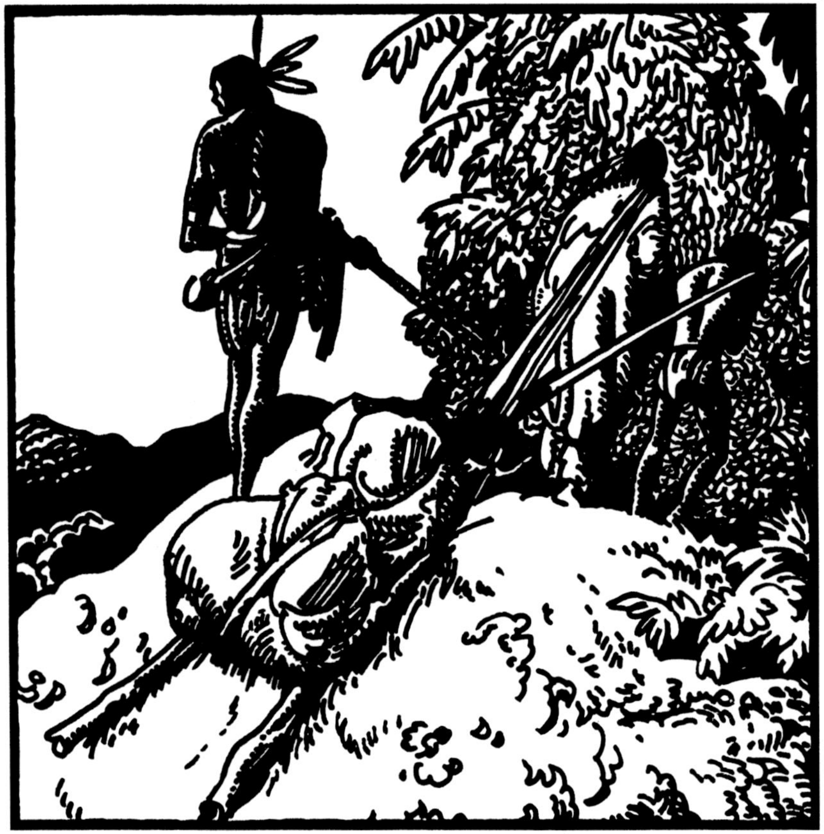

Dispossessed

the shallow headwaters of the Mad River, such as Cæsar Creek. The rail led north over this stream to Cedarville on Massie Creek, to the west of which large and interesting mounds are visible from the highway to Xenia (U.S. 42).

From Cedarville a branch probably led down Massie Creek to Old Town on the Mad River, a few miles due west where the Council Hill and the scene of Kenton's running of the gauntlet are definitely marked.[1]

From Cedarville, the main trail continued northward across the Little Miami at the mouth of Yellow Springs Creek (Ohio 72), and passing up through the modern town, led over the rolling dividing ridge down into the flats four miles below Springfield, to Old Piqua on the western side. Here is the Piqua of Logan, Harmar and Kenton. The town lay sheltered from the winds of winter under the northern bluff, and here, near the modern city, was the haunt of the dreaded enemies of the early Kentucky settlers.

From Piqua the route lay up the west bank of the Mad River, at the foot of the slope to the east, past modern Springfield, and following the steep wall-like bluffs of the wide flats that lead due north, it swung to the west at the mouth of

[1] Simon Kenton, Ohio's greatest border hero, is buried in Oakdale Cemetery in Urbana. He called himself Butler to evade difficulty under a false accusation of murder in Kentucky.

His remarkable escapes, in spite of numerous gauntlets run by him at Chillicothe Old Town, Maccocheek and Upper Sandusky, and his rescue from the stake at Wappatomica, indicate his hardy nature. At a bad curve on the modern road at Old Town there was once written upon the railroad bridge, by some local wag, words said to have been uttered by him before he ran the gauntlet: "Don't hit me too hard, I'm growing old!" The spot at Maccocheek where he also ran the gauntlet is visible just south of the famous Squaw Rock, where a squaw was killed by mistake during a skirmish and her baby was adopted by her slayer.

Nettle Creek, and moving diagonally up the slope, led west through St. Paris (U.S. 36). At this point the trail probably united with the trail that ran past the Maccochee Towns and up the Mad River Valley to join the Scioto Trail at Upper Sandusky, which will be discussed later.

Leading somewhat north of west, the trail climbed the long grade of Nettle Creek and reached the high flat land around St. Paris, and continuing (U.S. 36), left the present highway running to modern Piqua, at about the town of Lena; thence it led over the heads of several watercourses flowing south, to a point where, three miles northeast of Piqua, it descended abruptly a broken steep hillside into the bottoms of the Miami, where to the west, in a southern salient of the river, lay old Pickawillany at the mouth of Loramie Creek.[2]

Here it joined the trail up the Miami and the Loramie path to the portages of the Auglaize and Wabash. The trail in Indian days was undoubtedly a long, straight trace through dense and monotonous woodlands, and the path must have emerged unexpectedly upon the meadow bottoms of the old town and trading post.

The Pickawillany Trail begins at the Scioto and Ohio confluence as a semi-mountainous route, and ends across the prairies of the upper Miami, while in the Mad River region of Old Piqua it traversed a mild, pastoral, and gently rolling region.

[2] Celeron de Bienville, after descending the Ohio and planting at the mouth of its main tributaries a plate of lead, and nailing to a prominent tree a tablet of tin in the name of the French King, returned to Montreal by way of the Miami and St. Mary's Rivers to Fort Wayne and then via the Maumee and the Lakes. This was on account of low water in the Auglaize. He was thus able to visit Pickawillany, where he attempted to win over La Demoiselle or "Old Britain" to the cause of France against English influence in Ohio.

The Wappatomica Trail

The league formed by the Shawnees and Miamis with the Wyandots of the north, for defence of the Ohio Country, required a line of communication between the Mad River and Miami towns and the towns of the Sandusky region. It was over this route that many captives from Crawford's defeat were led to Wappatomica and Maccacheek.

The region of its northern extremity, the Sandusky Plains, is flat, but beautiful on account of the rich alluvial soil, which shows black amid the green of the crops, and which has caused to grow those dense woodlands which stand out in angular, blocky masses on the sky line.

The plain in Crawford's day was a waving prairie over which masses of birds flew like clouds, and upon the surface of which a few isolated "islands" of large tree clusters grew like the one that sheltered his beleaguered army. The boundaries of this region are clearly determinable today by the sudden change of color in the soil and the gentle but definite rise of the land, from flat to rolling, as the trail leads southward.

The trail led southwest from the Sandusky River opposite the Old Wyandot Town at a point where the present highway from Little Sandusky turns north to enter modern Upper Sandusky, about two miles south of the Court House (Ohio 67).

The trail almost immediately strikes a higher level; once it entered the gloom of the forest that surrounded the plains and defined their boundaries in a remarkable manner in early days. It crossed the Tymochtee at Marseilles on the present highway (Ohio 67) where today a byroad still leads southwest down rolling and descending ground to the vicinity of Pfeiffer, on the willow-grown banks of the Scioto. Here at the trail crossing, where the small Upper Scioto winds among low, muddy banks, Dr. Knight, the friend of Crawford, made his fortunate escape from his captors after the Sandusky defeat.

The modern byroads in this region permit an approximate tracing of the route over the flat, high valley of the Scioto until the land rises to Big Springs at the head of the Mad River Valley. Here the rocky ridge of the Bellefontaine uplift is met. The trail follows the improved road through Rushsylvania and down the ridge to the sudden, surprising outlook over Zanesfield, the home of Izaac Zane and his Indian wife, Myeerah, in the basin of the rocky upper Mad River.

Below Zanesfield the trail follows the lower slopes of the high western ridge, and where the valley narrows, about two and a half miles below, there projects from the western ridge a high promontory where stood Wappatomica. Around the stone shaft which marks the point, the ground still shows the circular depressed track made by Shawnee feet. Here Kenton was tied to be burned but was saved; others less fortunate died in sufficient numbers for the ground to tell the tale.[1]

The trail is well marked in this region by the well designed

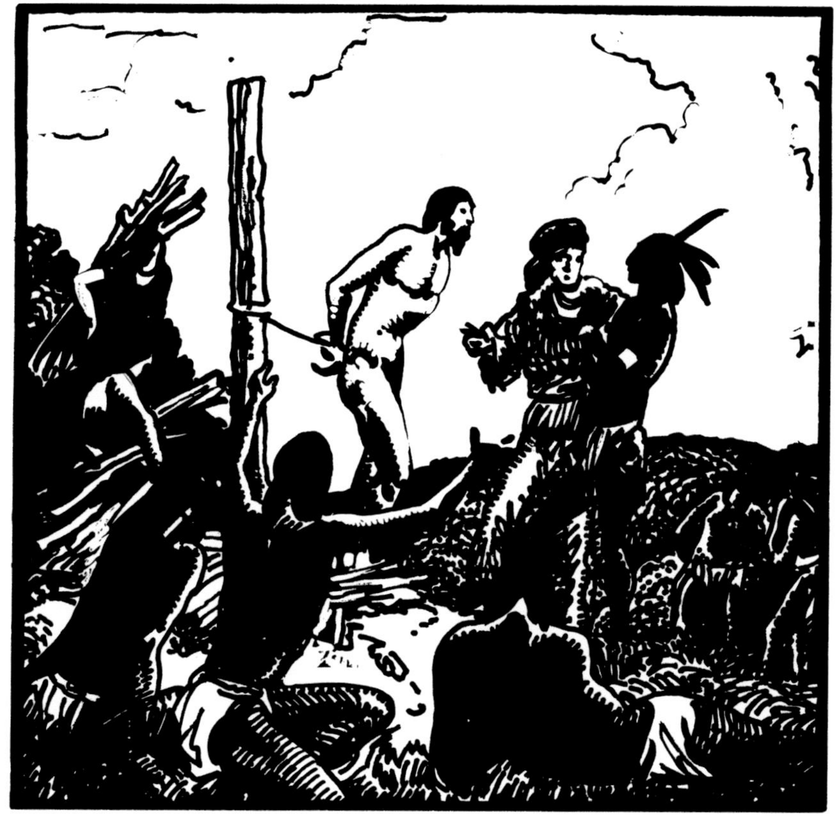

The Intercession

[1] During Logan's campaign in the Mad River Valley, in 1786, there were two towns destroyed; Wappatomica on the west bank and another northeast across the valley where lived the chief. An English blockhouse at modern Zanesfield was also burned. It was at Zanesfield that Zane later lived with his Indian princess for a wife. Logan on his campaign adopted an Indian youth called Spemica Lawba, or High Horn. The boy was educated by him and took his name, which is not to be confused with that of Logan, the Mingo. He fought in 1812 and was killed by British Indians on the Maumee.

guideposts that mark the Revolutionary Trails. It now leads across the narrow bottom above the wide flats around West Liberty, and taking to the eastern ridge, follows it southward, soon to drop into the beautiful little Macochee Valley past the Piatt Castle. It then led down this valley on the well beaten roads of this popular region to the other Piatt Castle, Castle Mackacheek, where the famous owner collected so much in the way of Indian relics. On the hill to the north appears Squaw Rock, where an Indian tragedy occurred in the days of frontier warfare, and at the foot of the hill, leading southward across the flats, is the mile-long gauntlet through the Indian camp at the mouth of the Creek, which was one of many that Kenton was forced to run.

Two miles eastward on the hill lie the Ohio Caverns, which, being unknown to the Indian, we will pass by, but from the hill there is a wonderful vista east and north over the deep but streamless valley. At the head of the valley five miles southeastward lies Mingo, once another Indian town.

The trail from Maccochee now runs southwest along the creek in the Mad River bottoms, and following the river southward, passes Urbana, the home of Kenton, where at the mouth of Nettle Creek it connects with the trail to Pickawillany from the mouth of the Scioto.

This trail is today as satisfactory to the student of historic lore as is the region of the Tuscarawas. It teems with stories of human interest and tales of hardship, romance and personal heroism that are almost legendary.

The Wappatomica Trail may be considered as connecting also with the Licking River of Kentucky. Retracing the route of the Pickawillany Trail back to Piqua below Springfield, it led on down the west bank of the Miami to Dayton, where it joined the Miami Trail to the site of modern Cincinnati, traversing thus the short distance between Dayton and Springfield to make the connection. This was the Revolutionary Trail from the Licking to Wappatomica.

The Miami Trail

Commencing at the water front of modern Cincinnati, the Miami Trail led out between Eden Park and the city, and passing over the hills east of Mill Creek, continued northeastward to Sharonville (U.S. 42) where it moved up the north side of Sharon Creek and over the heights through Mason and over Turtle Creek to Lebanon. Here it continued northwards. On the right five miles away lies the deep cut of the Little Miami (I 71).

As the valley receded on the right, a high plateau was crossed, the course continuing north until Holes Creek was met and the trail swerved eastward around the head and then dipped down into the flats east of Dayton. Crossing the flats of the Mad River, the path continued on the heights north of the city, keeping the Miami on its left, and descended into the flats northeast of Tippecanoe City (I 75); thence, crossing the river, it passed through Troy, and followed the west bank to modern Piqua (I 75). Traversing the site of that town, it soon passed the outlet of Loramie Creek (Ohio 66) across from which, on the flats in a southern salient of the Miami, stands the old Indian Agency of Sir John Johnson; opposite which but nearer at hand is the Johnson Burial Ground.

This was the Pickawillany of history, and here came Christopher Gist in 1750, when the French controlled the trade; it was also visited by the Englishman, Bird, in 1780, by Harmar in 1790, and by Wayne in 1794. From here a trail led eastward to the Shawnee towns, and one led northwest up Loramie to Loramie's store or trading post, and on past Celina to the St. Marys River.

Before discussing the western extension, which was properly part of it, we should consider the nature of the district. Undoubtedly the town of Pickawillany was easier of approach than many eastern points. The river was reported as treacherous, but there are no hills, properly speaking, in the Miami country and the trails are level when on the upper benches. Also, the wide meadows must have afforded natural forage for the pack trains so necessary for military expeditions. This remote point was known long before many places to the eastward. The Miami Valley does not give warning of its nearness, but one comes upon it suddenly in the flat plateau. Modern dikes, carried far up into the state, suggest the floods that may have rendered it so dangerous to the early explorers.

From Pickawillany, the Loramie trace led west onto the plateau, and turning north, led across the stream at Newport (Ohio 66), continuing to Fort Loramie at the west end of the modern reservoir.[1] This district today resembles Holland or northern Germany, with the spires of Minster clearly visible to the north and the canals around the outlet. There is little to suggest the Indian, but in his day it must have been a semi-wooded and marshy prairie.

[1] Loramie's Station was a trading post occupied by the English about 1750-51 and was then known as Pickawillany. In 1752 it was attacked by a French and Indian force. It later became Loramie's Station. In 1782 it was destroyed by General George Rogers Clark. In 1794 General Wayne built a fort here called Fort Loramie. It is an important point in the Greenville Treaty Line.

Pierre Loramie established his trading post, at the head of the creek bearing his name, 17 years after the sack of Pickawillany. He was highly esteemed by the Indians of the district, who remained loyal to his cause.

The sacking of Pickawillany by the French under Charles Langlade brought about the death of "Old Britain," the chief who was loyal to the English cause in the French and Indian War. This expedition started from Michilimackinac and arrived via the lakes and the Maumee and Auglaize Rivers.

The trail led northwest across the flat marshes to Celina (U.S. 127) (Ohio 32) at the foot of the modern St. Marys Lake or Grand Reservoir which is surprisingly large, but gives no warning of its nearness in the landscape. Crossing the outlet of the lake which enters the Wabash, it continued northwest to strike the lower St. Marys River in Indiana. (U.S. 33, 27.)

The territory between St. Marys and Loramie is the natural portage ground of the region. The streams meander slowly like canals and lead away from the district into the Auglaize, St. Marys, and Miami, that is, practically in every direction. Although there is so little to indicate it, it was a natural focal point for aboriginal travel by canoe or trail.

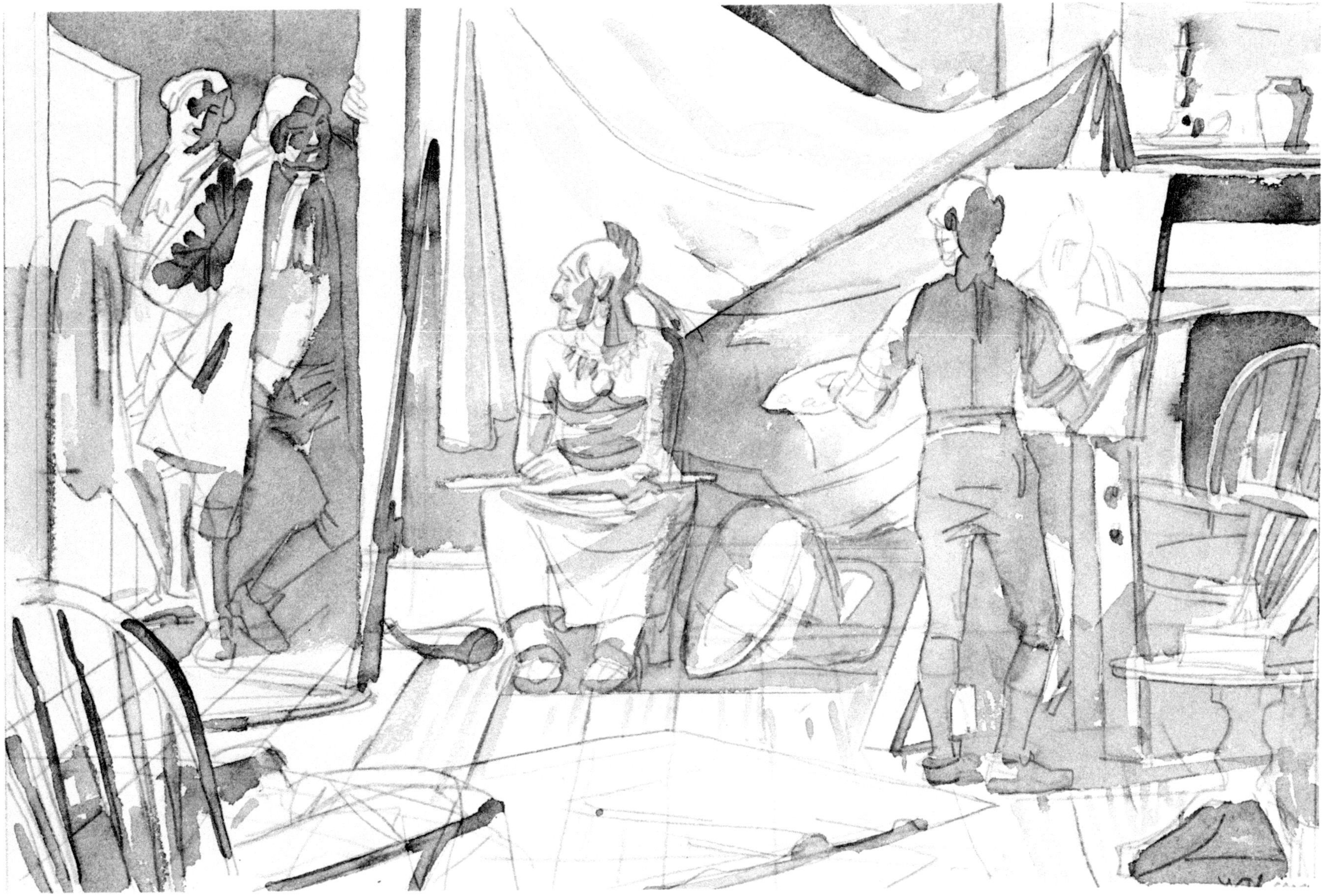

Little Turtle Has His Portrait Painted

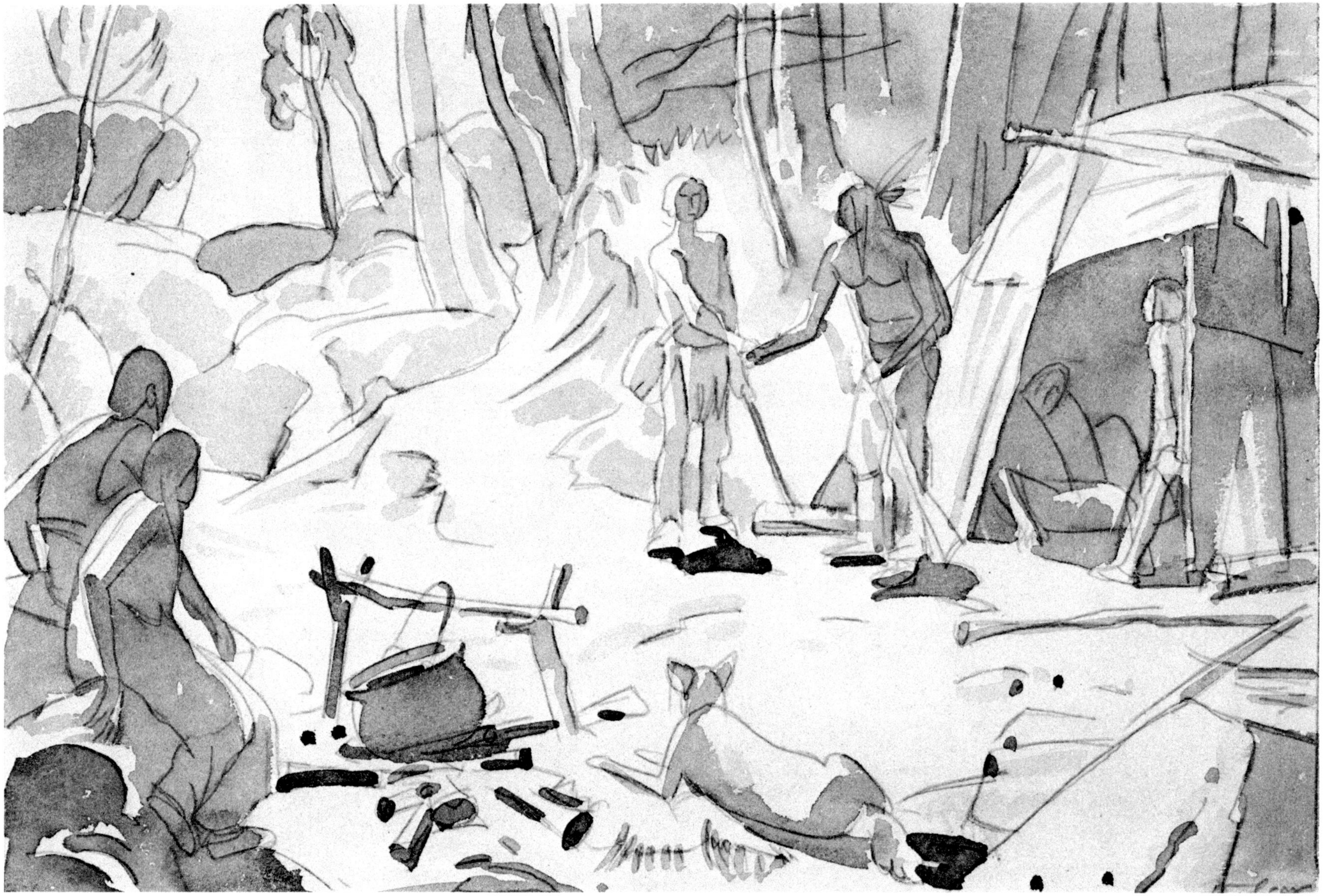

William Wells Takes Leave of His Foster Father, Little Turtle

The Wabash Trail

Before Ohio was a definitely bounded territory, the Miamis and other tribes wandered over the western area of Ohio and the Indiana country.

Little Turtle controlled the Wabash, and since that river rises in our territory, it was natural that a trail should lead out from Kentucky via the Licking, and to the headwaters of the northern and western waters. The Licking, opposite modern Cincinnati, was too far upstream to join the Miami, so the approach to Indiana lay up Mill Creek and northwest over the Miami Basin.

This is the route traversed in part by St. Clair, Wayne and others in their struggles with the retreating red men.

This trail led up the narrow valley of Mill Creek and followed the bend at Cumminsville; at Rockland it took the left-hand side, and mounting the hill (Ohio 4) led northwest to Hamilton, crossing the Miami at that place.[1] From Hamilton it led north, and crossing the Four Mile Creek at its mouth, followed through to Seven Mile (U.S. 127) northwest up the west side of that stream and through Eaton to its headwaters. This is an unusual stretch of trail in that it continues so far along the same stream without changing direction. The track must have been, however, much broken by sharp ravines unless the tracks were held fairly far from the river (U.S. 127). The path seems to have swerved well to the westward south of Eaton.[1]

[1] Fort Hamilton was built by General Arthur St. Clair in 1791 as a depot for supplies in his campaign against the western tribes. It stood on the east bank of the Miami at the east end of the bridge to Rossville at Hamilton. Fort Jefferson was an advanced depot in the village of Fort Jefferson, six miles south of Greenville.

[2] One mile west of Eaton is the site of Fort St. Clair. This fort was built on

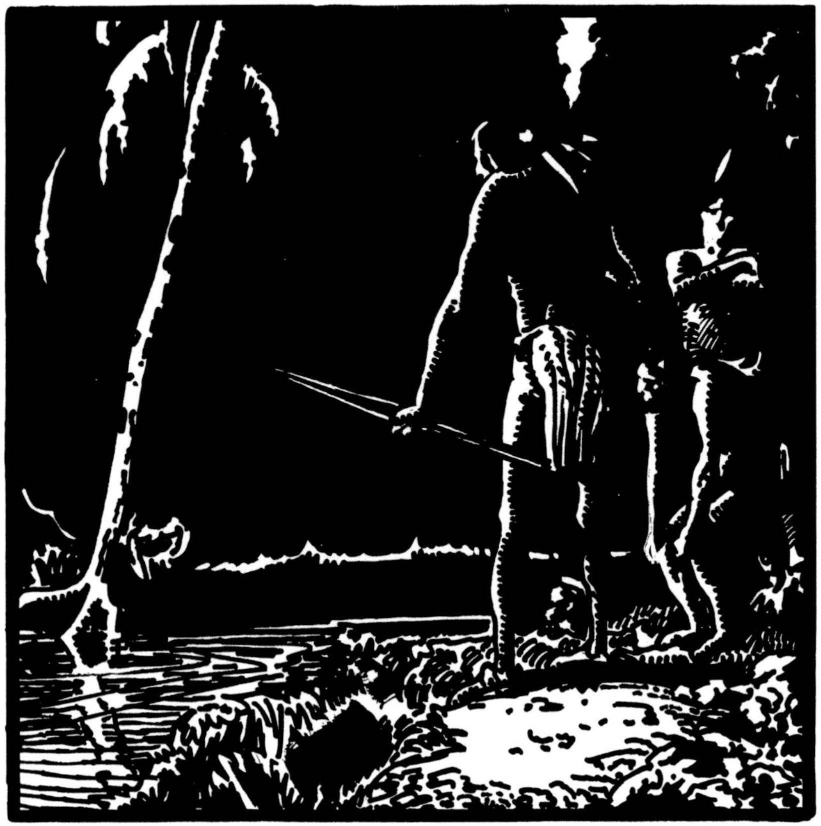

The Marksman

The course from Eaton was due north over headwaters leading southeast into the Miami Basin (U.S. 127) to a point about seven miles south of Greenville, where it bent to the westward into the Prairie outlet southwest of that town. Here, above a somewhat broken, marshy section to the west, where sand pits are now, stood Fort Jefferson. The records of St. Clair indicate that on this route he had some difficulty with swampy ground, and it appears that he was unable to bear west until the head of the outlet to the Prairies, the Whitewater River, was rounded.

The land along the Indiana line slopes perceptibly eastward in a long even grade, forcing the waters to settle in a trough parallel to the State line. The bottom of this trough, in the form of Mud Creek, led into the Greenville Creek just west of the town, and the attempt to cross the marshy land was apparently not made by the trail until Greenville Creek was passed. The probabilities are that the Indian trail did not swing west to Fort Jefferson, but continued directly to Greenville (U.S. 127).[2]

From Greenville, with its very broad, shallow valley and alluvial soil, the trail led northwest (Ohio 49) to Fort Recovery, the land maintaining at first its eastward slant into the Stillwater, but at Lightsville crossing the low divide and drifting down the gradual slope to the Wabash at Fort Recovery. Then it continued, after one mile down the river, into Indiana.

St. Clair's march against the northwestern Indians, and here was fought a sharp skirmish by part of his forces against savages under Little Turtle, whose activities centered about the site of modern Fort Wayne, Indiana.

[3] Forts Hamilton and Greenville were the most important posts on the route of St. Clair and Wayne, and grew into important towns in consequence.

Looking at the territory today, it is hard to realize the difficulties met by St. Clair in 1791, but without artificial drainage the heavy forest must have made it a flat, wet, and dark jungle where the sluggish watercourses gave little aid in direction. Wayne in 1794 had profited by the experience of his unhappy predecessor.

The Auglaize Trails

Near Fort Loramie the water courses of the prairie seem entirely motionless, but five miles to the north is visible the northward flow of the tributaries of the St. Marys River.[1]

The trail to the Maumee by way of the Auglaize led due north from the Fort through Minster (Ohio 66). Three miles beyond at New Bremen, it turned northeast around the head of St. Marys Lake, and passing through the present town, led to where the river bent to the west seven or eight miles beyond. It then ran over a low dividing ridge northeastward to where, at Spencerville, the Auglaize approached on the right (Ohio 66).

The path now followed the low-banked stream as it meandered with a markedly serpentine motion in the level country to where, about four miles beyond Delphos (U. S. 30) (Ohio 66), it reached the site of Fort Jennings (Ohio 190) at a sharp bend.[2] Continuing approximately parallel to the present highway, which has kept several miles to the west, it soon converged south of Oakwood and arrived at Charloe, the old Indian town; thence following the west bank, it continued into Defiance and its confluence with the Maumee (Ohio 66).[3]

[1] Pierre Loramie was a Canadian Frenchman who had established a trading post where the reservoir and stream bearing his name are seen today. This lay at the headwaters of the Miami, south of the portage to the Auglaize and St. Mary's.

His influence with the Indians led General Clark to destroy his station on his Miami Campaign in 1782. General Wayne built Fort Loramie here in 1794.

[2] Fort Jennings, or Fort Amanda, was built at the Auglaize Indian towns during Wayne's Campaign in 1812.

[3] Fort Defiance was built by General Wayne, in the heart of an ancient Indian territory and on the site of the Ta-en-da-wie of the Wyandots.

Fort Winchester was built in the War of 1812, one hundred yards south of old Fort Defiance, which was then probably in ruins. It was built to sustain the

Along this route are many points of interest going back to the War of 1812, and also to Wayne in 1794 and Bird in 1780, not to mention its associations with the French voyageurs at an early date. The route leads through perhaps the least picturesque or varied landscape in the state, so that a real interest in the historical associations is necessary to appreciate it. However, there are plenty of river scenes of pastoral beauty.

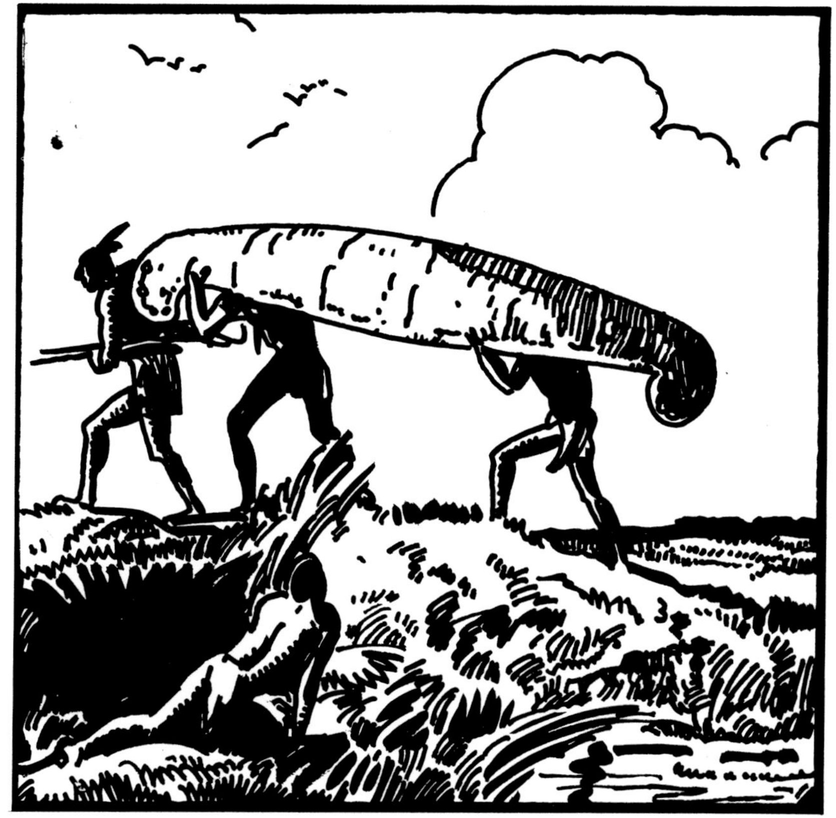

The Prairie Portage

advance of the American troops who met defeat at the Battle of the Raisin River, between Toledo and Detroit.

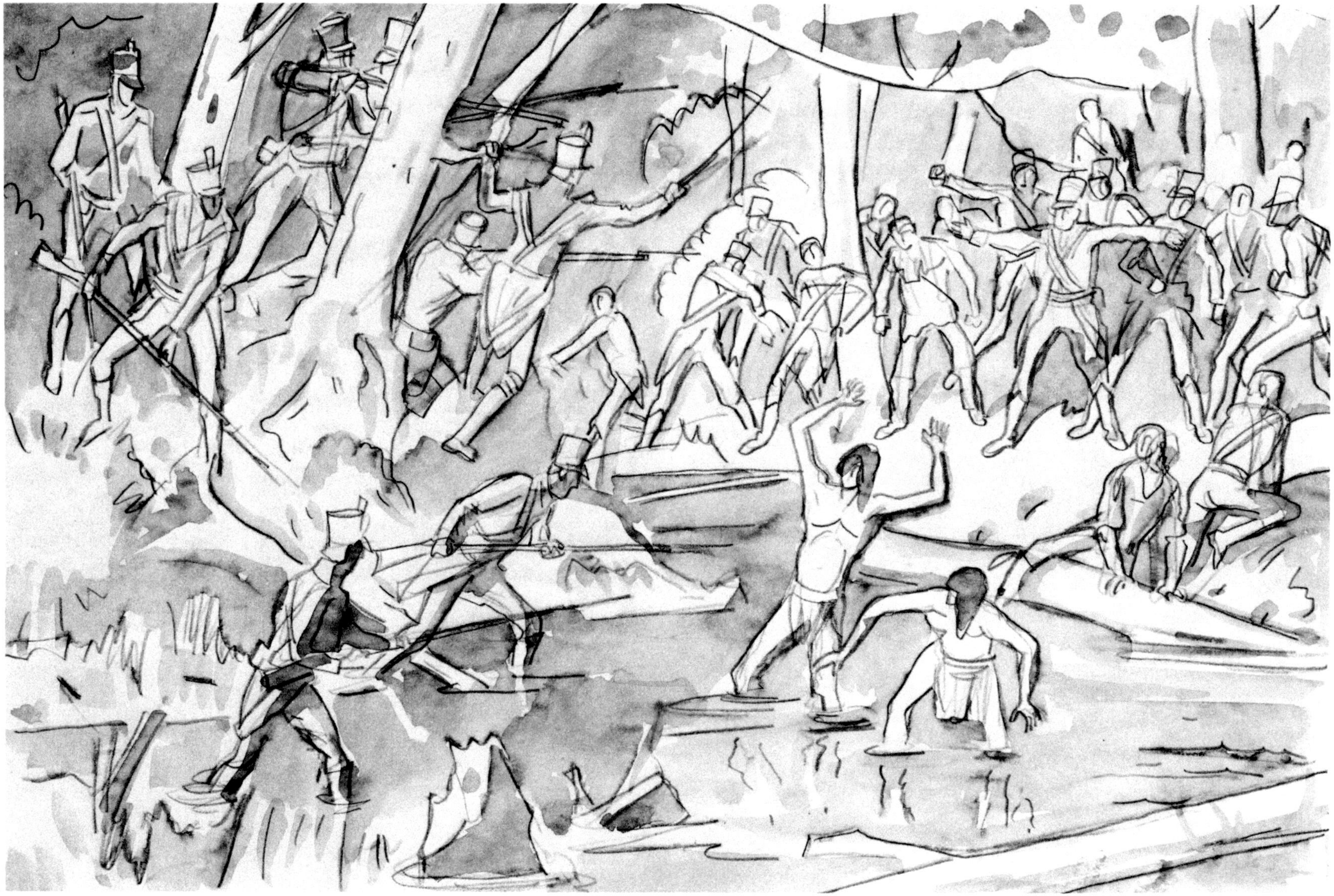

The Black Swamp Trail

Routes across the "Black Swamp" seem to indicate that many highways grew at an early day out of the meandering paths of the Indian through the damp, grassy or boggy land.[1] The surveyed roads, conforming to the section boundaries, are cut diagonally by the longer highways that suggest the old trails. Certain main streets or four-corners give credence to this idea.

The confederation of Indian tribes centering around Defiance and Fort Wayne undoubtedly utilized a route from the mouth of the Auglaize to the Sandusky region.

Evidences of a trail are traceable from Defiance southeastward. This trail led southeast through Ayersville and Pleasant Bend, over the head of the Turkey Foot to Leipsic, and through its winding main street (Ohio 113) to the southeast and the Blanchard River; it followed the north bank (U.S.224) (Ohio 17) to Findlay, where it probably crossed the river, and tracing the general course of the Big Four Railroad, led to Carey (U.S.23) (Ohio 568); from there it probably ran down Spring Run to Old Tymochtee, and south along the Sandusky to Indian Mill and the springs at present Upper Sandusky. A shorter route would have been from Carey, through Crawford, on the line of the Hocking Valley Railroad. This would seem probable in view of the fact that Crawford, according to record, was led to that place by a trail.

This trail could not have been other than a desolate route in Indian days, except in the pleasant, rolling Tymochtee

[1] When the Moravian Indians were first led to Detroit from Wyandot Old Town, Heckewelder mentions the very swampy ground at the head of the lake and the "deep cracks" that served for rivers. This region is described as barren, bleak, and having prairies miles in length.

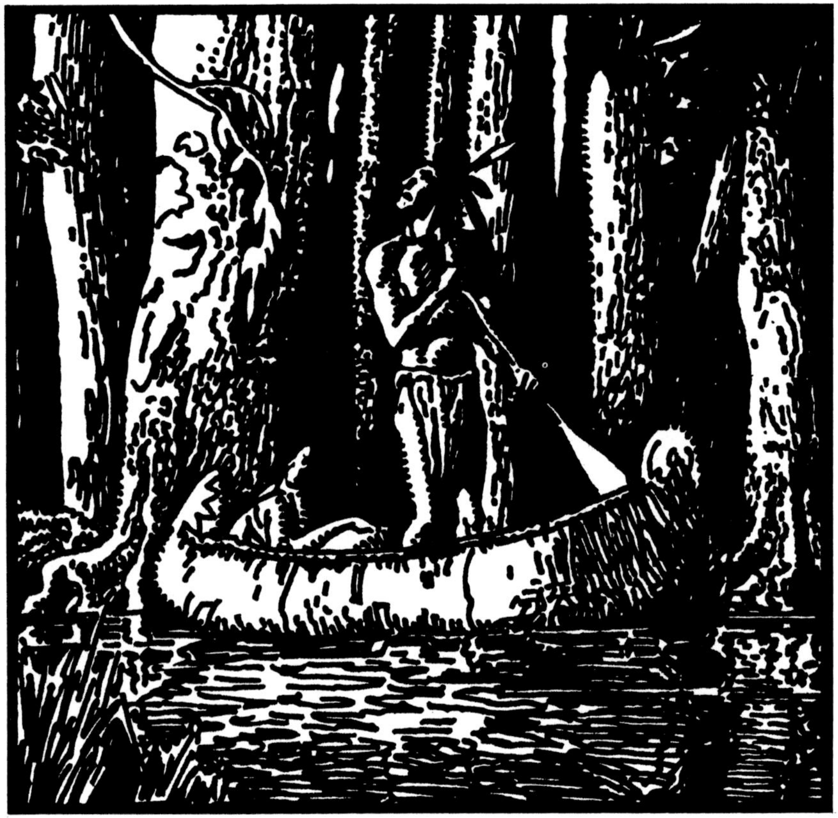

Forest Voices

Creek section where the low, broken hills bounding the wide Sandusky Plains on the west are not uninteresting.

The Maumee Trail

Starting from the Great Lake Trail, at the present site of Toledo (U.S. 24), the route from Detroit to the French and Indian settlements in Indiana led along the first ridge of the west bank of the Maumee. Its course was through the old post at Maumee City,[1] through the battlefield of Fallen Timbers to the south with its Turkey Foot Rock,[2] past the rapids and southwest to Waterville Station Island and Roche de Bout. Here was Fort Deposit.[3] It continued to follow the north bank until it crossed at Grand Rapids. This trail beside its rapid river and the vast amount of black timber which grew here, must have suggested Canada and the north even more than it does today. The river was choked with water-worn tree trunks cast on the shallows.

Following the southern bank, the trail continued westward to some small islands, where it crossed (U. S. 24) as it did also at the site of Napoleon. Thence it continued southward four

[1] Fort Miami, the oldest fort in Ohio, was built by order of Frontenac in 1680. It was rebuilt by the English in 1785 and held until the Indian Treaty of 1795. It was reoccupied in 1812, and after the close of that war became an American trading post.

Fort Miami lay north of the present Maumee City at a bend of the river. It served as an outpost of British authority at Detroit. Opposite Maumee City stands Fort Meigs, built by the Americans in 1812; just above are the rapids, west of which was fought the Battle of Fallen Timbers, where General Wayne broke the Indian power in Ohio under the eyes of the British Fort.

[2] Turkey Foot Rock, on the battlefield of Fallen Timbers, bears Indian petroglyphs suggesting turkey tracks. This type of sculpture representing the tracks of animals is common in Ohio.

[3] Fort Deposit suggests by its name its purpose, which was to preserve supplies in Wayne's Campaign.

There is a legend that an Indian, angry with his squaw because she had not saved his child from falling from the Roche de Bout, dared to cast her over. Her relatives retaliated in kind, and the feud continued until many were drowned. This incident is borne out by the discovery of many burials at this point.

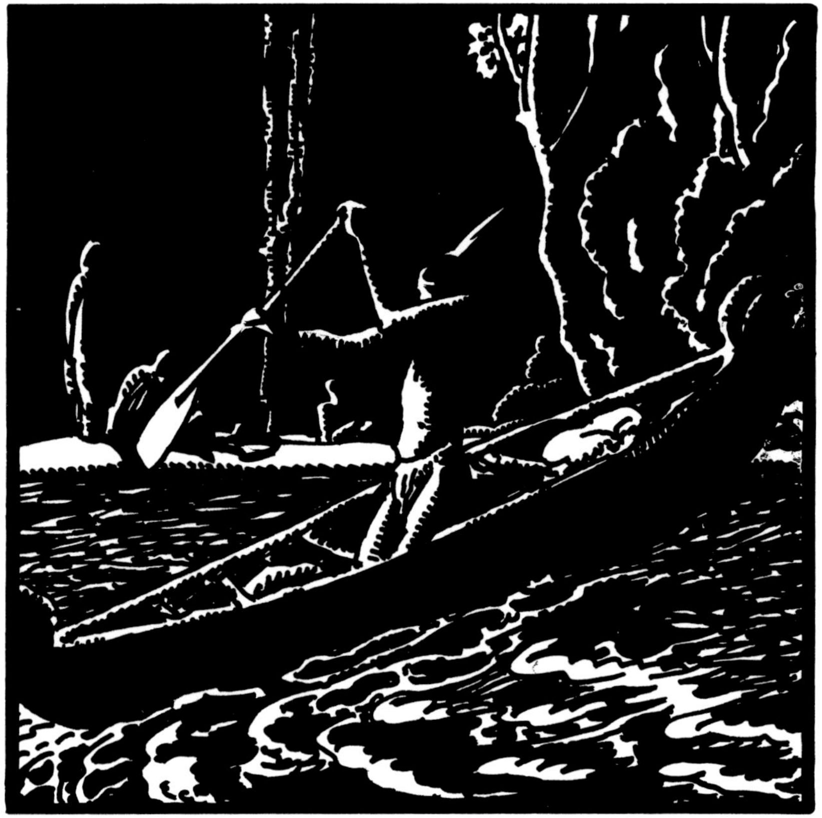

Miami of the Lakes

miles and turned southwest at the bend of the island named after Girty, the frontier renegade.[4] Continuing southwest and then west it passed through Independence, and old Ottawa village, and crossed the river at Defiance where it met the trail from Pickawillany and from the Scioto. Westward it followed the course of the B. & O. Railroad along the south shore of the Maumee to "The Bend," where it probably crossed to follow the northern salients of the river, over the state line, to the Turtle's village at Fort Wayne and beyond (U.S. 24).

[4] There were four Girty brothers: Thomas, George, James and Simon, of whom Simon was the most notorious. James was adopted by the Shawnees, George by the Delawares, and Simon by the Senecas or Mingos. George Girty lived five miles above Napoleon at Girty's Point, opposite an island where he is said to have hidden when out of favor. He was an Indian trader.

The particularly vindictive Simon Girty was active against his former allies at the siege of Fort Henry or Wheeling, at Bryant's Station in Kentucky, at St. Clair's defeat, at the attack on Colerain, and at Crawford's defeat. It is said that he was inactive only at Fallen Timbers. Much has been said of the influence of McKee and Elliott over these men, when young, in eastern Ohio.

After the capture of Hamilton by Clark at Vincennes, Simon Girty was engaged to take the scalp of Zeisberger. This plot was revealed to Heckewelder by Alexander McIntosh, the trader of Upper Sandusky. This was an attempt to destroy the imagined activity of the Moravian Delawares against their savage brethren and their Wyandot neighbors. Girty was probably actuated only by brutality, and McIntosh seems to have realized this. Pipe succeeded in causing a division among the Delawares, but on account of White Eyes, did not arouse prejudice against the missionaries.

An instance of Girty's cruelty is shown by his insistence upon the Sandusky Moravian Indians being driven like cattle to Detroit on their second pilgrimage there to the Commandant. They were, however, conducted by boat from Fremont.

Many of the Moravian Delawares, after their release at Detroit, accepted the invitation of their relatives on the Wabash to live there. This was a ruse to break the influence of the missionaries. They were deceived by the Medicine Man called the Prophet and brother of Tecumseh. He had burned Tatapachkse or Grand Glaize King as a witch, and also Joshua, the Moravian, and others of the congregation.

This trail was the theatre for the heroic and efficient deeds of "Mad Anthony" Wayne. The battle of Fallen Timbers was the only white man's victory in Ohio. The lower course of the river is impressive, and the route is full of interest and completely recognizable.

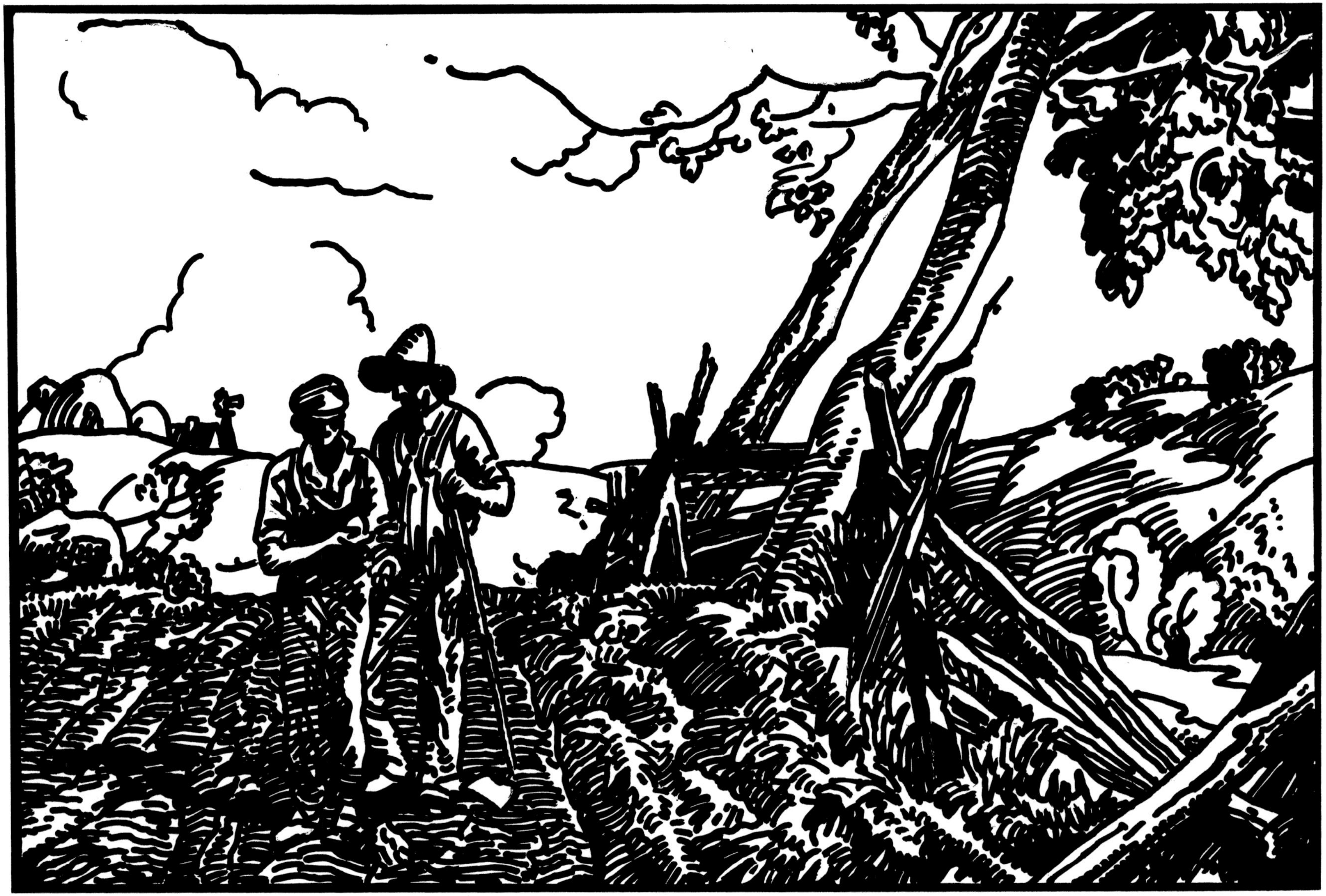

Finding the Arrowhead

In Conclusion

In concluding this description and outline of the Indian Trails of Ohio, it might be said that it is quite possible to glean a good idea of them from the present highways and improved roads. In some districts, even where routes are not numbered, they conform definitely to the trails, with the result that in many localities the Indian ways can be followed on their approximate paths.

The road map gives no idea whatever of the terrain to be crossed. Many considerable streams are not indicated, so that frequently, without any previous study, one may encounter a landscape that is a most pleasant surprise. The white spots on the road map are usually places where it is well to use caution in venturing too boldly, but every year the regions they represent are being cut up by new roads and additional portions of the trails may be followed.

It is pleasant, either before or after an exploring trip, to study the topographical charts. Many a jaunt may thus be preserved in memory that would otherwise be forgotten, and the relative positions of various points may be realized almost as though the journey had been taken by aeroplane; but no trip by air can instill in one an enthusiasm for Indian Trails. One of the most entertaining features of this kind of exploration lies in the fact that almost every denizen of a district, if approached properly, is glad to divulge information on local history and geography. Much can be learned in this way, and the byroads induce a mood for this study. It is surprising to discover how many devotees of Indian lore there are, from the youthful flint collector and amateur archæologist to the peruser of histories and the dealer in antiques

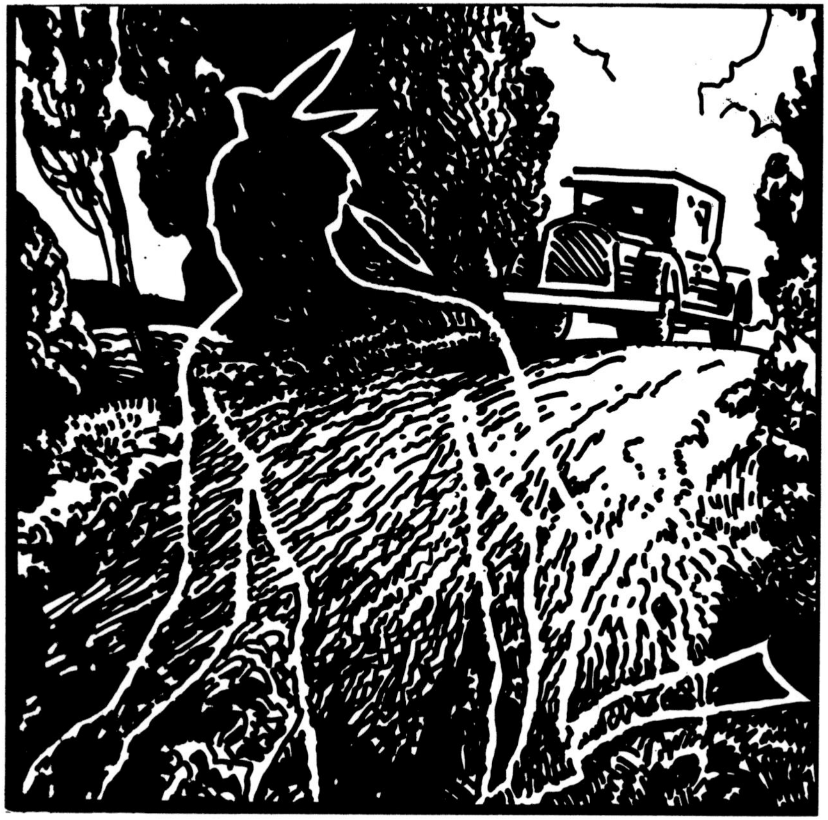

The Spirit of the Red Man

with a real interest in his stock. Many are they who might, a few years ago, have told us much that now will be forever lost.

On the byroad the best vistas of the country are to be seen. The modern highway, like the railroad of today, cuts the landscape down to a practicable level. On the wooded hilltop, far from the roar of speeding traffic, and undistrurbed by the confusing, and illusion-destroying, evidences of a practical and mundane modernity, one can best appreciate the country from the standpoint of the first explorer, and visualize the trails by which the Indian was wont to pursue his way.

Bibliography

BUTTERFIELD, CONSUL W.—
Crawford's Campaign against Sandusky

CROW, GEORGE H. AND SMITH, C. P.—
My State, Ohio

DUMAS, C. G. F.—
Historical Account of Bouquet's Expedition
Translated by Francis Parkman

FARRIS, JOHN T.—
On the Trail of the Pioneers

FOUSE, RUSSELL L.—
The Western Reserve and Early Ohio

HECKEWELDER, JOHN—
Heckwelder's Narrative

HOPKINS, CHARLES EDWIN—
Ohio the Beautiful and Historic

HOWE, HENRY—
Howe's Historical Collections of Ohio

HULBERT, ARCHER BUTLER—
The Ohio River

KENTON, EDNA—
Life of Simon Kenton

MCKNIGHT, CHARLES—
Simon Girty

MILLS, W. C.—
Archeological Atlas of Ohio
Ohio Archeological and Historical Society Publications

PALMER, FREDERICK—
Clark of the Ohio

PARKMAN, FRANCIS—
Conspiracy of Pontiac

POST, CHARLES W.—
Doan's Corners and the City Four Miles West

RANDALL, EMILIUS O.—
History of Ohio

ROGERS, ROBERT—
Journal of Major Robert Rogers

ROOSEVELT, THEODORE—
The Winning of the West

SHETRONE, HENRY CLYDE—
The Mound Builders

TAYLOR, JAMES W.—
History of the State of Ohio

WHITTLESEY, CHARLES—
The Early History of Cleveland

Ohio Rivers and Associated Trails

	River	Trails
A.	Ashtabula	Ashtabula
		Lake
	Auglaize	Auglaize
		Black Swamp
B.	Beaver	Great Trail
		Mahoning
	Little Beaver	Great Trail
		Moravian
	Blanchard	Black Swamp
C.	Chippewa	Cuyahoga
		Muskingum
	Conotton Creek	Moravian
	Cuyahoga	Lake
		Muskingum
		Mahoning
G.	Grand	Lake
		Ashtabula
H.	Hocking	Ohio
		Belpré
		Coshocton
		Standing Stone
	Huron	Lake
		Mohican
		Watershed
		Great Trail
		Mahoning
		Huron
K.	Killbuck	Killbuck
		Walhonding
		Cuyahoga
		Great Trail

	River	Trails
	Kokosing	Walhonding
		Owl River
		Cuyahoga
L.	Licking	Coshocton
		Muskingum
M.	Mad	Wappatomica
		Shawnee-Miami
		Pickawillany
	Mahoning	Mahoning
		Ashtabula
		Tuscarawas
		Salt Spring
	Maumee	Lake
		Maumee
		Auglaize
		Black Swamp
	Mohican	Walhonding
		Cuyahoga
		Great Trail
		Huron
	Miami	Wabash
		Miami
		Pickawillany
		Auglaize
	Little Miami	Pickawillany
		Shawnee-Miami
	Muskingum	Muskingum
		Mingo
		Coshocton
		Moravian
		Walhonding
		Great Trail
		Mahoning
		Watershed
		Lake
N.	Nimishillen	Tuscarawas
		Great Trail
O.	Olentangy	Owl River
		Cuyahoga
		Walhonding
P.	Paint Creek	Pickawillany
		Shawnee-Miami
	Portage	Lake
R.	Rocky	Lake
		Mahoning
		Watershed
S.	Sandusky	Scioto
		Black Swamp
		Huron
		Lake
	Little Sandusky	Scioto
		Wappatomica
	Sandy	Great Trail
		Moravian
		Muskingum
	Scioto	Pickawillany
		Scioto
		Standing Stone
		Shawnee-Miami
		Kanawha
		Belpré
		Coshocton
		Walhonding
		Cuyahoga
		Owl River
		Wappatomica
		Huron
		Black Swamp
		Lake

	River	Trails
	Little Scioto	Standing Stone
	Stillwater	Shawnee-Miami Scioto
	Sugar Creek	Great Trail Muskingum
T.	Tuscarawas	Muskingum Cuyahoga Tuscarawas Great Trail Moravian Mingo
	Tymochtee	Wappatomica Black Swamp Scioto
V.	Vermilion	Lake Watershed
W.	Wabash	Wabash Miami
	Walhonding	Walhonding Mohican Killbuck Muskingum
	Walnut Creek	Cuyahoga Walhonding
	Whetstone Creek	Cuyahoga Owl River
	Wills Creek	Mingo Muskingum

Ohio Towns and Villages Related to Trails

	Town	Trail
A.	Alliance	Tuscarawas
	Akron	Cuyahoga
		Muskingum
		Watershed
	Amanda	Belpré
	Arkoe	Pickawillany
	Ashtabula	Ashtabula
	Aurora	Western Reserve
	Austinburg	Ashtabula
	Avery	Watershed
	Ayersville	Pickawillany
B.	Bath	Watershed
	Barberton	Cuyahoga
	Barretts Mills	Pickawillany
	Beech Flats	Pickawillany
	Bedford	Mahoning
	Belpré	Ohio
		Belpré
	Berlin Heights	Lake
	Big Prairie	Mohican
	Big Springs	Wappatomica
	Birmingham	Mohican
	Bloomingdale	Mingo
	Bloomingville	Lake
	Bolivar	Great Trail
		Muskingum
		Tuscarawas
	Botzum	Muskingum
	Bowerston	Mingo
	Brecksville	Muskingum
	Brinkhaven	Mohican
C.	Cadiz	Mingo
	Calcutta	Moravian
	Canfield	Salt Spring

	Town	Trail
	Cannon's Mills	Moravian
	Canton	Western Reserve
	Carey	Black Swamp
	Carrollton	Moravian
	Castalia	Great Trail Mahoning Watershed
	Cedarville	Pickawillany
	Centerburg	Walhonding
	Centerville	Kanawha
	Chagrin Falls	Western Reserve
	Charloe	Auglaize
	Cheshire	Ohio
	Chester	Ohio
	Chester Hill	Belpré
	Chesterville	Owl River
	Chillicothe	Scioto
	Cincinnati	Miami
	Circleville	Scioto Shawnee-Miami Kanawha Belpré Coshocton
	Clarksfield	Mohican
	Cleveland	Lake Muskingum
	Coolville	Ohio
	Corning	Belpré
	Coshocton	Coshocton Muskingum Walhonding
	Cranmer	Muskingum
	Crawford	Black Swamp
	Crystal Springs	Muskingum
	Cumberland	Mingo
	Cumminsville	Wabash
	Cuyahoga Falls	Mahoning Watershed
D.	Dayton	Wappatomica Miami
	Deersville	Mingo
	Defiance	Maumee Auglaize Black Swamp
	Delaware	Scioto Cuyahoga
	Dellroy	Moravian
	Delphos	Auglaize
	Dennison	Moravian
	Dover	Muskingum
	Doylestown	Cuyahoga
	Drinkle	Belpré
	Duke	Pickawillany
	Duncan Falls	Muskingum
	Dungannon	Great Trail Moravian
E.	Eaton	Wabash
	Elmore	Great Trail
F.	Fairport	Lake
	Fitchville	Huron
	Findlay	Black Swamp
	Fort Jefferson	Wabash
	Fort Recovery	Wabash
	Fort Seneca	Scioto
	Frazeysburg	Coshocton
	Frederickton	Cuyahoga
	Fredericktown	Owl River
	Fremont	Scioto
G.	Galena	Walhonding

	Town	Trail
	Gambier	Walhonding
	Gavers	Moravian
	Genoa	Great Trail
	Girard	Mahoning
	Gnadenhutten	Muskingum
		Mingo
	Goshen	Muskingum
	Gratiot	Coshocton
	Greenville	Wabash
H.	Hamilton	Wabash
	Haynes	Standing Stone
	Helmeck Station	Killbuck
	Hemlock	Belpré
	Henley	Pickawillany
	Highland	Pickawillany
	Hinckley	Watershed
	Hiram Rapids	Western Reserve
	Holmesville	Killbuck
	Hopedale	Mingo
	Howard	Walhonding
I.	Ira	Muskingum
	Irondale	Moravian
	Independence	Muskingum
	Ironville	Great Trail
	Iron Bridge	Watershed
J.	Jackson	Kanawha
	Jeromesville	Mohican
K.	Kanauga	Kanawha
	Kelleys Store	Muskingum
	Kent	Mahoning
		Western Reserve
	Kingston	Kanawha
L.	Laceyville	Mingo
	Lancaster	Coshocton
		Standing Stone
	Latham	Pickawillany
	Lebanon	Miami
	Leipsic	Black Swamp
	Leonardsburg	Cuyahoga
	Limestone	Great Trail
	Lindsey	Great Trail
	Lisbon	Great Trail
	Lightsville	Wabash
	Little Sandusky	Scioto
	Lock Seventeen	Muskingum
	London	Shawnee-Miami
	Loramie	Miami
	Lore City	Mingo
	Loudonville	Mohican
	Lucerne	Cuyahoga
M.	Macedonia	Western Reserve
	Malvern	Great Trail
	Mansfield	Great Trail
	Marion	Owl River
	Marietta	Muskingum
	Marseilles	Wappatomica
	Massillon	Muskingum
	McKinley Crossing	Great Trail
	Mechanicstown	Moravian
	Medina	Watershed
	Midvale	Mingo
	Milan	Mohican
	Millersburg	Killbuck
	Millport	Moravian
	Millwood	Walhonding
	Mineral Ridge	Mahoning
	Minerva	Great Trail

	Town	Trail
	Minster	Auglaize
	Mohicanville	Cuyahoga
	Monroeville	Great Trail
	Momeneetown	Great Trail
	Mound Crossing	Standing Stone
	Mount Gilead	Owl River
	Mount Liberty	Walhonding
	Mount Sterling	Shawnee-Miami
	Mount Union	Tuscarawas
	Mount Vernon	Walhonding
	Montrose	Watershed
	Munroe Falls	Watershed
	Munson Hall	Ashtabula
	Myersville	Western Reserve
N.	Napoleon	Maumee
	Nash Corners	Scioto
	Nashport Station	Coshocton
	Navarre	Muskingum
	Negley	Great Trail
	New Bremen	Auglaize
	Newcomerstown	Muskingum
	New London	Watershed
	New Philadelphia	Muskingum
	Newton Falls	Mahoning
	New Washington	Huron
	Niles	Mahoning
	Nimisila	Muskingum
	Northfield	Mahoning
	Northampton	Western Reserve
	Norwalk	Mohican
O.	Oak Harbor	Lake
	Oakwood	Auglaize
	Ohlstown	Salt Spring
	Olentangy	Scioto
	Olivesburg	Great Trail
	Old Town	Pickawillany
	Old Tymochtee	Black Swamp
P.	Painesville	Western Reserve
	Parkman	Western Reserve
	Parral	Muskingum
	Pekin	Great Trail
	Perrysville	Cuyahoga
	Pfeiffer	Wappatomica
	Philadelphia Road	Mingo
	Philo	Muskingum
	Piedmont	Mingo
	Piqua	Miami
	Pleasant Bend	Black Swamp
	Pleasant City	Mingo
	Pleasantville	Coshocton
	Plymouth	Great Trail
	Pomeroy	Ohio
	Portsmouth	Scioto
	Port William	Pickawillany
R.	Ray	Standing Stone
	Rainsboro	Pickawillany
	Reeds Mills	Mingo
	Rempel	Kanawha
	Revenge	Belpré
	Richfield	Muskingum
	Richmond Dale	Kanawha
	Rockbridge	Standing Stone
	Rockland	Wabash
	Rome	Great Trail
	Roscoe	Walhonding
	Royalton	Coshocton
	Rushsylvania	Wappatomica
S.	Salineville	Moravian

	Town	Trail
	Sandyville	Great Trail
	Schoenbrun	Muskingum
	Sciotoville	Standing Stone
	Sebring	Tuscarawas
	Seven Mile	Wabash
	Sharonville	Miami
	Shawnee	Belpré
	Silver Lake	Watershed
	Sinking Springs	Pickawillany
	South Woodbury	Cuyahoga
	Spencerville	Auglaize
	Springfield	Miami
	St. Marys	Auglaize
	Stockport	Muskingum
	Streetsboro	Western Reserve
	St. Paris	Pickawillany
	Stringtown	Muskingum
	Struthers	Mahoning
T.	Thornville	Coshocton
	Tippecanoe City	Miami
	Tobias	Owl River
	Toledo	Lake
	Trinway	Muskingum
	Tuppers Plains	Ohio
	Twinsburg	Western Reserve
U.	Uhrichsville	Moravian
	Upper Sandusky	Wappatomica Scioto Black Swamp
	Urbana	Shawnee-Miami
V.	Vincent	Belpré
W.	Wakefield	Scioto
	Wakeman	Mohican
	Waldo	Scioto
	Walhonding	Walhonding
	Warsaw	Walhonding
	Washingtonville	Salt Spring
	Waterville	Maumee
	Waverly	Scioto
	Westfall	Scioto
	West Liberty	Wappatomica
	Weymouth	Huron
	Wilson Mills	Western Reserve
	Wooster	Great Trail Cuyahoga
	Wyandot	Owl River
X.	Xenia	Pickawillany
Y.	Yellow Springs	Pickawillany
Z.	Zanesfield	Wappatomica
	Zanesville	Muskingum
	Zuck	Walhonding

Historic Indian Towns in Ohio

Indian Name	Modern Name	County
Amanda	Amanda	Pickaway
Anioton	Venice	Erie
Beaver Town	Bolivar	Tuscarawas
Big Son's Town	Streetsboro	Portage
Blue Jacket's Town	Defiance	Defiance
Buckongehelas Town	St. Marys	Auglaize
Charloe	Charloe	Paulding
Chillicothe	Chillicothe	Ross
Chillicothe	Slate Mills	Ross
Chillicothe	Spunkeytown	Pickaway
Chillicothe	Old Town	Greene
Coashoskis	Howard	Knox
Conchake	Killbuck	Holmes
Cornstalk's Town	Circleville	Pickaway
Cornstalk's Town	Westfall	Pickaway
Crow's Town	Cadiz	Harrison
Delaware Town	Bridgeport	Belmont
Dunqueindundeh	Fremont	Sandusky
Goshgoshing	Coshocton	Coshocton
Gnadenhutten	Gnadenhutten	Tuscarawas
Green Town	Perrysville	Ashland
Grenadier Squaw Town	Haysville	Pickaway
Half King's Town	Indian Mill	Wyandot
Hell Town	Perrysville	Ashland
Hurricane Tom's Town	Richmondale	Ross
Jeromesville	Jeromesville	Ashland
Junandat	Fremont	Sandusky
Kanauga	Kanauga	Gallia
Killbuck Town	Big Prairie	Holmes
Kiskeminetas	Pomeroy	Meigs
Koshkoshkung	New Matamoras	Washington
Kuskuskies Town	Youngstown	Mahoning
Le Baril	California	Hamilton
Little Turtle Town	Defiance	Defiance
Lichtenau	Coshocton	Coshocton
Logan's Town	Ira	Summit
Logan's Town	Mingo Junction	Jefferson
Logstown	Junction of Ohio with Beaver, Pa.	
Loramie's Station	Loramie	Shelby

Indian Name	Modern Name	County
Lower Sandusky	Fremont	Sandusky
Lower Shawnee Town	Portsmouth	Scioto
Maccacheek	West Liberty	Logan
Maguck	Circleville	Pickaway
Margaret's Town	Royalton	Fairfield
Miami Town	Maumee	Lucas
Mingo Town	Ghent	Summit
Mingo Town	Delaware	Delaware
Mingo Town	Columbus	Franklin
Mohawk	Mohawk Village	Coshocton
Mohican John's Town	Mohicanville	Ashland
Mohican Town	Newville	Richland
Muskingum	Millersburg	Holmes
New Comer's Town	Newcomerstown	Tuscarawas
New Hundy	Zuck	Knox
Old Tuscarora Town	Tuscarawas	Tuscarawas
Onandaga Town	Aurora	Portage
Onandaga Town	Geauga Lake	Geauga
Ostionish	Akron	Summit
Old Pipe's Town	Old Tymochtee	Wyandot
Old Town	Letart Falls	Meigs
Ottawa Town	Southpark	Cuyahoga
Ottawa Town	Northampton	Summit
Owl's Town	Mount Vernon	Knox
Painted Post	Dungannon	Columbiana
Pettquotting	Milan	Erie
Pecowick	Yellowbud	Ross
Pilgerruh	Southpark	Cuyahoga
Pickawillany	Piqua	Miami
Pipe's Town	Long Pond	Summit
Pipe's Town	Wyandot	Wyandot
Pipe's Town	Jeromesville	Ashland
Piqua	Springfield	Clark
Piqua Town	Westfall	Pickaway
Pluggy's Town	Olentangy	Franklin
Saguin's Post	Willow	Cuyahoga
Salem	Milan	Erie
Salt Lick Town	Niles	Trumbull
Salt Lick Town	Columbus	Franklin

Indian Name	Modern Name	County
Schoenbrunn	New Philadelphia	Tuscarawas
Senaca Town	Twinsburg	Summit
Shawnee Town	Lima	Allen
Silver Lake	Silver Lake	Summit
Squaw's Town	Westfall	Pickaway
Standing Stone	Lancaster	Fairfield
Tapacon Town	Dover	Tuscarawas
Three Legs' Town	Midvale	Tuscarawas
Tontoganee	Tontogany	Wood
Tullihas	Mount Vernon	Knox
Tuscarawas	Bolivar	Tuscarawas
Tymochtee	Old Tymochtee	Wyandot
Upper Sandusky	Upper Sandusky	Wyandot
Waccachalla	Andersonville	Ross
Wakatomika	Dresden	Muskingum
Walhonding	Walhonding	Coshocton
Wanduchale's Town	Waverly	Pike
Wanduchale's Town	Hockingport	Athens
Wapogkanetta	Wapakoneta	Auglaize
Wappatomica	Zanesfield	Logan
White Eyes' Town	West Lafayette	Coshocton
White Woman's Town	Warsaw	Coshocton
Will's Town	Duncan Falls	Muskingum
Wyandot Old Town	Upper Sandusky	Wyandot

Topical Index

Amherst or Wilkins' Expedition, 13, 32
Appleseed, Johnny, 12
Bailey, Ann, 101
Ball, Capt., 72
Battle Island, 6, 71
Belpré, 95
Big Bottom, 50
Big Prairie, 84
Big Spring or Buffalo Wallow, 81
Bird, Commander, 10, 16, 113, 121
Black Fork of the Mohican, 85, 86
Black Hand Gorge, 91
Blennerhassett Island, 95
Blue Hole of Castalia, 9, 13, 31, 47
Blue Jacket or Buckongehelas, 12, 70
Brokensword Creek, 87
Boone, Daniel, 10, 70
Bouquet, Col., 9, 13, 43, 79, 82
Bouquet's Spring, 79
Bradstreet, Gen., 9, 13, 32
Brady, Daniel, 10, 34
Brodhead, Col., 10, 50, 82
Buckongehelas, 12, 70
Buffaloes, 71, 83
Buffalo Wallow or Big Spring, 81
Burning Mound, 70
Burr, Aaron, 95
Buskirk's Battle, 65
Camp Bouquet, 43
Carpenter Episode, 55
Camp Charlotte, 14, 74, 99
Camp Lewis, 70
Canals and Trails, 17, 18, 31, 44, 53, 114
Captives among Indians, 51, 70, 75, 79, 83, 87, 108, 111, 123, 126
Carter, Lorenzo, 28
Castalia, 9, 31
Catfish Camp, 34
Cats or Eries, 7, 27, 40, 77
Celeron de Bienville, 33, 77, 109
Clark, Gen. George Rogers, 10, 14, 16, 114, 120
Clay, Gen., 16
Congo Creek, 70
Copley Swamp, 40, 77
Copus Massacre, 85
Cornstalk, 10, 12, 101
Council Rock, 50
Crane, The, or Tarhe, 12, 70
Crawford, Col. Wm., 11, 13, 14, 16, 17, 65, 66, 71, 87
Cresap's War, 9
Cresswell, Nicholas, 14, 44
Croghan, George, 9, 14
Decoy Boats on Ohio, 69
Delawares, 7, 10, 12, 19, 70, 75, 82
Demoiselle, The, 109
Difficulties of Early Travel, xiv, 16, 83
Doan's Corners, 28
Drainage, Effect of, 6, 19, 27, 118, 120, 123
Duncan Falls, 67
Dungannon, 44, 55
Dunmore, Lord, 9, 14, 99, 101
Dunqueindundeh, 47, 72, 74
Duquesne, Fort, 33
Eries or Cats, 7, 27, 40, 77
Elliot, Mathew, 11, 51, 55
English Posts, 9, 10, 79, 111, 125
Fallen Timbers, Battle of, 25, 125, 127
Fire-lands, 85
Flint Ridge, 6, 20, 91
Fort Hill, 6, 105, 106
Fort:
  Amanda or Jennings, 120
  Ball, 72
  Defiance, 120
  Deposit, 125
  Greenville, 118
  Hamilton, 117, 118
  Harmar, 49
  Jefferson, 117
  Jennings or Amanda, 120
  Laurens, 3, 10, 12, 44, 51
  Loramie, 12, 114, 120
  Miami, 125
  Meigs, 125
  Pitt, 9, 13, 33
  Recovery, 11
  Stephenson, 72
  St. Clair, 117
  Wayne, 11, 12
  Winchester, 120
Freese's Landing, 31
French House, 37
French Margaret's Town, 89
French Traders, 7, 17, 33, 36, 37, 39, 47, 73, 103
Gauntlet, Kenton's, 108, 112
Girty, Simon, 10, 16, 50, 126
Gist, Christopher, 9, 13, 14, 73, 89, 113
Gnadenhutten, 10, 11, 13, 50, 56
Goshen, 50, 65
Grand Glaize King or Tata-pachkse, 126
Great Salt Lick, 59, 60
Greentown, 85, 86
Greenville Treaty, 17
Grenadier Squaw Town, 70, 74
Half King, The, 11, 55
Hamilton, 'The Hair Buyer', 10
Harmar, Gen., 11, 14, 16, 108, 113
Harris, Mary, 79
Harrison, Gen., 13, 16
Heckewelder, The Missionary, 9, 13, 33, 50, 55
Helltown, 75
High Horn or Spemica Lawba, 111

Hurons, 7, 19
Indian Battles, 9, 10, 11, 12, 13, 40, 65, 72, 83, 120, 121
Indian Cross Creek, 65
Indian Ferry, 28
Indian Legends, 40, 67, 72, 77, 79, 91, 108, 125
Indian Massacres, 11, 56, 83, 85
Indian Migration, 7, 9, 12
Indian Mounds, 69, 70, 105
Indian Petroglyphs, 91, 125
Indian Village Sites, 20
Iroquois, 7, 27, 63
Jerome, Jean Baptiste, 45, 84
Johnson, John, 12, 113
Joshua, 126
Kendall's Ledge, 36
Kenton, Simon, 10, 13, 16, 32, 108, 112
Killbuck, 45, 76
Knight, Dr., 14, 111
Lakes:
  Buckeye, 89, 91
  Chippewa, 41
  Geauga, 62
  Long Pond, 52
  Loramie, 114
  Odell, 76, 81
  Silver, 34, 39
  St. Mary's, 114, 120
Leatherlips, 70
Leesville, 83, 87
Lewis, Col., 9, 14, 70, 101
Lichtenau, 50, 53, 82
Little Turtle, 12, 117, 118
Logan Elm, 10, 14, 70, 102
Logan, The Mingo, 9, 12, 70
Logan, Col. John, 14, 16, 108, 111
Logstown, 43
Loramie, Pierre, 7, 114, 120
Louis Phillipe, 50
Loyal Indians, 70, 114
Maccacheek, 112
Maguck, 70, 73, 102, 103
McIntosh, Col., 13, 55
McKee, 11, 55
Miamis, 19
Mingos, 7, 19, 70, 76
Mingo Bottom, 65
Mohawks, 76
Mohawk Village, 79
Mohicans, 7, 14, 19, 76, 84
Mohican John, 84
Moravians, 9, 36, 51, 65, 78, 82, 83, 123, 126
Monuments, Historic, 28, 70, 79, 83, 99, 101
Munseys, 82
Myeerah, 111
Navarre, Pierre, 47
Navigation, Early, 3, 17, 24, 28, 31, 33, 72, 109
Negley, 43
Nelson Ledges, 63
Neutral Nation, 72
New Comer, 79
New Hundy, 79
Newville, 75
Ogontz, 31
Old Britain, 9, 109, 114
Old Maid's Kitchen, 39, 62
Old Portage, 39, 40, 52, 63, 75
Old Towns:
  Letart Falls, 95
  Tuscarora, 44, 50, 58
  Upper Sandusky, 11, 12, 14, 71, 83
  Xenia, 108
Old Smith Road, 40, 41
Olentangy Battle, 83
Onondaga George's Lookout, 40, 52, 63
Ostionish, 40, 63
Ottawas, 5, 7, 19
Painted Post, 44, 55, 59
Petroglyphs, 91, 125
Pettquotting, 31, 51
Piatt Castles, 112
Pickaway Plains, 6, 14
Pickawillany, 9, 103, 113, 114
Pigeon Roost, 89
Pilgerruh, 36
Pioneer Roads in Ohio, xiv, 12, 13, 16, 17, 18, 27, 40, 52, 56, 58, 59, 60, 61, 89, 123
Pipe, Capt., 12, 50, 75, 82, 84
Pipe's Towns:
  Ashland County, 82, 85
  Summit County, 52, 53
  Wyandot County, 74
Piqua, Old, 108
Point Pleasant, Battle of, 10, 14, 25
Pontiac, 9, 12, 32
Ponty's Camp, 32, 62
Portage Path, The, 39, 40, 77
Portages:
  Auglaize, 7
  Cuyahoga, 12, 39, 40, 52, 63, 71, 77
  Huron, 87
  Mahoning, 33
  Scioto, 71, 83
Prairies, Natural, 6, 14, 19, 25, 70, 72, 84, 102, 110, 114, 124
Prophet, The, 51, 126
Raven Rock, 105
Railroads and Trails, 24
Ring Hunting, 25
Roche de Bout, 125
Rock House, 93
Rogers, Robt., 9, 13, 32
Ruffner Massacre, 85
Saguin's Post, 37, 53
Salem (Tuscarawas), 50
Salt Springs:
  Franklin County, 78
  Jackson County, 94
  Trumbull County, 59, 60
Sandusky Plains, 6, 72, 83
Scenic Points on Trails, 31, 37, 43, 49, 50, 61, 63, 66, 69, 70, 72, 76, 79, 81, 84, 85, 89, 91, 94, 99, 102, 105, 106, 111, 112, 114, 125
Schoenbrunn, 10, 13, 50, 56, 57
Senecas, 76
Serpent Mound, 105
Shawnees, 4, 7, 12, 19, 99, 103
Shelby, Gen., 14, 16
Sinking Springs, 106
Smith, James, 31, 87
Spemica Lawba or High Horn, 111
Squaw Rock, 108, 112
Standing Stone, 93
St. Clair, Gen. Arthur, 11, 16, 117, 118, 119
Tarhe, The Crane, 12, 70
Tatapachkse or Grand Glaize King, 126
Tecumseh, 12
Teutonic Names of Indian Towns, 36, 50, 75
Treaty Tree, 36
Tuendawie, 120
Turkey Foot Rock, 125
Union Lane, 28, 53
Wakatomika, 53
Walhonding, 79
Wappatomica, 110, 111
Wayne, Gen. Anthony, 11, 16, 32, 114, 117, 119, 120, 121, 127
Wetzel, Lewis, 12
Weymouth, 40
White Eyes, 55, 56
White Eyes, Capt., 12, 55, 56
White Woman's Town, 53, 79
Williamson, Col., 11, 13, 51, 65
Wyandots, 5, 7, 12, 19, 76, 78, 87
Zane, Ebenezer, 14, 89, 111
Zane, Isaac, 111
Zeisberger, The Missionary, 13, 50, 51, 65